# Explorations in World Ethnology

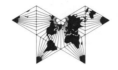

## ROBERT B. EDGERTON and L. L. LANGNESS
University of California, Los Angeles

General Editors

# STRUGGLE FOR CHANGE IN A NUBIAN COMMUNITY

## An Individual in Society and History

JOHN G. KENNEDY

*(with the assistance of Hussein M. Fahim)*

 Mayfield Publishing Company

*No social study that does not come back to the
problems of biography, of history, and their
intersections within society has completed its
intellectual journey.*

C. Wright Mills

Library of Congress Catalog Card Number: 76-28115
International Standard Book Number: 0-87484-321-9

Manufactured in the United States of America
Mayfield Publishing Company
285 Hamilton Avenue, Palo Alto, California 94301

This book was set in Aster by Chapman's Phototypesetting
and was printed and bound by Malloy Lithographing.
Sponsoring editor was Alden C. Paine, Carole Norton
supervised editing, and Barbara Pronin was manuscript
editor. Nancy Sears designed the text and cover, and
Michelle Hogan supervised production.

# CONTENTS

# ACKNOWLEDGMENTS

The author's field crew from the Social Research Center of the American University of Cairo deserve high praise for their individual and collective efforts in behalf of the research reported in the pages that follow. The diligent effort, intelligent observations and comments of Hussein Muhammad Fahim and Omar Abdel Hamid, who assisted in studying the life of the village men, and of Samiha el Katsha and Sohair Mehanna, who worked with the village women, not only provided the basic information for this study but served as a constant check on my own field work as well. Dr. Fahim merits special thanks for his role in gathering material for this book.

Laila Shukry el Hamamsy, director of the Social Research Center, provided intellectual sustenance and moral support throughout the course of the work and has shown unusual patience in waiting for the results of the Nubian research project to appear. Robert Fernea, director of the Ethnological Survey of Egyptian Nubia from 1962 to 1966, played an important part in all our research, and it has been a pleasure to work with him. The survey itself was supported by the Ford Foundation through the Social Research Center.

Robert Edgerton and Lew Langness of UCLA, who encouraged me to finish this book, have both offered numerous valuable editorial suggestions and comments. I am very grateful to Mayfield Publishing Company for seeing this book through the editorial process while I was out of the country doing field work in Yemen and unable to answer the many queries that arise in the production of a book. My special thanks go to Alden Paine, Carole Norton, and Barbara Pronin.

In assigning credit for this book, perhaps our greatest debt is to the people of Kanuba, who have been so generous with their time, good will, and Nubian hospitality, and to Shatr Muhammad Shalashil for placing the events of his life at our disposal. The names of our village, of our protagonist, and of his fellow villagers have been changed in the interests of preserving their anonymity.

To all the above, my profound gratitude.

# EDITORS' PREFACE

Rapid social change is having an impact on almost everyone on earth and now seems to be accelerating. For many years anthropologists have shown great interest in the process by which traditional communities, particularly those in the Third World, undergo significant social change. Anthropological studies have emphasized many of the social, political, and economic factors involved in such change, but for the most part the role of individual leaders has been neglected. Moreover, residents of these traditional communities have usually been studied in terms of their reactions to new conditions imposed on them from the outside. Rarely do we see how individuals in remote towns and villages take an active part in shaping the course of the changes that can so profoundly affect life in their communities.

This book, by John G. Kennedy, allows us to see how important social changes in a remote village in Nubia were brought about, at least in part, by the leadership of one man—Shatr Muhammad Shalashil. Professor Kennedy allows this man to speak for himself in an autobiographical account that begins with his childhood and concludes with his successes in guiding important changes in his village. These changes are obviously related to a series of dam constructions on the Nile which resulted in the resettlement of whole villages, just as they are related to basic changes in the government of Egypt and to economic and political factors throughout the Middle East. But without the personal force of Shatr Shalashil, the village of Kanuba would not have responded in the ways it did. Professor Kennedy allows Shatr to tell his own story, but he also provides the historical background and social context necessary to understand his story. Since so little has been written about life in Nubia, this background material has a unique value in its own right.

Professor Kennedy was trained in anthropology at the University of California, Los Angeles, where he received his Ph.D. in 1962, and where he has been a member of the faculty since 1967. He has done fieldwork with the Tarahumara Indians of Northern Mexico which resulted in, among other scholarly publications, a book entitled *Isolation and Alcohol: Ecology of a Mountain Tarahumara Community*. He also spent four years doing research and teaching in Egypt; in addition to this book, he is the author of *Nubian Ceremonialism: Studies in Religious Syncretism and Culture Change*. He has recently concluded almost two years of anthropological field research in Yemen, the first ever conducted in that country.

Robert B. Edgerton
L. L. Langness

# STRUGGLE FOR CHANGE IN A NUBIAN COMMUNITY

# THE NUBIAN PROJECT

# 1

BACKGROUND

The village of Kanuba is situated outside the region that is traditionally called Nubia—a region that extends southward along the Nile from the first cataract at Aswan, Egypt, to the fifth cataract in what is now Sudan—and is composed of people who emigrated from Nubia as a result of the second raising of the Aswan Dam in 1933. Although Nubia had always been economically poor, the progressively rising lake created by the construction of the first Aswan Dam in 1902 and by successive heightenings in 1912 and 1933 destroyed most of its limited agricultural land and palm trees. Just before their removal from their homeland in 1933, most Egyptian Nubians were pursuing a subsistence level of existence.[1]

The consequences of labor migration—split families and disproportionate numbers of women to men—had been common features of Nubian life for more than a century before the first dam was erected. But in 1933, as in 1902 and 1912, the major form of adaptation to increased land deprivation was simply to increase the numbers of migrants. Afraid of urban life, many had used their small compensation payments and whatever other resources they possessed to establish new village communities in rural areas of Upper Egypt along the Nile north of Aswan, usually on the peripheries of such larger towns as Aswan, Daraw, Kom Ombo, Isna, Idfu, Luxor, and Qena.

Kanuba is one of these self-relocated Nubian communities located about three kilometers from the market center of Daraw and consid-

*Sheikhs of tribes,
Old Diwan,
before 1933.*
Courtesy
Sheikh Abdel Galil.

ered administratively to be a part of the larger town. The majority of
Kanubans came from the southern Nubian administrative district of
Diwan and speak a Mahass dialect in addition to Arabic; but the village
also contains families from the Mahass-speaking administrative districts
of Tongala, Tomas, Abu Handl, and Derr, and there are, in addition, relatively large numbers from the Kenuz-speaking district of Abu Hor.

The Ethnological Survey of Egyptian Nubia of the Social Research
Center of the American University of Cairo was inspired by the catastrophic effects on the Nubian population of the High Dam at Aswan.
In 1960 Robert Fernea and Laila Shukry el Hamamsy, both members
of the Social Research Center, determined to gain more information on the
Nubians before resettlement had irrevocably altered their culture; they
also wished to provide authorities in Egypt with information that might
assist the government in carrying out a more enlightened resettlement.

Funded by the Ford Foundation and directed by Fernea, the survey's major components included sociological studies of Nubian migrants
in Cairo and Alexandria, an ecological survey of Old Nubia, community
studies with emphasis on salvage ethnography in the major linguistic-
cultural areas of Egyptian Nubia, and a study of land and irrigation in
Adindan. My assignment was to study one of the Nubian groups that
had been relocated as the result of a raising of the dam, and I was interested not only in the changes brought about by the resettlement but by
the process of change itself. To inquiries made on survey trips to the
Nubian villages of Dahmit and Ballana and in the towns of Aswan and
Daraw, I was often directed to Kanuba, many informants referring to
the people of this village as Kushaf (hereditary rulers of Nubia from
Mamluk times).

KANUBA

My assistant Hussein Fahim and I entered Kanuba for the first time around 2 P.M. on a sun-drenched afternoon in January 1963 and were at once impressed by both the nondescript appearance of the village and the exceptional quietude of its streets. Here was none of the elaborate architectural decoration characteristic of Old Nubia; only the mosque was relatively imposing compared with those in traditional Nubian villages south of Aswan. As in most villages in this part of Egypt, the walls of the houses along the street joined in a single continuing plastered face so that it was difficult to discern where one residence ended and another began. Because other towns and villages that we had visited in Upper Egypt had been full of people busily pursuing their daily tasks, we were surprised to find ourselves totally alone, without even the bands of curious children who usually surrounded us.

*House with dried jackal, Kanuba.*

After some time a young man emerged from one of the houses and led us to the entrance of what was identified in Arabic as the village club. Shortly thereafter another lone man wearing a long brown and white striped robe and a turban greeted us with a handshake, asking us to wait while he brought from his house the key to open the club. Reappearing a moment later with a long runner of carpet draped over his arm and a large wooden key in his hand, he unlocked the club door and led us into a small room opening onto an arched courtyard, where, seated on a long wooden bench on which the carpet had been spread, we were served tall glasses of a delicious drink made from the fruit of the doom palm. Our host, who owned a store in the village, was Sheikh Muhammad.

In the course of time several other men arrived to whom we explained the nature of the Nubian project, said that we had been referred to Kanuba by other Nubians, and added that we might wish to spend some time here for the purpose of studying Nubian customs. These explanations did not appear to be fully accepted. Most of our questions about the size, occupational structure, and history of the village elicited politely evasive answers, and we continued to be treated in a cautious, restrained manner, as if the group were uncertain how to handle the situation.

A half-hour later there appeared with several young men a rotund and unprepossessing individual about forty years of age, round of face and fairly light-skinned for a Nubian, who was greeted as Shatr effendi. He was wearing a wrinkled and dirty gallabeya, the loose, comfortable gown of Egypt, puffed out in front by his protruding belly. His small bright eyes darted here and there in curiosity, his voice was high and thin, and many of his remarks in Nubian drew laughter from the others. Soon, however, he dominated the interrogation, occasionally issuing orders in Nubian to the children who had by now collected about us.

From the beginning, Shatr Shalashil told us about the village's troubles—about the termites that had eaten away the wooden parts of many houses and about a rising salinity which had not only made the fields infertile but which, seeping upward through floors and into walls, had made uninhabitable a whole section of wooden houses. We were shown the crumbling roof beams, door jambs, and window shutters of several nearby buildings, were led on a tour of the ruined parts of the village, and were given water to taste from a salty well. We were also told how the village founders had come to Kanuba when their land in Old Nubia had been flooded as a result of the 1933 raising of the Aswan Dam.

Instead of attempting to rebuild on the rocky cliffs overlooking the widened river, many people who had seen their houses engulfed by the rising water had migrated to this area near Daraw, where they had expected to reproduce their farming existence in Old Nubia. The people from the district of Diwan had sent out their tribal leaders to find a suitable area in Upper Egypt, and this particular piece of land had been purchased for purposes of agriculture from the Kom Ombo Valley Company. Almost the entire financial resources of the village founders had been used to obtain the 426 feddans (one feddan is roughly equal to one acre) that constituted the unfarmed area surrounding Kanuba, and the company had promised that the government would soon build canals to irrigate it.

Bitterly the men described their treatment at the hands of both the previous government and the Kom Ombo Valley Company. The government had not compensated them adequately for their losses. They had been given only four Egyptian pounds for each room built of mud brick and only thirty pounds for each feddan of land they had lost. The immensely expensive cattle-driven water wheels of Old Nubia, built with the capital and labor of several families, had not been compensated at all. For their precious palm trees, which had taken so long to grow and which yielded the greatest percentage of their income, they were compensated a mere five piasters to one pound per tree according to its yield. Orange trees were compensated at the rate of sixty piasters each. "It was a disaster for us and an injustice too," said Sheikh Muhammad.

Unlike the recent well-planned resettlement project of the Nasser government, which had provided land and cash compensation for the migrating Nubians, as well as houses, schools, medical units, and other service facilities,[2] no mosques, schools, or even houses had been prepared for them in 1933. The Kom Ombo Valley Company had never furnished the promised water for the undeveloped land they had bought and, further, had profited at their expense—first, by buying the land from the government at twenty piasters a feddan; then, by selling it for as much as eighteen pounds a feddan and five pounds for land farther from the Nile. The deal had been negotiated by the notorious Sidqi Pasha, prime minister of Egypt in 1933, who had not only reduced the amount of compensation to be paid to the Nubians but was chairman of the board of the Kom Ombo Valley Company at the time.

Walking near the village outskirts, we noticed that only a narrow strip of land on its immediate periphery was cultivated with wheat. Beyond this strip, which was not more than thirty to forty meters wide, the desert began. In the distance against the horizon we could see the tents and camels of a camp of the Heganna, the border patrol of Egypt. The reason for the village's silence and deserted quality now became apparent. Unlike the inhabitants of most villages in Egypt, these people were not farmers but had been forced into other occupations elsewhere.

Their attempts to make the land fertile by digging wells and building water wheels had failed. Water was scarce and deep, and their lifting devices could water only a few feddans. To compound the problem, the wells soon developed a high salinity which tended to decrease productivity of the soil. Most people had abandoned these attempts after a few years, though some had hung on, eking out a bare subsistence from agriculture for several more seasons. Later, people returning from the cities (including the protagonist of this book) had invested their money in modern pumps, but these attempts had also failed. They were able to reclaim from the desert only a small fraction of the land they had bought.

As the afternoon wore on the village became more animated. Young men returned from their jobs in Daraw, Kom Ombo, and Aswan, soon changing their business suits to greet us in gallabeyas; the children were out of school; women in black emerged from the plastered walls to draw water from the public tap or to gossip in groups along streets entirely free of vehicular traffic. At the end of the afternoon our portly guide conducted us to the exhibition room of the village club, where he proudly showed us an impressive array of traditional Nubian handicrafts and asked us to sign the club's guest book. As we left for our waiting taxi we were startled to hear applause and my name being shouted by a crowd of women and children. In the background we heard the ululating female joy cries, called *zaghareet*, that are typical of this part of the world.

*Women at water tap, Kanuba.*

Courtesy Samiha El Katsha.

*Showing official the quality of Kanuban crafts.*

## THE FIELD EXPERIENCE

At this time I had no idea that I would later return to Kanuba to live there for nearly a year; but after surveying other, earlier-settled Nubian villages in Aswan and Qena provinces and after visiting Kanuba again, I was impressed by the extent to which it differed from these as well as from the agricultural villages surrounding it. Although the people of Kanuba had experienced great setbacks, hardship, and disillusionment, they appeared dynamic, optimistic, and progressive compared with those in the surrounding communities of Upper Egypt. I wanted to know whether the appearance reflected the fact and, if so, how this adaptation had come about—how Kanuba had apparently surpassed its long-settled neighbors in adapting to the changing pattern of Egyptian society so far as to exhibit many urban characteristics.

My research team consisted, apart from my wife and children, of two Egyptian male assistants (Hussein and Omar) and two Egyptian female assistants (Samiha and Sohair), most of whom had had no previous experience in anthropological field work. Before long, however, they came to understand exactly what field work involved—no specific

7

daily working hours, no Sundays off, and a relentless, tedious writing of notes—until, through close living conditions, constant discussion of individual observations, and sharp questioning of my purposes and methods, they were gradually transformed from translators and interviewers into ethnographers.

As there was, understandably, no house available for us in Kanuba when we first began our research, we settled instead in Daraw, a nearby market town of nearly 14,000 people and the administrative center of which Kanuba was then technically a part. Our house was of the characteristic Kenuz type, with a high vaulted roof, ceilings twelve or more feet high, and a spacious pebbled courtyard with a large open verandah. During the long hot season when the temperature exceeded 100° F, we were obsessed with a fear of scorpions, whose often fatal sting brought to the Daraw hospital an average of thirteen people a day.

Until our mail began to arrive from Cairo and our presence in Daraw became a more accepted part of the everyday scene, we were somewhat troubled by our visible uniqueness in the community. On market day, especially, Daraw offers a fascinating kaleidoscope of ethnic types: the proud Ga'afras in their dark brown gallabeyas; sheikhs of the Ababda tribe riding quick-trotting donkeys and protected from the sun by white umbrellas; the Bisharin with their wild woolly hairdos, long rifles, and blue robes crossed in front by long, full, white cloths, who come with other desert tribesmen to trade camels at the Daraw market and to sell smuggled goods from Sudan. There are other groups as well, including natives of the area called the Awlad al-Sheikh Amer, three types of Nubians from Upper Egypt and Sudan, and a gypsylike traveling people called the Hallab.

Although our study had been legitimatized through the proper political channels, this was also a period of political tension, especially with the U.S. Congress cutting off wheat aid to Egypt from time to time; and from the local point of view, the sudden appearance of an American family accompanied by four Egyptian city types with no business except the alleged purpose of studying a nearby village was a "first." A few days after settling in Daraw we were summoned to the police station and, after prolonged interrogation, ordered never to leave the town, even for Kanuba, without first reporting to the police. Within two months, however, our presence in Daraw had become normal, and by the time our mail was being delivered we were no longer required to check out with the autorities.

Kanuba was culturally subdivided into two sections—one-third Kenuz and two-thirds Fadija. While Samiha visited women in the Fadija section and Sohair worked with the Kenuz women, Hussein and I visited the two village sheikhs, both of whom were storekeepers, and some old men who no longer worked regularly (all the other working men held jobs outside the village). Our general pattern of work was to drive to Kanuba in the early morning before the heat became stifling and to return to the Daraw house for lunch and a rest, often going back to Kanuba in late afternoon when the heat had begun to subside. At this time, the girls visited more women while Hussein and I sat with the men, whose habit it was to congregate in front of Sheikh Muhammad's store every evening until seven or eight. (Omar was soon called back to Cairo and returned to Kanuba thereafter only for several one-month assignments.)

At the beginning of our research, we were frequently frustrated in any attempt to go beyond a discouragingly superficial level of information. Although we came to the village every day, were ceremoniously ushered into the club by Sheikh Muhammad and given drinks made from the doom palm while a group of men answered our questions, our reception remained formal, the answers remained politely evasive, and for two-and-a-half months not one Kanuban invited us into his home. When we later succeeded in winning their trust, we learned that this had been Shatr Shalashil's planned strategy for dealing with us—a strategy intended to obstruct our work in numerous and subtle ways.

When the Nubians did not wish us to understand them, for example, they would switch from Arabic to one of their native dialects, just as we, under the same circumstances, would switch from Arabic to English. When we resorted to this tactic on one occasion, however, after several months in the village, Shatr suddenly interrupted us to make a point. It was at the very least disconcerting to realize that he had been monitoring our private conversations all along, having learned English when he had worked with the British Army. It was the more disconcerting to discover later that four of the village men were conversant in our language, although their abilities proved useful in time since I could now interview them and use them as translators of Nubian and Arabic.

For another example of Shatr's purely obstructional tactics: we were sitting in front of Sheikh Muhammad's store one day, getting nowhere, when I reverted to the anthropological ploy of taking genealogies, usually the most innocuous means of getting to know people during the early stages of research. After obtaining a few names from members of one family, we were suddenly cut off, as Shatr had told them in native dialect that it was a "shame" to give out the names of their women. On another occasion he decided that it was a "shame" for women to be photographed, with the result that we were prevented from shooting pictures of women for months. In reality, there was no shame connected with these matters, and when we had finally won acceptance and trust in the village we were given full genealogies and allowed to shoot any pictures we wanted.

In June 1963 we left Kanuba for Cairo and returned to the village three months later, much clearer about our specific goals. After some debate, the village association allowed us to rent a house in Kanuba, having by this time developed a proprietary interest in us coupled with a pride that we had "chosen" them for study, although we continued to be entertained only at the club. Our Kanuba house had a large courtyard and high ceilings but lacked the vaulted roof of the typical Kenuz structure. Our meals were prepared by Am Ibrahim, a hired cook, on a kerosene stove; our water was delivered daily by a man who hauled it in skin bags by donkey; our toilet was a hole in the ground; our lights were pressurized kerosene lanterns. Flies were ubiquitous; to be free of them during mealtimes, we ate in a cloud of DDT. Fresh meat and vegetables were available once a week at the Daraw market and were supplemented by special foods and canned goods sent to us from one or another of our assistants' homes. The life was hard in many ways, but we all adapted to it and, in time, even found it exhilarating.

Our presence in the village as a household seemed to catalyze the village's acceptance of us and our work. The fact that I had brought my family with me had legitimatized our living arrangement, and, in addition, my roles as husband and father were easier to identify with than the roles of professor and anthropologist. Since we were no longer commuters from Daraw, the villagers could observe our behavior at close range, as we could observe theirs; and so the barriers began to fall one by one.

*House in Abu Hor, Old Nubia.*

Walking in the village one afternoon, Hussein and I met Hakim Kamel, a villager who, in the perfunctory formula of the area, asked us in for tea. Aware that the invitation was not meant to be accepted, we nevertheless accepted with alacrity, our rudeness born of desperation, so overjoyed were we at having finally been invited into a home. Visibly embarrassed, Hakim led us into his guest room while his wife hastily prepared tea—a small event but for us a heart-lifting breakthrough, as soon afterward all the families in the village would be vying with one another to invite us in their turn. To be sure, there were some who maintained until the day we left Kanuba that we were spies, but these were a small minority. In general, people began to realize that no great purpose was served by concealment. Among those who saw us as fitting in with their plans to publicize the village, there were a few who expected us to bring about tangible benefits as well.

As field work progressed, I came to realize that many of the changes taking place in the village were being engineered largely by one man, Shatr Shalashil. This had not been immediately apparent because we had been told that other older men, such as Sheikh Muhammad and Hag Abdullah (the imam of the mosque) were the village leaders and that Shatr had originally been summoned to deal with us only because, having lived a long time in Cairo, he had had contact and experience with strangers before. In addition, Shatr's personal qualities did not correspond to our stereotypes of leadership. He seemed timid and vacillating rather than aggressive and decisive, and he often played the clown, making people laugh at or with him. He was the butt of much ridicule and joking and always publicly disavowed any desire for leadership or authority. It took months before we discerned that behind the clownish and dissembling mask was a clever, ambitious leader playing multiple roles while exercising a decisive influence on all decisions of village importance.

A good part of this book is devoted to Shatr's own account of his life and views, and it is in that respect a kind of autobiography. The life history is an old established genre in anthropology, and many of those to be found in the literature are of outstanding quality, not only as fine literature but in providing insight into a society's inner workings and a window on the meanings that life in a particular cultural setting has for the particular actor.[3] At the same time, however, much potential insight may be lost to the reader who lacks knowledge of the sociocultural setting and historical background of the events described. For this reason, I have placed Shatr's life story and philosophical observations within the cultural and historical framework of a particular Nubian village in Egypt, hoping that this will not only make his own actions more intelligible but will provide another set of data relating to how Nubian culture is perceived and used by its members during a period of significant change.

*11*

The material in the book arises from three main sources. The historical and cultural background of the Nubians is a distillation of travelers' reports, comments of historical scholars, and recollections of older informants. Material on village social life was gathered during our residence there in 1963–64. The life history was taken during the course of the field work, which included the usual methods of informant interviewing, participant observation in village activities, and formal interviews of samples of men and women.

Shatr told his story to Hussein Fahim in a series of interviews several evenings a week for more than three months. Although it took some time to establish the necessary relationship, once he had finally consented to give his story he became very cooperative—indeed, expansive—increasingly engrossed in expressing his views and in recalling past events. Before each session I would go over previous material with him, raising various questions and points to be covered. Immediately afterward I would review what had already been said, again taking notes and raising questions to be covered in later interviews. Though a student at the time with no previous experience in this kind of research, Hussein was very skillful in eliciting material in unobtrusive ways.

The following account is thus an attempt to portray the intersection of one man's life with the history and culture of his ethnic group within the environment of his community and society. As such, it is an affirmation of the view that stands as the epigraph of this book. To that, C. Wright Mills adds: "Neither the life of an individual nor the history of a society can be understood without understanding both. . . . By the fact of his living, [an individual] contributes, however minutely, to the shaping of his society, and to the course of its history, even as his is made by society and by its historical push and shove."[4]

Although each individual does contribute to the shape of his culture and society, the contributions are not of equal magnitude. We were especially fortunate to obtain our life history from a Nubian who has played a unique role in, and made a disproportionate impact on, the life of his community, a very unusual Nubian village in Upper Egypt. It is in large part due to his vision and efforts to convert his dreams to reality that the village of Kanuba in the region of Aswan has achieved its reputation for progress and success.

# NUBIAN HISTORY AND CULTURE

# 2

FROM THE BEGINNING TO THE NINETEENTH CENTURY

The portion of the Nile Valley that is historically known as Nubia extends from the first cataract at Aswan, Egypt, to the fifth cataract near Dongola in what is now Sudan. Before construction of the High Dam brought about the resettlement of all Nubians, Egyptian Nubia occupied some three hundred miles between Aswan and Wadi Halfa and included several linguistic subgroups. Between Aswan and Sebua were the Kenuz speakers; between Sebua and Korosko lived a Nubian group that spoke only a special dialect of Arabic; and from Korosko to Wadi Halfa were the Mahass speakers called the Fadija or Nubieen.

Because of its lack of economic potential, Nubia has been culturally and economically a marginal area from the beginning of the civilized history of the Middle East. Although it has been the site of several petty states and has even enjoyed political autonomy at times, economic poverty generally prevented the growth of large populations that could be organized into powerful kingdoms and also made the area undesirable as a site on which empires might establish important subcapitals. Often it has served as a buffer area between military kingdoms or as a frontier for the enrichment of others. The Egyptians exploited the region for gold, building stone, and copper, all of which were to be found in the eastern Nubian Desert, and also traded with its people. The mines at Wadi Allaqi supplied much of the gold of ancient Egypt and were often a source of conflict during the Christian and Islamic periods.

*13*

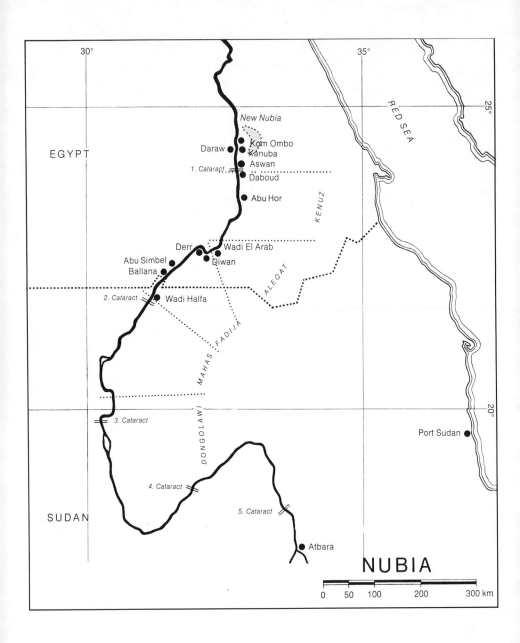

The first cataract at Aswan has always formed a boundary separating Upper Egypt from the less fertile lands of Nubia. To what extent
racial and linguistic differences existed between the peoples of the two
regions is unclear, but that the culture of Egypt dominated in early dy-
nastic times is evidenced by the many Egyptian temples and forts dotting
the Nubian Nile as well as by the great variety of Egyptian pottery and
other artifacts found in graves of the early periods.

Those who were probably the ancestors of today's Nubian speakers are believed to have entered and begun farming this area around the beginning of the fourth century A.D., when the political dominance of Roman Egypt to the north and the Great Kingdom of Meroë to the south was on the wane. Before this time the area had been abandoned for nearly seven hundred years, partly because of its use as a buffer zone between Egypt and Meroë, partly because the low level of the Nile had made agriculture a precarious pursuit. The immigrants appear to have been the "Nubatae" reported by Byzantine historians—a mountain or desert people from somewhere west of the Nile in present-day Sudan.

As the empires of Egypt and Meroë fell into weakness and decline, Nubia experienced a cultural and political flowering that would persist through most of the Christian period, until, in the late fourteenth century, the Arabs finally Islamized Nubia and reduced the area to a petty province of Egypt. Although the Ballana culture, which flourished from roughly A.D. 250 to A.D. 500, was strongly marked by Byzantine influences, a degree of cultural independence had developed among Nubian speakers who had occupied the area during the Roman-Merowitic period. A measure of political autonomy arose as well when the Nobatian kings, with capitals at Ballana and Qustal, were able to consolidate at least a portion of Lower Nubia into an independent state. This could not be called a unified autonomy as there were many petty chiefdoms; it was not until the early centuries of the Christian Era that unification was made possible by the larger populations that developed as a result of sakkia water-wheel irrigation.

The Christianization of Egypt began around 323, ten years after the Edict of Milan had established Christianity as the religion of Egypt. In 390 Emperor Theodosious 1 issued an edict for compulsory conversion of the country, but Nubia was still relatively independent of Egypt at this time. In 540 two rival missionaries left Constantinople for the purpose of converting the Nubians. The Monophysite (Jacobite) mission sent by Empress Theodora was more successful than the Melkite (Orthodox) mission sent by Emperor Justinian. Monophysite Christianity became the official religion of Nubia in 543, and, despite the seventh-century onslaught of Islam on Egypt, it remained the religion of the Nubians for almost a thousand years.

For Nubia, the early Christian period (c. 543–850) was one of great turmoil though not without its compensations. When King Merrcurious of Makuria conquered the Nobatia, Makuria and Nobatia merged into one kingdom, and between 650 and 710 the region from Aswan to Dongola was united under one ruler on a larger scale than ever before. This unification enabled Nubia to withstand Arab raids and thus better resist Islamization. The Classic Christian phase of Nubia (c. 850–1100), a period of relative autonomy and prosperity, coincided with the completed

Muslimization of Egypt, but the Muslim conversion of Nubia would be a gradual process over several, mostly embattled centuries. Arabs penetrated the area throughout the Christian period, and, if there were many battles between them, they had also been peacefully infiltrating Nubia from as early as the eighth century.

The period of Fatimid rule (909–1171) seems to have been an era of fairly peaceful relations between the two kingdoms. As early as the mid-tenth century there were Arab settlers in the area south of Aswan, and Muslims were working the gold mines in the eastern Nubian Desert. During Fatimid times, too, there was increased culture contact between Egypt and the "land of the blacks" south of Aswan owing to the use of black troops by the Fatimids and also because of an extensive slave trade, which, by reducing the number of young able-bodied Nubian men and by giving Arab traders a knowledge of the country, had the effect of aiding Arab influence on, and penetration of, the region.

The movement was not exclusively one-sided, however. The Nubians stoutly resisted Islam, and their armies made many incursions into Upper Egypt, even capturing Upper Egypt as far north as Idfu around 962. But the forces of history were against them. The Arab tribes that had settled in Upper Egypt maintained a constant pressure that finally resulted in extensive Islamic influence in the region. The capitulation of the area to the south of Mans is inscribed in the mosque of Dongola and dated 1317. But the Christian faith was not completely eradicated in the area for many years, and Christian Nubian pilgrims were reported in Palestine as late as the fifteenth century.

For much of the area, conversion was accomplished less by the sword than by Arabs marrying into powerful Nubian families. It is surprising that, despite the adoption of a patrilineal kinship system and of the many legal, religious, and moral customs of the Muslims, the Nubians managed to retain their indigenous languages, which persist as their first languages to the present day. How these social changes came about at the same time that the invaders were assimilating the indigenous culture and languages is a matter of conjecture. That Nubian Christianity had been only a thin veneer over indigenous folk beliefs and practices would help to explain the equally superficial substitution of Islam as an official religion. In addition, Arab immigrants were probably few in number compared with the indigenous population. Apparently Nubian wives transmitted to their children their own culture and languages instead of those of the conquerors.

The Mamluk period between the thirteenth and sixteenth centuries is obscure in Nubia. Although at least part of the area was abandoned for perhaps two hundred years, it appears to have been a time of both local rule and of continued gradual Arabization and Islamization. In the time of the Ottoman Sultan Selim I, who conquered Egypt in 1517, members of the Gharbiya tribe in Nubia are reported to have requested aid against their enemies, the Djoberae. In response, the sultan dispatched a force of several hundred Bosnian soldiers under the command of Hassan Koosy.

After driving the Djoberae to the south, Hassan Koosy set himself up as the governor of Lower Nubia, while he and other soldiers from Circassia and Kurdistan took Nubian wives and established themselves as a local gentry. The great variations in skin color and the occurrence of reddish hair which are still to be found among people of the Derr and Ibrim areas is continuing evidence of the absorption of these soldiers into the Nubian population. The descendants of Hassan Koosy—called Kushaf, a title for Ottoman Turkish provincial governors—continued to govern much of the area until the twentieth century and were largely left alone by the central government of Egypt as long as they paid their taxes.

The Nile Valley was one of the principal routes by which slaves were transported to the north, and for several centuries the Kushaf and wealthy merchants throughout Nubia participated actively in the trade, thereby adding to the general complexity of the Nubian experience. Many female slaves became concubines of Nubians, and further genetic admixtures occurred when groups of desert nomads, such as the Bisharin and Ababda, settled near the Nubians along the river and merged with them.

Thus, subject for centuries to many diverse racial, cultural, political, and economic influences, Nubia remained an economically marginal area and, after medieval Christian times, never regained its political autonomy but reverted again to the position of a subordinate buffer zone between more powerful states. Ecological poverty together with its political-geographical position placed Lower Nubia at the mercy of even small military forces. It was often devastated by maurading armies from north and south alike, intervillage warfare was frequent in times of political weakness, and population growth was further checked by the despotism of local rulers and by periodic epidemics. Conditions of instability and unrest continued through the late nineteenth century when the Mahdi Rebellion against the British in Sudan brought British troops to the area. From the seventeenth century onward there are fairly reliable reports of increasing numbers of Nubians in the large cities of Egypt.[5]

THE NINETEENTH AND TWENTIETH CENTURIES: ECONOMY

Before the Aswan dams of 1902, 1912, and 1933 diminished Nubian farmland, the Nubian economy was based on a subsistence agriculture whose nature had been determined by the area's topography. At their widest, the fields that could be cultivated along the banks of the Nile extended inland no more than two kilometers. In many places the huge pale yellow sand dunes of the desert encroached on the river's edge, making long stretches uninhabitable. Rocky bluffs often extended several kilometers, separating the villages from one another. The rough topography made extensive canal irrigation impossible, and the summer flood did not inundate vast tracts, enriching the soil with alluvium, as it did in more northern parts of the Nile Valley. Only tiny strips and a few islands were made eternally fertile by flooding; most of the land required water to be lifted day and night by oxen-powered water wheels.

In summer the unceasing desert sun of Nubia is relentless in its intensity, the heat sometimes reaching 52° C (125.6° F); as the Nubians say, "The ground is like fire and the wind like flame." Surprisingly, however, in winter people must dress warmly during the day to ward off the penetrating cold. Even during the summer months the desert cools to a remarkably reasonable temperature at night, making it possible for people to escape the heated mud-brick or stone houses to sleep under the open sky in their courtyards. Rain is so infrequent that people tend to recall the years in which it occurred. The archaeologist Budge has reported several violent rainstorms at Aswan near the turn of the twentieth century, and at Derr people remember a cloudburst in 1933.

Thus fields were small but the combination of constant sunshine, absence of strong winds, and great fertility of soil made it possible for the pre-dam visitor to Nubia to find the vast desert bleakness relieved by green patches, palm groves, and small fields of millet and barley along

*Harvesting millet, Old Nubia.*

the edges of the Nile. Breads made from millet and barley constituted the staple foods of the Nubians, and it was possible for them to harvest two and sometimes three crops of these grains per year. Millet was planted in September and October, just after the annual flood had subsided, and was harvested in late December or January. Barley and beans were planted in January and harvested around the middle of March. After the fruit of April, another crop of millet was planted in the most fertile areas to be harvested in July just before the annual flood, which generally lasted from late July through most of September.[6]

If millet was the staple, dates were the wealth of the Nubians, and their rich palm groves are what older people remember most vividly from pre-dam days. The palms were often thinly stretched along the banks of the Nile with the desert immediately behind them, but some regions, such as the plain of Diwan and Derr, were thick with trees—one Kanuba emigrant from that area said nostalgically, "The groves were so dense that you needed a lantern to find the river in the daytime." The almost total lack of rain, the great summer heat, and the closeness of the groves to the Nile produced a quality of date that was highly prized in Egypt and the Middle East. Trading as much as two-thirds of their date crop was the principal means by which the Nubians obtained needed goods for their own relatively deprived area. Indeed, the reduction of field area in recent times caused grain to become so scarce that even more dates had to be traded for such staples as wheat, beans, and millet.

The Nubians distinguished at least twenty-four different varieties of date, each of which was qualitatively rated on a value scale, each having its distinct uses. Dates were not a major food source, but they supplemented and diversified the simple Nubian diet with a molasses or "honey" made from dates, a date vinegar that was poured over boiled greens, and a variety of date that was kept in butter and eaten as a delicacy. Combined with the fermented dough of kabbid bread, made from millet, dates were used in the preparation of an alcoholic drink known as *harissa*. Since no sugar cane was grown in old Nubia, dates also provided the source of sugar in the diet. Dates were useful, too, because they could be dried and stored.

In addition to its importance as a source of commercial fruit, the date palm had many other uses in the Nubian economy. The fronds were woven into distinctive mat plates and sitting mats and were also used in the construction of beds. The solid parts of the trunk made the large timbers of sakkia water wheels and the roof beams of houses, while the fiber from inside the trunk was used for rope and cordage.

That the date palm was extremely important economically was reflected in the symbolic values attributed to it. The fruit symbolized the Nubian virtues of goodness, hospitality, and generosity and was associated with wealth and the good life in general. Weddings were frequently planned to coincide with the date harvest because people could better afford the expense at this time and also because men would return from the city to oversee the picking and sale of their fruit. To the present day the Nubian host sets before the guest in his house a large basket plate of dates and popcorn.

The Nubian diet was given additional variety by a number of other plants. Chief among these were lentils, the small loubia bean whose leaves were cooked as a green, a grass called *kasherengeg* which was also cooked as a green, and a species of summer melon. A popular tea called *karkedee* was made from a shrub. The Nubians also grew tobacco and, principally between Afia and Abu Simbel, a small amount of cotton.

After the dams had reduced their farmland, some of those who were least affected by the lake took up limited livestock breeding, which provided some compensation for their loss of land, although ecological limitations made the maintenance of large herds impossible. For the most part, livestock was scarce in Old Nubia, and except for very special occasions animals were seldom slaughtered for food. It was customary to sacrifice animals on the first, seventh, fifteenth, and fortieth day after a death and on other feast occasions, such as saints' days, marriages, and circumcisions. Although sheep or goats were most commonly slaughtered on these occasions, a family of any standing would slaughter cattle, which suggests that there may have been a few surplus cattle during the nineteenth century when the fields were larger. Camels, though often owned by wealthy families and used for processions in Nubian weddings and circumcisions during the nineteenth century, have been virtually non-existent in the area except for those belonging to Ababda and Bisharin nomads.

Because of the lack of clover, the few cattle that were necessary to run the water wheels had to subsist on dry millet stalks for most of the year. But cattle were essential because they made effective irrigation possible, and effective water-wheel irrigation was the cornerstone of Nubian agriculture. Many nineteenth-century travelers to Nubia have mentioned the ceaseless creaking of the wooden gears that kept them awake at night in their boats moored along the Nile banks.

Along the edges of the river, the thin strips of fertile soil that were annually inundated by the summer flood comprised a productive area too small to support a population of any size. Irrigation of the rich soils that lay a little farther from the river was accomplished to some degree by the ancient shadouf, a simple counterweighted lever-and-bucket water-lifting device. But this relatively inefficient instrument was used only for fruit trees and vegetable gardens along the edge of the richer soil area. For the irrigation of grain a more efficient means was necessary, and the sakkia water wheel, introduced to Nubia sometime during the late Ptolemaic or Roman period in Egypt, provided the solution.

*21*

*Washing a goat, Old Nubia.*

*Driving the sakkia, Old Nubia.*

*Carrying fodder, Kanuba.*

While the shadouf can lift water to a level of only eight or ten meters even when three of them are used in sequence, the sakkia can raise a much greater volume of water almost any distance if the vertical shaft can be sunk from the alluvial surface to the water level.[7]

Until the 1963–64 relocation, the sakkia remained Nubia's most important irrigation device. During the first few centuries following its introduction the Nubian population increased by more than threefold what it was just before abandonment. For the past 150 years the area has maintained a consistent population level at about 100,000 people while the population of Egypt has increased almost fifteen times over the same period.[8] The Nubian population has increased too, but the excess has been drained off to Cairo, Alexandria, and Khartoum.

Thus the paramount occupation of Old Nubia was farming. Men worked in the fields, planting and harvesting the millet and dates, hoeing the weeds, irrigating the two or three crops a year, working the shadoufs and sakkias. In contrast to the practice in Upper Egypt where the economic activities of women are more restricted than they are in Lower Egypt or Nubia, Nubian women also worked in the fields, weeding,

*23*

gathering animal fodder, caring for the animals, and helping to harvest the crops though seldom participating in the heavy work of planting or irrigation.


OCCUPATIONAL SPECIALIZATION

Of the few economic specializations to be found in Old Nubia, perhaps the clearest was that of the boatmen who either sailed their own boats or those owned by a family, tribe, or village. Overland transportation between Aswan and Wadi Halfa has always been difficult since there was no road between them until the recent resettlement. Most of the overland caravans from the south carrying slaves, ivory, and various trade goods to Lower Egypt passed over routes farther out in the Nubian Desert. The railroad constructed by the British in the twentieth century stopped at Aswan but recommenced its southward course below Wadi Halfa. Most of the trade in Nubia involved the transport of dates, henna, and other goods to Lower Egypt, and for the Nubians the most convenient artery was the Nile.

Before steamers between Aswan and Wadi Halfa were introduced in the late nineteenth century, sail-powered feluccas were the principal mode of transport in Nubia. Almost every village had at least one family that owned a boat; some districts were known for their skilled boatmen whose feluccas carried goods between the first and second cataracts. In addition to their participation in trade, the boats were used to carry people and animals to saints' festivals, weddings, and funerals within the local area or to transport villagers to relatives across the Nile. (For the most part the Nubians disdained fishing, an occupation dominated in Nubia by the Sa'idis, Upper Egyptians who lived among them.) As late as the recent evacuation there were still many felucca owners supplying transport services in Nubia.

In more recent times the only regular means of public transportation in Nubia was supplied by the postboat, which stopped at one village in each district once a week to take on or disembark people traveling to or from the city, to bring the mail, or to deliver such precious goods as tea, kerosene, and cigarettes. The arrival of this old riverboat with a large barge lashed to each side was the high point of the week for these districts. There were itinerant peddlers in Nubia as well, and until the 1963–64 resettlement they could be seen in all the villages traveling on donkeys, camels, or by boat, supplying people with sugar, salt, oil, metal tools, beads, and cloth. After the introduction of the postboat and the increased use of powered barges, a few men in each district were able to set up small permanent stores in competition with the peddlers and boat merchants.

*Nubian felucca, Old
Abu Hor.*

Nubian building techniques were passed down through families from generation to generation, but a few men were regarded as specialists. Some of these were responsible for local carpentry needs—for sakkia repair, the manufacture of beds, wooden chairs, donkey saddles, and the like; some were masons; and, in the Kenuz area especially, there were men who possessed the traditional skills for building the barrel-vaulted domes typical of the houses in this northernmost part of Nubia. House building was traditionally an activity of the extended family with all relatives taking part in the festive occasion, in exchange for only food and drink, under the direction of the owner and a master builder.

Before the recent resettlement, Nubian houses were notable for their beauty and sculptural qualities, especially in the Kenuz area where many elaborations of the vaulted structure could still be seen. The arched roofs were made of mud brick and then plastered over, eliminating the need for wooden ceilings, and when facing north were perfectly designed to catch even the slightest breeze. The placement of vaulted rooms in various positional combinations around a courtyard gave a very distinctive appearance to Kenuz housing compounds, but these houses were far more spacious and imaginative than those more typical of Nubia before the twentieth century.

Although there were families in Old Nubia who specialized in weaving and pottery making, the production of ordinary clothing and of everyday cookware was generally a domestic occupation. Informants report that most people fired their own bowls and water jars. Johann Burckhardt, a Swiss traveler passing through Nubia in 1813, noted that most of the homes had looms. Women wove gowns from wool, shirts from cotton, and baskets and mats from palm fronds.

Finally, a few specializations arose out of health and religious needs. The village barber, who also circumcised the boys, was a specialist at healing the sick—at applying suction to a patient's back by means of a heated bottle and at making the small facial slits (whose scars are still a distinguishing feature among many Nubians) that were supposed to treat eye disease. The female counterpart of the barber was the midwife, who, in addition to her role in childbirth, was expected to perform the clitoral excision ceremony for girls. Still another specialist was added in the late nineteenth century when Koranic schools for children, introduced by the Egyptian government into most districts of Nubia, were run by a local holy man, often blind or aged, whose principal task was to advance the memorization of the Koran.

It should be emphasized that most of these areas of expertise were sideline specialties and not full-time occupations. All Nubian men were farmers. Even long-term city migrants, attempting to preserve the illusion that urban service work was merely a temporary and inconvenient necessity, regarded their primary occupation as farming. But this condition would be permanently altered in the twentieth century by the construction and successive raisings of the Aswan dams, which, by destroying the traditional economic base of Nubian life, effected significant changes in Nubian society and culture as well.

The first Aswan Dam, constructed in 1902, inundated Lower Nubia as far as Dakka, which is about one hundred kilometers upstream from Aswan. After the first raising in 1912, the lake reached Sebua; after the second raising in 1933, the farmland of Nubia was submerged as far as the district of Ballana near the Sudanese border. The most recent dam, completed in 1970, has created a lake reaching the third cataract, two hundred kilometers into Sudan. Lower Nubia is now totally eliminated, and its population has been split into two resettlement projects. The

Egyptian Nubians have been removed to Kom Ombo in Aswan Province, while their brethren in Sudan now live in Khashemengerba near the Ethiopian border. Both groups were compensated by their respective governments with cash, new houses, and farmland. Whether the Nubians will remain in their new homes or whether in a few years some of them will return to their old country, finding sites for new villages when Lake Nasser has reached its final limits, remains to be seen. Past experience suggests that many may return, although the comparative lucrativeness of their new land and its proximity to schools, hospitals, movies, and other new facilities may keep most of them in the resettlement areas.

Whatever the future may hold for the Nubians, there can be no question that the succession of dams has brought about increased migration to cities, closer access to the changes accompanying the growing modernization of Egypt, and greater access to the various influences of Europe that are increasingly being felt throughout the Middle East. The building of the railway from Cairo to Aswan, the institution of the post-boat and of the Sudanese express boats that sailed the Nile between Aswan and Wadi Halfa, the continued movement up and down the river of the many feluccas and barges—all such regular means of transportation greatly facilitated the shipment of goods, increase in communication, and movement of people throughout Lower Nubia. At the same time, however, they have brought about a significant demographic shift.

Although Nubians had been migrating to the large cities of Egypt and Sudan for centuries, a core of young men had always remained in the villages, while a much greater percentage of the total population had remained in Nubia as a whole. After the catastrophic effects of the 1933 raising of the dam, however, the only agriculture permitted in the area was a marginal four-month crop. After 1933 the dam was closed down from October to June with the result that most of the arable land from Dabout to Ballana was underwater during the winter period; while from July to the beginning of October each year the water was down to its pre-dam level, allowing the Nubians only the briefest growing season. Since they could not cultivate traditional grains but were limited to growing animal fodder, cucumbers, and melons, Nubian farmers experienced great difficulties. The Kenuz were the hardest hit, but the hardship was felt in even the southernmost communities.

With their palm trees gone, their crop area radically reduced, and the growing season made brief and unpredictable despite irrigation projects here and there, thousands of Nubians unable to support themselves from the land alone had to seek livelihoods elsewhere. Many moved their entire families to urban centers, significantly changing both the age and sex ratio of Nubia since women, children, and old men could now perform the few tasks necessary for summer floodplain agriculture. Many who remained in Nubia moved their houses, clinging tenaciously to the dunes and cliffs along the river, but became totally dependent on remittances from husbands, fathers, and sons in urban centers.

The effects of migration were mitigated to a certain extent by the development after 1933 of government pumping stations at Allaqi, Gurta, Dakka, Tushka, and Ballana. In most cases, however, Nubian owners of this land either allowed it to lie uncultivated or leased it to Sa'idi share-croppers who moved to Nubia from Upper Egypt to cultivate it. That the absentee owners preferred to remain at their city jobs as doormen, cooks, and waiters indicates that the labor migration rate was attributable not only to a dam-related lack of economic resources in Nubia but to the allurements of the city as well.

Indeed, in view of the situation created by the dam, it is surprising that so many Nubians remained in Nubia at all. It was apparent at the time of the recent resettlement that many Egyptian Nubians, especially young adults, eagerly anticipated moving in order to live closer to their wives and husbands and to have greater opportunity to participate in the modernizing changes occurring in Egypt. Sixty years of Aswan dams had eroded loyalty to Nubia and softened the impact of resettlement.


SOCIOPOLITICAL ORGANIZATION

Before Islamization of the area south of the first cataract, Nubian tribal organization was matrilineal, inheritance passing from the brother to his sister's son. The patrilineal tribal structure, in which descent is reck-oned through the father's side with the resulting groups of relatives act-ing as cooperative units in economic activities and defense, became more widespread with the influx of Arab tribes into the region after the twelfth century. Marrying into Nubian ruling families and passing their inher-itance to their children according to the patrilineal mode of Islam cre-ated a means by which Arab chieftains could take over Nubian land and authority. From at least the fifteenth century, Nubian tribal structure has been organized on this basis.

Marriage within the local community was primarily a secular mat-ter involving a contract between two families. Although for the first mar-riage Nubians preferred to marry the daughters of their paternal uncle, the more important requirement was that the marriage partner be a relative—preferably a close relative from within the lineage but at all events from within the tribe; it was far less important that a second wife, whether acquired simultaneously or serially, be either a cousin or even a close relative. Although Nubians claim that very few men had plural wives in Old Nubia, the polygamy and easy divorce of Islam have long been Nubian customs.

Nubian tribes were broken down into lineages, at the head of which

*28*

were chiefs, or sheikhs, who held a number of financial and administrative responsibilities for the group—their most important duties including settling disputes within the lineage or representing their members in conflicts with members of other lineages. Although Nubian villages usually became mixtures of several tribes, loyalty at this time was to the lineage or tribe rather than to the village.

Thus each of the thirty-two districts of nineteenth-century Nubia contained a number of villages made up of several localized, patrilineal, generally endogamous tribes, one of which was usually wealthier and stronger than the others and tended to dominate them. Yet one cannot speak of a single political system characterizing Nubia as a whole because there were important differences in this respect between the Kenuz and the Fadija. The Kenuz in Upper Nubia tended to have autonomous tribes and districts with a certain equality among them, while in the Fadija region of Lower Nubia a definite system of social stratification came to modify the Arabic-style tribal structure common elsewhere.

Richer economic resources south of the Kenuz enabled some Fadija tribes to become wealthier and more powerful than others in each local district, and the arrival of the Kushaf after 1517 added still another level to the top of the social pyramid. A highly despotic ruling elite, the Kushaf imposed heavy taxes on the peasantry, often appropriating the land of those they had thus ruined and dividing it among their followers. At the same time they forced men of means to give themselves and their sons their daughters in marriage, by this means appropriating much of the wealth of their fathers-in-law. The local tribes into which the sons married were thereby elevated socially, ranking themselves according to their degree of closeness to the Kushaf families.

At the bottom of this stratification was a slave caste that varied in size with the waxing and waning of the slave trade between Egypt and Sudan. The genetically hybrid group that arose from the concubinage of slave women to Nubian men was noted earlier. Until slavery was finally abolished in Egypt in the late nineteenth century, much of the agricultural labor of Nubia had been performed by slaves, enabling many men the more easily to migrate to Cairo. Not surprisingly, slaves were more numerous among the Fadija, where they not only labored on farms but served in the homes of the wealthiest Kushaf rulers.

Although stratification continued to be an important determinant of status and behavior patterns among the Fadija, the power of the Kushaf diminished greatly during the nineteenth century; the rights of former slaves substantially increased; kinship ties and tribal structures weakened; and people became more dependent on reciprocal dyadic relationships.[9] By the time of the 1964 relocation, the local residential community and individual families had supplanted lineage and tribal structures in importance.

Throughout Nubia, disputes between the tribal members of local districts were regarded as tribal matters and were usually adjudicated by responsible members from both sides. There were reports of conflicts between districts as late as the early nineteenth century. Burckhardt reports a skirmish between Dabout amd Shalall when he passed through the area in 1813,[10] and older informants in Abu Hor have told me of battles with other districts in which their own fathers participated. This evidence coupled with the strong persistence of the Kenuz tribal system to the present day suggests an absence of supratribal political control in the north of Egyptian Nubia. In the southern area, petty-state governments had taken some judicial functions from the heads of tribes by the time Burckhardt reached the area, but tribal customs were still intact.

> If one Nubian happens to kill another he is obliged to pay the debt of blood to the family of the deceased, and a fine to the governors of six camels, a cow and seven sheep: or they may be taken from his relations. Every wound inflicted has its stated fine consisting of sheep and dhurra [millet], but varying in quantity according to the parts of the body wounded. This is an ancient Bedouin custom. . . .[11]

With the advent of the successive dams at Aswan, Nubia was brought increasingly within the administrative system of the central government of Egypt. District heads were appointed, and governors for cities, towns, and villages were elected. Growing numbers of Egyptian officials were sent into the area as directors of pumping stations, agricultural advisers, teachers in the new national schools, doctors, and medical assistants. These changes came about very slowly, however, and were not accelerated until after the 1952 revolution.


CEREMONIAL LIFE

Although urban Egyptians have long regarded them as primitives having little understanding of religion, the Nubians have for centuries been devout Sunni Muslims of the legalistic school of Maliki. In reality, however, the Nubian religious pattern combines elements from several sources. Until the 1930s a "popular" Islam that centered around saints' cults and the Sufi zikr ritual was prevalent in most areas. As labor migration brought increased urban contact around the turn of the twentieth century, orthodox Islam began to exert a greater influence in Nubia as in Egypt as a whole, although eliminating pre-Islamic pagan practices has remained a continuing problem for those attempting to complete the Islamization of the area.

In this century, significant numbers of Nubians have begun sharply to differentiate these patterns, and the most marked recent trend has been a progressive shift from pagan to more orthodox practice. The shift was furthered when a few Nubians educated at Al-Azhar schools from the Islamic University in Cairo returned to their villages and introduced religious reforms. In recent years, pressure toward greater orthodoxy in Nubia has been increased by members of the Ansar al-Sunna movement which has attempted to purge Islam of both its popular and pagan elements. In some villages the trend toward greater orthodoxy has produced factionalism and a widening divergence between men and women with regard to ritual and belief. Although a great overlap of religious patterns continues to characterize the area, popular Islam and traditional pagan practice are now found only among Nubian women, while orthodox religion is largely the prerogative of men.

The Nubian religious pattern is nevertheless predominantly ritualistic and places little emphasis on theology or doctrine. Indeed, during the nineteenth and early twentieth centuries, Nubian life was characterized by an almost continual round of ceremonial occasions. The most important of these were the Large and Small feasts, the rituals of Ramadan, the feast on the Prophet's birthday, and the many annual ceremonies commemorating the birthdays of saints. The cycle was enriched by rituals of Ashura, rituals of the twenty-seventh day of the Islamic month of Rageb, and rituals of a portentous evil day called Arba Maidour. These regular calendrical ceremonies were augmented by frequent family rituals on the occasions of birth, circumcision, marriage, and death. Even arrivals to and departures from a village, so common in a society dependent on labor migration, were ceremonialized.

POPULAR ISLAM

Throughout most of Nubia, popular Islam centered on saints' cults and the Sufistic zikr ritual. Each cult was associated with the shrine of an individual reputed to have been exceptionally pious during his lifetime. The holy man's miracles were frequently recounted; his relics were believed to bestow a blessing of miraculous power; and vows were made to the saint, who was asked to cure sickness, to relieve barrenness, to return a husband from Cairo, and so forth. Most Nubian shrines were not only the sites of an annual feast but of individual pilgrimages throughout the year. Some of the shrines were ancient ruins; others exhibited the traditional dome of mud brick; many others were simply circles of stones surrounding clay pots that had to be kept filled with Nile water. Offerings were made in the form of money, the burning of votive candles, or in the form of service—for example, carrying water to fill the pots.

The annual celebrations commemorating the birthdays of saints, usually held during the Arabic month of Shaban, involved a gathering of tribal members and friends from an entire district and its neighboring districts. The area around the shrine was decorated with painted flags, villagers were dressed in their brightest clothing, and each felucca bringing more guests was greeted with gunshot and song. Prayers of thanks were made to the saint for fulfilling requests; an animal was sacrificed that had been provided by members of the family, lineage, or tribe conducting the celebration; while feasting, dancing, singing, and processions to the Nile continued day and night.

In its purely religious aspects, the veneration of saints reflected practices widespread throughout the Muslim world. In Nubia, however, and especially among the Kenuz, the extraordinary elaboration of these cults was carried to such a degree that in many areas children built their own shrines and carried out elaborate annual celebrations of their own that were taken quite seriously by the adult community.

The Sufistic zikr ritual—a repetitive chanting of one of the names of God or of one of the adjectives referring to Him—was the other major pattern of popular Islam in Old Nubia. A revolt against the formalistic, legalistic aspects of orthodox Islam, Sufism originated during the eighth century A.D. and became a widespread movement emphasizing the individual mystical experience. During the fourteenth century, different ways of performing the zikr ritual, each stressing certain features of Islamic belief, began to spread over the Islamic world. Some "ways" became elaborate organizations with large followings and tight leadership hierarchies; others remained loosely organized and retained an emphasis on simple ritual and ascetic living. The Mirghanni way, brought into the Nubian region from Sudan around 1817 by its founder, Uhman el-Mirghanni, had little success north of Aswan but became the dominant Sufi order in Nubia.

As it was practiced in Nubia, the zikr ritual involved reciting a long poem from the Mirghanni book praising the Prophet Muhammad and recounting events of his life, chanting various phrases with repeated body movements and synchronized breath control. After reading some of the poetry, men gathered in a semicircle, swaying their bodies in unison and gradually increasing the tempo until some of them had achieved a state of trance. At a signal from the leader they would chant *"Allah hi! Allah hi!"* ("God is alive"). Incense would be passed around continually so that each participant could enhance his ecstatic communion by inhaling the smoke. Women were not permitted to participate in the zikr ritual, but they formed the audience and at various points in the chanting would utter wavering joy cries, some of them occasionally becoming possessed and dancing around the performers.

Zikrs were an integral part of Nubian life-cycle ceremonies and saints' festivals, of the Friday mosque service, and of other calendrical ceremonies. They were also performed separately and in some districts were performed regularly on Mondays and Thursdays. On certain occasions, such as the Prophet's birthday, the zikr was preceded by a feast and followed by recitations from the Koran. Both the performers and watching guests were served cinnamon tea before and during the chanting period.

## ORTHODOX ISLAM

In spite of their avid practice of popular Islam, the Nubians also possessed the common repertoire of orthodox Islamic customs. In addition to the regular Friday mosque service, orthodox observances included the Small Feast, the Large Feast, and the observances of the holy month of Ramadan. During Ramadan, generally a month of reduced economic activity, people fasted from sunrise to sunset, abstaining from food, drink, tobacco, and sexual intercourse. A mosque service was held each night, which most people attended immediately after breaking their daily fast with dates and water. Later in the evening they gathered at the homes of neighbors where special festive foods were served, and, as the water pipe passed from hand to hand, jokes, stories, and experiences were recounted far into the night.

The Small Feast that followed the month of Ramadan emphasized a happy spirit of friendship and communal solidarity. In the predawn of the first morning of the feast, the women of a Nubian village gathered at the cemetery chanting, "Greetings to you, inhabitants of the grave. May God forgive and rest your souls," and reciting the opening verse of the Koran for each dead relative. Newly cut palm fronds and bowls of water were placed at the ends of recent graves, and water and perfume were sprinkled over them, to appease the ghosts of the dead. Dates, wheat, and sweets were distributed to the children or left for the village poor to collect later. On the same morning, the village men gathered in the open air near the cemetery for a predawn prayer led by the imam. At the conclusion of the imam's speech, all the men would rush toward him believing that the first to shake his hand would receive the special blessing of the feast. When each member of the crowd had embraced those near him, tea and sweets were brought by young girls and unmarried youths.

In another custom of the Nubian Small Feast, all the men of the village, followed by the children dressed in new clothing, would visit each house in their own and neighboring villages where they would be offered special cookies, plates of sweet noodles, popcorn, dates, and small glasses of cinnamon tea. The holiday greeting was "live and see holidays," to which women replied, "You, too, live and see them."

For the Muslim Large Feast, which commemorates Allah's sparing of Ismail's life from sacrifice by Abraham, the Nubian custom was for every adult male in each household to sacrifice a sheep for the ram that Allah had miraculously substituted for Ismail. Again, a communal prayer was made in the open air at dawn, graves were visited, and new apparel was worn. Around midday a ceremonial food made from Nubian bread and the meat of the slaughtered animal was served to groups of neighbors gathered in several houses throughout the village.

SPIRIT BELIEFS

A good deal of Nubian daily behavior was directed toward recognizing, placating, or avoiding the hosts of good and evil spirits by whom they believed themselves to be surrounded. The demons, or jinn, who were associated with mountains and desert rather than with the Nile, were believed to occupy empty houses and to hover around garbage dumps and ashes awaiting their chance to occupy a human body, in which they produced symptoms of physical illness or insanity. Hence when embarking on a trip, crossing a threshold, or approaching a repository of garbage or ashes, Nubians uttered the opening verse of the Koran—"In the name of God, the merciful, the compassionate"—to protect themselves.

The good spirits, usually spoken of as angels, were believed to have been created at the same time as the Prophet Adam. To the Nubians, the most important of these were protectors of individuals who are deferred to in certain ritual gestures during Muslim prayer. The members of another group, called "angels of the Nile" or "people of the river," are mostly feminine and take a favorable attitude toward human beings (although river monsters who eat people and steal dates are also believed to inhabit the Nile), and these play a part in many Nubian ceremonies, especially those relating to the life cycle.

In addition, the ghosts of saints were believed to hover about their shrines at certain times and the ghosts of the dead to return to their graves during the Small Feast, when food, water, and palm fronds were placed at the cemetery for them. Indeed, much of the symbolism that pervades Nubian ceremonial life is aimed at pleasing or dispelling spirits. White clothing, green palm leaves and branches, gold, henna, incense, perfume, Nile water, ritual foods, animal sacrifices, and sharp iron objects—all were believed to be protective when used in conjunction with a symbolism built around the numbers three, seven, and forty.[12]

Although the Nubians were skilled at using hundreds of plants and mineral substances in various combinations, as well as in employing such techniques as cupping, bloodletting, searing with hot irons, making bodily incisions, and bonesetting, most of these techniques were also linked with supernatural treatment rituals. While a holy man might recommend that a person with a pain in his lower body rub his legs with oil or that one with persistent headaches submit to the pressure of a red-hot nail to his forehead, he might also perform a divination, make a charm, or recommend a visit to a shrine. Protective devices for fending off evil spirits that caused illness included such charms, knives, or other sharp pieces of iron. Widows and mothers giving birth kept sharp nails under their mattresses and needles under their pillows, and brides sewed needles into their shoes.

A principal method of dealing with emotional disorders, especially when all other remedies had failed, was the zar ceremony in which women dancing in a state of trance felt themselves to be possessed by angels of the Nile or by spirit holy men from places as distant as Cairo or Sudan. Zar rituals differed from other ceremonies in featuring a special drama enacted by the Sheikh of the Zar, a specialist who had himself been similarly cured of a serious mental disorder; by a great deal of wish-fulfillment behavior and an acting out of ordinarily repressed desires; and by fortunetelling and clairvoyant reports relating to the anxieties and wishes of people in the audience.

## LIFE-CYCLE CEREMONIES

The ceremonies attending birth, circumcision, marriage, and death in Nubia were lengthy and complex affairs mobilizing the whole community, involving great expense to the responsible families, and generally reflecting most of the elements of Nubian ceremonialism already described.

*Birth* Many ritual observances were held at the time of a birth and for forty days afterward while the mother was considered to be in a state of sacred vulnerability. Spirits of the Nile were believed to be particularly in evidence at this time, and the mother attempted to present to them as pleasing an image of herself as possible. Especially on the birth of her first child, she had to wear clean white clothing and her best golden ornaments. Immediately before and after the birth she was bathed in Nile water; when delivery was imminent, her hands and face were rubbed with henna and her eyes made up with the black cosmetic, kohl.

Before the delivery, knives or nails were placed under her pillow to defend against the jinn; dates, wheat, and perhaps an eggplant were placed in a bowl near her head; the midwife also lighted a bowl containing cotton and oil near her head to create a pleasing illumination for the Nile spirits; and close relatives made a ritual procession to the Nile where they threw food made of grain and milk to the Nile angels to assure an easy birth. During labor, the mother grasped two palm branches hanging above her, which were afterward kept in the room throughout her forty-day confinement.

When the baby was born, the midwife put onion and kohl in its eyes for cosmetic reasons as well as to protect them from disease; the baby's eyebrows were also marked with kohl to ensure that the eyes would be beautiful. Among other rituals, the midwife would bite into a fresh date and spit the particles into the baby's face seven times to assure beauty, health, and a melodious voice. On the third day after the birth another procession of neighborhood women went to the Nile, and similar processions were made on the seventh and fortieth days.

*Circumcision and excision*   The most common explanation for the customs of circumcision and clitoral excision is that they are religious obligations prescribed in the "Traditions," a body of sayings about the deeds and utterances of the Prophet Muhammad and his companions. Circumcision is also claimed to be a prophylactic measure promoting cleanliness, general bodily health, and fertility, and some believe that it purifies the boy for future participation in prayers. The excision operation for girls is an extreme measure taken to prevent the loss of virginity or a shameful premarital pregnancy that might otherwise result from what was believed to be the inherent sexual wildness of girls. For boys and girls alike, the preferred age for this ritual operation was between three and five.

Although a girl's excision was occasionally scheduled to coincide with a boy's circumcision, her ceremony was generally conducted quietly by women in the neighborhood. According to older Nubian informants, before the 1930s, boys' circumcision ceremonies were the greatest of all Nubian ritual events, though in terms of time, organization, and complexity they were generally less elaborate than weddings.

The four-day celebration of a circumcision was an important indicator of family prestige, and preparations were begun about fifteen days in advance. The large amounts of grain necessary to provide bread for the guests, the many baskets of dates that were passed out to the crowds, the perfume that was sprinkled on the celebrants, the provision of new clothing for the immediate family, the procurement of a camel and donkeys for processions to saints' tombs, and especially the provision of sacrificial animals, in some areas as many as four cattle—all constituted a considerable burden on family finances. Paternal relatives aided the father and his brothers and sisters in defraying initial expenses, while some of the other costs were made up by the obligatory small gifts of money, grain, or sugar given to family members during the ceremony.

On the first day of the celebration a sheep or cow was killed as an initiation of the feast activities, and singing and dancing continued throughout the evening. Early the next morning the boy was bathed and dressed in a long white gown of a very lightweight material to prevent irritation of the wound. Special gold necklaces belonging to his female relatives were hung around his neck while an elderly woman of the family put henna and kohl on his eyelids. Sometimes a woman's veil was placed over his head. These and other ritual actions were taken against jinn, who were believed to attack fertility, and to propitiate the Nile spirits, who could be dangerous if not pleased.

As the ritual preparation proceeded, the customary gifts of dates, sugar cones, wheat, and millet were presented, each loudly acknowledged and carefully recorded by a slave. In the courtyard, musicians performed and women danced while the boy in his ceremonial dress sat on a mat with his mother on his left and his father on his right. A plate of henna was placed before the mother and a bowl of water before the boy. The mother stuck a piece of henna onto the boy's forehead; the father affixed a gold coin to it, and the water in the bowl was used to wash the henna off. Then the mother's sister or an older female relative came forward to hold him for the operation.

Chanting "in the name of Allah, the compassionate, the merciful," the barber severed the foreskin, which shortly thereafter would be cast together with an old coin into the Nile to pacify the river spirits. The mother, who had been holding the boy's face away so that he would not become sterile by looking at his wound, cracked three eggs into a small bowl and held them to his nose to prevent fainting while the women intensified their dancing and drumming, uttering long joy cries, and at intervals calling out "congratulations to the groom." Followed by the singing and drumming crowd, the mother (or his sister if she was adult) carried the boy to the Nile where he was bathed.

After the operation, a procession was undertaken to a nearby saints' tomb, headed by the boy's father carrying a sword and the boy riding a donkey. At the shrine, a caretaker greeted the crowd, then slaughtered a cow for the ritual meal, following which the procession returned singing and dancing to the village, where festivities and zikr rituals continued for three days. At the culmination of the event, two cows were slaughtered for a large feast that was served to the crowds that had continued each day to gather from more distant villages.

For ten days after the celebration, the boy, under various taboos, was confined to the house, where he dined alone on pigeons, chickens, and eggs, which were believed to enhance virility and fertility. On the seventh day, a small ceremony was held featuring a zikr ritual in the evening and a meal for the guests. For forty days thereafter the boy was required to observe many precautions that would protect him against spirits.

The excision ceremony for girls was a measure of far greater severity and reflected a Nubian belief in the inherent wantonness of women. On the eve of the operation the child was dressed in new garments and adorned with gold, her eyes made up with kohl, and her hands and feet dyed with henna. On the following morning a few neighborhood women gathered at the house. A bowl was placed beneath the girl to catch the blood, and while several women spread her legs apart the midwife quickly excised the clitoris, the labia minora, and part of the labia majora with a razor, following which the wound was washed, raw egg and green henna were applied, and her legs were tied together.

While the ordeal was in progress, incense was burned to frighten away jinn, and the women chanted: "Come, you are now a woman; you become a bride; bring her groom now; bring her a penis, she is ready for intercourse," and so on, punctuated by joy cries interspersed with protective Koranic incantations. Afterward, the mother and closest female relative distributed dates, candy, popcorn, and tea to the visiting women and sprinkled them with perfume. Everyone congratulated the girl, some giving small gifts to her and her mother. The child's legs might remain tied together for forty days following the operation, but she was usually regarded as healed after seven days. The healing process generally provided scar tissue for the complete closure of the vulva except for a small urination orifice kept open by a match or reed tube.

*Marriage*   Perhaps no life-cycle event held greater importance for the Nubians than marriage, which symbolized both family unity and community solidarity. Weddings were usually scheduled to coincide with the date harvest, partly to assure the attendance of men who would be returning from the city to oversee their annual economic affairs. Hence marriage was symbolically associated with the abundance of harvest and with the pleasurable anticipation of seeing returning loved ones again.

Marriage also validated adult status and ushered the individual into full social standing. A person was regarded as not fully Muslim and thus not a completed social being until married. Until this threshold had been crossed, men had no vote in community affairs and women could not prove their maturity or social 'worth. Indeed, in those villages in which women outnumbered men by two to one and where most resident men were either children or elderly retirees, marriage was the major preoccupation and high point of a woman's life.

Finally, a wedding offered the supreme opportunity for a family to demonstrate its prestige, and it was incumbent for each to display as much wealth and generosity as possible. The size of the marriage payment, the number and types of animals slaughtered, the abundance of festive foods, the quality and amounts of new clothing and jewelry, the frequency with which perfume was sprinkled on the guests, the amount of incense burned, the number and social ranking of guests and the distances they traveled to arrive—all were carefully observed. The custom of giving small gifts to be repaid on similar occasions reinforced the network of obligatory reciprocal ties that underlay the social organization of the Nubian community.

The official betrothal, marked by a visit to the bride's house of a delegation of male members and friends of the groom's family, sometimes took place several years before the wedding and was often preceded by a prior understanding between the couple's parents. From the betrothal until the wedding, however, the Nubian bride and groom were required to avoid seeing each other, as contacts were believed to augur evil for the marriage and to endanger the chances for offspring.

Preparations were begun about a month before the wedding. Millet was ground, bread and ceremonial dishes were made, and the wedding chamber at the house of the bride's father was whitewashed. For fifteen nights before the wedding, people gathered near the groom's house to dance. The first dancing line was made up of older women with the younger girls remaining decorously in the background; but slaves also danced in the front lines and were often prominent in performances in which women danced individually within a circle of clapping hands. Older female relatives of the betrothed carried canes which they shook aloft in rhythm.

On the eve of the ceremony (called "the night of the slaughter"), a slave carried to the bride's house as a gift from the groom a mat basket full of sweet noodles and one or two cones of sugar, which the bride's mother refilled with millet or wheat for return to the groom's house. On the afternoon of this day, certain of the village men publicly butchered the groom's cow and the slaves prepared a feast, while another cow was slaughtered and cooked at the bride's house. After the evening feast, the groom, accompanied by a slave carrying a water pitcher and a bowl, and by a child with a pot of burning incense, mounted a camel, and a procession was formed to sing and dance its way to the bride's house.

The bride, who had been veiled and secluded all this time, was seated on a mat in her parents' bridal chamber while henna was applied to her body, hands, and feet by an older female relative. The following morning, henna was again applied to the bride, her hair curled into tiny ringlets by a specialist in hairdressing, and her lips tattooed with designs. Neighborhood women continued to contribute small gifts, and while these were being recorded the groom sat on a chair outside the house, his hands mounded with henna. Before dawn, he ran to the Nile to wash off this henna as an offering to the river spirits while the women sang and gave joy cries.

On the day of the wedding, an important noon meal was held at the groom's house and another at the house of the bride. The groom's lunch was the more important because this was the occasion of signing the marriage contract and of finalizing the amount of the marriage payment—generally cloth and clothing, silver bracelets, and an amount of money varying between five and thirty Egyptian pounds—by the village marriage official. When the negotiations had been concluded, a procession of men moved to the bride's home where the groom awaited them in his festive clothing. Before the second lunch, the marriage official examined the young man's knowledge of the Koran, asking him to recite several verses from the holy book. The official then observed, "Your son knows the Koran well. What will be his reward for this?" The father (or other male relatives) and mother replied that they would give him a certain number of palm trees planted in a certain area, or they might say in an exaggerated manner that they would give him twenty sakkias in such and such a place.

Dancing recommenced near sunset, the two families involved in the wedding each slaughtered a sheep, and still another procession moved from the groom's to the bride's house amid great shouting, gunshot, and drumming. (In earlier times there was at this point a mock battle between the two families in which the groom and his escort were thrashed with whips.) Before entering the house, the groom was greeted by the bride's family and offered sweetened water or milk symbolizing a happy wedded life for the couple. As he and his friends watched from an honored place, from time to time signaling for perfume to be sprinkled on the guests, singing and dancing continued outside the house.

At this time the bride—newly bathed, dyed with henna, and wearing new underclothing, a colored gallabeya with a blue dress over it, two colored veils, and a white shawl—awaited the groom in the decorated bridal chamber, which was divided into two parts. The bride stayed behind a curtain that would remain up for forty days after the wedding and was attended by a special slave who brought her food and drink, dressed and undressed her, and generally looked after her needs during her period of seclusion. In the front of the chamber the groom received his guests during this period.

During the evening, the groom and a few of his friends were permitted to penetrate the bride's chamber by means of a ritual in which they attempted first to bribe the slave guarding the door with a few coins but finally forcing entry into the bride's presence. As the groom burst through the door, the bride's mother spat on him and splashed him with milk, symbolizing the bride's purity, then demanded payment for allowing him into the room. After more bargaining, he gave a few coins, but the bride still refused him permission to see her face on this first night. After the refusal, he touched her forehead with his sword, pulled off her white shawl, spread it on the floor, knelt upon it and prayed. In some districts, he then sprayed Nile water over her veiled face from his mouth, and, placing his foot upon her, made several slight incisions in the calf of her leg. Before leaving the chamber, the groom and his friends scattered

*Sleeping room for married couple, Old Diwan.*

millet and sometimes dates over the bride to promote life and fertility, then passed the night in another room joking until morning. Several of the friends and relatives of the bride joined her in her own chamber through the night since consummation of the marriage had to await the next day.

Until relocation, the following customs were preserved in the Kenuz and Arabic-speaking sections of Nubia and, according to some older informants, among the Fadija as well. In the morning, the bride and groom went to separate places on the Nile in the company of friends and relatives. The groom stepped over some burning palm leaves in the doorway and, carrying his sword before him, dipped it three times into the Nile before handing it to his attending boy and washing some of the henna from his hands, feet, and forehead. In the Kenuz area, and probably among the Fadija also, boys chased and beat him lightly with whips as he approached the river. A short distance away, the bride bathed her hands, feet, and face while girls sang, gave joy cries, and danced. On returning to the house, the groom again stepped over the fire and tapped the door lintel three times before entering. As her attendants scattered Nile water and palm fronds into the doorway before her, the bride joined him.

*Decorations for sleeping room of bride and groom, Dahmit, Old Nubia.*

The bride now reentered her own quarters, replaced her veils, and sat quietly on her mat. The groom returned shortly thereafter and repeated the bargaining ritual, this time attempting to persuade her to speak to him. Shaking her head, she coyly refused his coins while he continued to increase the offer until he had reached a pound or two. Finally, at the urging of her attendant, the girl, with feigned pouting reluctance, removed her veils. Everyone then left the quarters except the attendant, who, because of the girl's excision closure, might be needed to assist the groom in deflowering her. Before the consummation could take place, a special leather belt with fine leather strings hanging down in a skirtlike fashion had to be removed from the bride. This garment, which symbolized virginity, had been worn by the girl up to the time of the marriage. Some informants claim that this was worn under the dress, though there is evidence that it was the principal outer garment of unmarried girls in the past.

Wedding
procession,
Kanuba.

Courtesy Samiha El Katsha.

Consummation was often a traumatic event for bride and groom alike, whose fears were magnified by a belief that genital blood attracted spirits dangerous to virility, fertility, and health. For several years the girl had been conditioned to look forward to the occasion that would make her the center of village attention. It had been emphasized during her childhood and at her excision that on her marriage she would take her place as a woman with adult rights and greater freedom to determine her own affairs. At the same time, however, largely ignorant of what to expect from her husband during private moments, conditioned to feel shame about sexual matters, and frightened of intimate contact with a man, girls were often so terrified that, although the groom was honor bound to perform intercourse on the wedding night, consummation was sometimes delayed for several years.

Although the bride was required to remain in the bridal chamber for forty days and to sit on a mat behind the curtain for seven of them, the groom was strictly confined for only seven days. The process of marital adjustment was aided by this custom, for, under many taboos, they were absolved of all normal obligations and could therefore devote their attention to learning to know each other. After some time had elapsed, the guests again assembled to congratulate the couple, the bride's attendant sometimes exhibiting a bloodstained cloth as proof of the girl's virginity. Guests were offered food or candy and sprinkled with perfume or incense to disperse any lingering spirits. As a goodwill offering, the groom sent ceremonial food to various houses in the neighborhood while the women continued to sing, dance, and utter joy cries outside the bridal chamber.

When the groom's period of confinement was over, he appeared each morning before the curtain to accept his guests' congratulations. To symbolize his role as groom, as well as to ward off evil spirits, he carried a sword, wore a dagger strapped to his upper arm, and was also equipped with a whip, which, if a circumcision had taken place at the same time as the wedding, was carried by the circumcised boy who accompanied him on his brief visits around the village. Ceremonies carried out on the third, seventh, fifteenth, and fortieth days after the wedding involved continuing processions between the houses of the two families as well as singing, dancing, animal sacrifices, and feasts.[13]

*Death*    Like other Nubian life-cycle occasions, funerals were tremendously important social events that mobilized the entire community in support of the bereaved family and involved everyone in a lengthy complex of ceremonials. On no other ceremonial occasion were the social obligations of such compelling force as at death, however, and people who failed to conform to custom were socially ostracized.

When a death occurred in Old Nubia, a piercing wail by nearby women immediately informed the village of the event and its location. Women dressed themselves in black and hurried to the home of the deceased, whose family had gathered in their courtyard to accept condolences; the village men followed when their other activities had been concluded. Women of the family removed all jewelry, dressed in black, tied ropes around their waist, and lashed rolled-up mats to their back together with some garment of the deceased; they also unbraided their hair, smeared mud on their heads, and applied blue dye to their faces. During the death dance, older female relatives waved green palm sticks.

On entering the house each woman blackened her hands and face with ashes from a pot near the door and offered condolence by embracing members of the bereaved family and crying alternately on each shoulder. Joining the circling death dance, they beat their breasts, tore their clothing, and poured dust over their heads—actions aimed at placating the ghost. A man, who was required to be more dignified, simply pressed his face to the shoulders of the bereaved, repeating, "It is God's will." Loosening his turban, he then joined the other men in a special mourning area composed of palm branches and mats. The close male relatives of the deceased wore their turbans hanging loose for seven days (during which they were prohibited from shaving or entering their own houses), then left an end of turban hanging down their backs until forty days had been completed.

*Funeral condolence, Kanuba.*

While a group of older men sewed the shroud, older relatives of the same sex as the deceased washed the body, rubbed it with henna, and sprinkled it with perfume. After a final purification with incense, the corpse was placed in the shroud, which was tied with three knots, and was then placed on a bed made from palms, with green palm fronds arching over the head and feet. Followed by men, women, and children in

*45*

procession, four close relatives carried the bier to the cemetery, where a grave had already been dug by men sent ahead of the procession. When the mourners arrived, the body was wrapped in a blanket, lowered into the cavity, and placed facing Mecca.

During and after the burial, the imam of the mosque read verses from the Koran, an animal was sacrificed, and women continued their wail from some distance away. The grave was humped with dirt, a flat stone was placed upright at each end, and parts of the sacrificed sheep or goat were left on top. Grains of millet placed on top of the grave were watered for forty days afterward, and a clay bowl placed at the foot of the grave had to be kept filled with water for the spirit for the same forty days. After the burial, each person recited the opening verse of the Koran, and the group returned to the house of the bereaved to fulfill their post-burial obligations.

Because the soul of the deceased was believed to linger nearby for forty days—going afterward to a large tree where it awaited entrance to Paradise or to a deep well where it remained until it descended to Hell—various rituals were performed and taboos observed during this period. Babies under forty days of age and recently circumcised children were believed to be in danger. Menstruating women, banned from participating in the funeral, were also prohibited from visiting graves. Women of the family could not go to the market for forty days, and close relatives refrained from attending weddings, circumcisions, or feasts for the coming year.

A widow was placed under the severest constraints of all. Dressed in black, her head shaved, she sat and slept on a special mourning mat for four months and ten days, at the conclusion of which she offered the mat to the water spirits of the Nile. For the first three days she fasted; for the first seven days she could neither walk nor change her clothing. The only exception to her long seclusion was a requirement that she visit the cemetery on each of the first forty days to water her husband's grave, change the green palm fronds, and place dates or grain upon it.

On the third day after the death, a sheep was slaughtered and special ceremonies were performed. Men read parts of the Koran in their mourning area and made a procession to the grave where they chanted "La elaha eh la Allah" seventy thousand times, on each repetition dropping upon the grave a tiny stone that symbolized the prayer. When the grave had been sprinkled with water, close relatives replaced their turbans, leaving one end hanging over the shoulder. The group then returned to the mourning area to continue the vigil, the women distributing dates and sweets to children or to passing strangers after the men had left the cemetery.

At the Nile, women washed the deceased's clothing, which was left on the bank for passing travelers; afterward washing their faces to cool the face of the spirit and sitting quietly for a few moments to help relax the body in the grave. The river spirits were offered food and henna accompanied by the incantations of women who were believed to have relationships with them. Returning from the Nile, each woman picked up a palm frond, which, while repeating the opening verse of the Koran, she cast into the doorway of the house, to disperse the jinn, before entering.

On the evening of this day—as well as on the seventh, fifteenth, and fortieth days if the bereaved family could afford it—a ritual feast was made from the sacrificed animal, and dates and cinnamon tea were served. After this, the male mourning mats were ritually rolled up and guests from distant villages began their return home, although close relatives or special friends might stay until the seventh or fifteenth day. For fifteen days after burial, close female relatives of the decased, each carrying an offering of seven dates, visited the grave and sprinkled water on it. On the fortieth day the women placed palm fronds at each end of the grave, passed incense over it, and poured libations of water on it. This ceremony bade farewell to the spirit, which would not return again except for the Small Feast or for any annual commemorative feast held in its memory.

# SOCIAL LIFE IN KANUBA

## 3

Separated from one another by rocky hills and dunes, the typical villages and hamlets of Old Nubia ranged in proximity from several miles apart to the immediate adjacency of settlements in the small flood plains. Until the 1963–64 resettlement, no road had penetrated Nubia. The railroad from Cairo to Aswan constructed by the British in the late nineteenth century renewed its southward course below the Egyptian border, so that the people of Lower Nubia remained remote from even Wadi Halfa and Aswan. In contrast, after their resettlement near Daraw in 1933, the Nubians of the village of Kanuba found themselves in a busy, bustling world whose pace of life would be even more accelerated after the Nasser revolution of 1952.

The Nubians who settled on the eastern edge of Daraw, about three kilometers from its center, were to some extent compensated for the loss of the river as a means of easy transportation by the construction of a highway, paved in the 1950s, that connected Idfu with Aswan. A regular bus service now facilitates travel to these towns and to Kom Ombo, while for the longer trips to Cairo and Alexandria the railway station at Daraw is a great convenience. Although the residents of Kanuba still rely on donkey and foot travel in the immediate vicinity of Daraw, the highway and railroad have given them a considerable advantage in geographical mobility over their relatives who remained in Old Nubia.

Until recently, Kanuba was administratively a part of Daraw, a town of more than 14,000 people loosely united by a governmentally imposed administrative structure with its town officials, school, hospital, police station, post office, telegraph office, and train station; by two shrines whose presence has made Daraw a minor religious center in Upper Egypt; and above all by a large market which is the town's economic base. In addition to its many permanent stalls offering a range of goods from vegetables and meats to cloth and tinware, the Daraw market is one of the locations of the rotating market system of southern Aswan Province, as well as a livestock market and transfer point for camels brought from Sudan.

Daraw is composed of several identity groups whose individual customs are not sufficiently distinctive to warrant use of the term subculture. Although there is considerable overlap and mixing among them, each section of Daraw is made up predominantly of one such group; each has relative autonomy over its own internal affairs; and marriages are generally kept within them. With respect to numbers and prestige, the dominant identity groups are the Ga'afra, the Sons of Sheikh Amer (the original inhabitants), and the Ababda.

A proud, disdainful people who claim links of close descent with the family of the prophet Muhammad, the Ga'afra, with about 4,000 members, constitutes the most numerous and highest ranking group in Daraw. Next is a large Sa'idi clan whose more than 3,000 members are called the Sons of Sheikh Amer, a saint from whom they claim descent. A group of Ababda, who claim almost as long a continuing residence in the area as the Sons of Sheikh Amer, number around 1,400 and are concentrated in two separate enclaves. Most of the Ababda in Egypt and Sudan still live the life of camel nomads in the eastern desert. The branch in Daraw, however, became sedentarized many generations ago, and, until the 1952 revolution removed the large tracts of land that were the basis of their power, they had provided the head men of Daraw during the twentieth century.

The Nubians, who comprise the next most numerous segment of the Daraw population, divide among themselves according to their subcultural regions of Nubia. The largest and most firmly rooted group in Daraw consists of the more than 1,400 Kenuz, largely from the district of Abu Hor, who migrated when their lands were flooded by the first raising of the Aswan Dam in 1912. The second major group is made up of the inhabitants of Kanuba—in effect a separate village of some 496 individuals of both Kenuz and Fadija origins—who founded their village after the second raising of the dam in 1933. The Mahass speakers, or Fadija, constitute the dominant group of nearly 350 people in Kanuba. The Kenuz in Kanuba, who migrated from Nubia in 1933 instead of 1912, number about 146 people and are related to the Kenuz of Daraw proper.

After the Nubians, the next largest identity group in Daraw is composed of about 1,000 people, called the Muhagereen, who are mostly descendants of those who migrated to the area as a result of the disorder accompanying the Mahdi Rebellion in Sudan during the late nineteenth century. In addition to the Sons of Sheikh Amer, two other groups of Saudis in Daraw—the Quftia and the Kaliheen, both from the region near Qena—are represented by only a few families and probably constitute no more than 500 people. The Kaliheen have founded a miniature village on a small piece of purchased land just south of Kanuba, while the Quftia have caused a problem for some of the Nubians by squatting on their land.

The colorful human variation in Daraw is also enriched by the frequent appearance of the Bisharin and Rashayda, groups of nomadic herdsmen living in the deserts of southern Egypt and northeastern Sudan, who come to the Daraw market with camels from the south; and by the Hallab, gypsylike traders and tinkers who settle on the outskirts of towns and large villages for months at a time. All these various affiliations are of great importance because, as the bases of personal identification and community status of individuals, they determine the course of local politics in Daraw, where voting in elections is solidly along identity-group lines.

RURAL-URBAN CIRCULATION

Although Kanuba is not unique among Nubian villages in its intricate linkages with urban life, it is difficult to convey adequately the degree to which its residents surpass the residents of other Egyptian villages in urbanity and sophistication or the extent of their greater involvement with matters and people outside their immediate community. So greatly does Kanuba encompass both rural village and urban Egyptian worlds that its society might even be termed bicultural.

Conditions of sexual imbalance arising from the effects of labor migration are partly responsible for this. In Old Nubia, just before the 1933 resettlement, there were about two females to each male, but the males remaining in the villages were for the most part either children or old men. Today in Kanuba there are approximately ten females to seven males. The situation is less extreme than it was earlier because a core of vital young men has been able to find good jobs in the area. As table 1 illustrates, however, the sexual composition of the village remains imbalanced.

Many women have lost husbands through death or divorce, while more than one-third of the women currently married have husbands working in the city. These men return to Kanuba two or three times a year for Islamic feasts, weddings, vacations, or emergencies. About once a year their wives, or one of their children, visit the urban center. Hence a constant pressure to travel in both directions, coupled with the easier access to travel offered by the railroad connecting Aswan with Cairo, results in frequent urban-rural exposure and communication.

TABLE 1    *Sexual imbalance in Kanuba*

|  | Fadija | Kenuz | Totals | Total | Approx. % |
|---|---|---|---|---|---|
| Widows | 43 | 15 | 58 | 72 | 47% |
| Divorcees | 12 | 2 | 14 | | |
| Husbands away working | 20 | 8 | 28 | | |
| Husbands in village | 34 | 20 | 54 | 82 | 53% |
| Total women married at least once | 109 | 45 | 154 | | 100% |

Before resettlement, the rural-urban trip could be made only by the expensive, time-consuming means of taking the postboat to Aswan and then the train to Cairo. Because of its proximity to Aswan, Kanuba has been a convenient way station for travelers in both directions of this two-stage travel pattern since 1933. As the visiting relatives of one or another family stopped for a few days in transit north to Cairo or Alexandria or south to Nubia, the Kanubans were able to keep more abreast than their Upper Egyptian peasant neighbors of events both in the cities of Egypt and in their country of origin.

Rural-urban circulation has also been increased by the presence in the city of close relatives who, because of their kinship ties, remain involved in the Nubian system of reciprocities. Our study revealed the names and locations of 122 primary relatives (parents, children, or siblings) of Kanuban adults living outside the village. This does not adequately reflect the dispersion of families, however, because we were told of 89 other primary relatives whose names and locations we could not obtain, and there are probably 12 to 15 more who eluded our count. It is safe to say that at least 200 primary relatives of Kanuban adults live outside the village, surprisingly few of them in Nubia. This nonresident shadow population of Kanuba must nevertheless be regarded as a socially real part of the village because its members not only visit frequently but

TABLE 2   *Primary relatives of adults living outside Kanuba*

|  | Siblings | Children | Parents | Total |
|---|---|---|---|---|
| Cairo | 16 | 43 | 1 | 60 |
| Alexandria | 10 | 25 | 1 | 36 |
| Suez | 0 | 4 | 0 | 4 |
| Other cities north of Aswan Province | 4 | 6 | 0 | 10 |
| Aswan | 2 | 2 | 0 | 4 |
| Nubia | 2 | 6 | 0 | 8 |
|  |  |  |  | 122 |

have claims to property, form part of the pool within which village marriages are arranged, and are obligated in the reciprocity system of familial relationships.

Within Kanuba there are to be found three types of viable residential units—that is, groups of people living together and having some degree of mutual economic interdependence. Table 3 indicates the high frequency of partial family households found in the village, which in turn reflects the effects of labor migration and of an imbalanced sexual ratio.

The travel patterns of Kanuba residents provide still another touchstone of the village's degree of urban involvement. Our study revealed that for village men over thirty years of age, the average length of urban experience in Cairo, Alexandria, Suez, or Port Said was fifteen years; there was no man of working age who had not spent at least two years in an urban center. Two adult Kanuban men had never visited their villages of origin in Nubia, and none who had grown to adulthood after the 1933 migration had returned to their villages in Old Nubia for more than a few weeks.

Kanuban women have had less contact with the urban milieu than men, but their experience is surprisingly extensive and does not conform to the stereotype of immobile women that is commonly associated with peasant village life. A representative sample of one-third of the adult women of the village revealed that nine had lived their entire lives in the city before moving to Kanuba, usually after marrying a village man or losing a husband. Only two of those interviewed had never visited Cairo or Alexandria. Among those who had not grown up in the city, the average number of prolonged urban living experiences was four. Two women had lived in the city for more than fifteen years; eleven had lived there more than five years; twenty-five had lived in a city from one to five

TABLE 3 *Households in Kanuba*

*Independent living units with economic interdependence among members*

| | Fadija | Kenuz | Totals |
|---|---|---|---|
| 1. Nuclear families | | | |
| a. Married man, wife, and unmarried children | 13 | 5 | 18 |
| b. Man and wife only | 2 | 0 | 2 |
| 2. Compound families | | | |
| a. Spouses with children and one or more of their parents and/or unmarried brothers, sisters, aunts, uncles, etc. | 20 | 8 | 28 |
| b. Brothers and/or sisters with or without spouses and children | 2 | 0 | 2 |
| 3. Incomplete families | | | |
| a. Widows or widowers with or without children | 16 | 5 | 21 |
| b. Divorcees with children | 0 | 0 | 0 |
| c. Widows or divorcees alone | 8 | 2 | 10 |
| d. Wives with husband away working and children | 8 | 0 | 8 |
| e. Bachelors or spinsters alone (includes village doctor) | 2 | 0 | 2 |
| f. Grandparents and grandchildren | 0 | 1 | 1 |
| | 71 | 21 | 92 |

years. Only five of those interviewed had had less than one year of urban experience.

Finally, degree of urban involvement is also reflected in the general educational level of the Kanubans. In sharp contrast with the less than 30 percent literacy typical of Egypt as a whole at the time of our study, the literacy rate of Kanuba men was almost 90 percent—only six adult men were illiterate. Ten men had completed secondary school or higher. Twelve of the older men had attended the traditional Koranic schools in Nubia in which only reading, counting, and Koran recitation were taught; but these—as well as fourteen men who had attended but not completed primary school—were functionally literate, having extended their reading and writing skills in the course of their urban work. Four men in Kanuba knew enough English to carry on simple conversations with me, and one of these was a teacher of English at the intermediate school in Daraw. Women, on the other hand, were far less educated. Seventy-seven percent of them could neither read nor write, and none had gone beyond a primary school education.


MARRIAGE PATTERNS

That the Nubians have maintained their own languages and traditions over centuries of close contact with dominating foreign cultures is partly attributable to their zealous attempts to keep intact their traditional rules governing marriage. The patrilineal parallel cousin is the preferred marriage partner, but, since not everyone can marry a paternal cousin, the imperative is to marry among one's relatives, especially among one's close relatives, following a scale of diminishing desirability.

TABLE 4  *Scale of marriage desirability*

*Near relatives*

    1a. Father's brother's daughter or his sister

    1b. Father's sister's daughter or son

    1c. Mother's brother's daughter or son

    1d. Mother's sister's daughter or son

    2a. Near relative of father's family—e.g., father's brother's daughter or son or their children; father's sister's son or daughter or their children

    2b. Near relative of mother's family (other than category 1)—daughter or son or their children, or mother's sister's daughter or son

*Distant relatives traceable*

    3. Distant relative of father's or mother's side

    4. Member of tribes that have traditionally provided wives but that are not already in categories 1, 2, or 3

    5. Nubian of same culture—e.g., Kenuz, Fadija, or "Arab"

    6. Nubians of another subculture

    7. Non-Nubian Muslim

*54*

The ideal combination is between people related in two of the preferred ways—i.e., a man who marries a woman who is both his father's brother's daughter and his mother's sister's daughter has made the perfect match. This is rare but its chances of occurrence increase with each generation of intermarriage. Since Kanuba is too small to produce many eligible partners to choose among, spatial proximity means little in marriage choice. The Nubians view their entire network of relatives as the marriage pool; eligible individuals in Cairo, Alexandria, Aswan, or Old Nubia are all included.

In support of their customs of endogamy (in-group marriage) and arranged marriage, the Nubians advance three arguments; (1) that an alien woman or outsider cannot understand a man's customs and habits; (2) that partners should be of the same basic economic status; and (3) that cousin marriage makes it possible for property to be kept under family control. The essential idea is to preserve and control family and tribal harmony but also to minimize chances of sexual infidelity or betrayal, a fear that has some basis in reality in view of the long marital separations enforced by labor migration. Nubians believe that women who have not been infibulated are likely to seek sexual contact outside marriage. Indeed, the men of Kanuba joke about the sexual propensities of other nationalities and ethnic groups and say that Nubian men and European women make good partners because the sexual desires of each are strong compared with their counterparts in their own groups. As one informant put it: "Our women can endure the absence of their husbands for years at a time. European women are not like that. We Nubians know; we have worked in the houses of foreigners."

In Kanuba the traditional pattern of marriage has begun to change. The young men and some young women, too, now hold the view, which is gaining ground in Cairo, that people should have freedom of choice in their selection of mates. At the time of our study, one marriage in Kanuba fulfilled the ideal conditions, and another young couple stood in this traditionally enviable relationship. In the second case, however, the young man resisted the pressures of both his family and the village and eventually married a girl of his own choice (who was still a cousin on one side). Among those who are attempting to change many of the traditional patterns toward patterns more in keeping with an urban model, this was regarded as a triumph for modernity.

In another instance, a man who had been given a list prepared by his mother of some twenty related girls from among whom to select a bride had chosen from the list a girl his mother had not favored. He viewed his selection as an act of free choice, and it is true that such behavior is quite a change from that of the past, when choice was much more rigidly determined by parents and when potential mates were required to avoid even seeing each other before marriage. Nevertheless, the extent to which

TABLE 5 *Numerical breakdown of 111 first marriages*

| Relationship | Fadija (71) | Kenuz (40) | Totals (111) |
|---|---|---|---|
| Father's brother's daughter | 6 | 10 | 16 |
| Mother's brother's daughter | 7 | 5 | 12 |
| Father's sister's daughter | 1 | 2 | 3 |
| Mother's sister's daughter | 8 | 4 | 12 |
| First cousins | 22 (30%) | 21 (52%) | 43 (39%)+ |
| Other close relatives (father) | 7 | 8 | 15 |
| Other close relatives (mother) | 5 | 2 | 7 |
| | 12 (17%) | 10 (25%) | 22 (19%)+ |
| Distant relationship (not precisely traceable) | 25 | 5 | 30 |
| No relationship | 12 | 4 | 16 |
| Totals of distant or no relationship | 37 (52%) | 9 (13%) | 46 (41.5%) |

the ideal model persists in Kanuba is surprising. According to our observation and inquiries, the data obtained are not only typical of Kanuba but are fairly representative of Nubians as a whole.

As table 5 indicates, of 111 first marriages in Kanuba on which we obtained data, 39 percent were between first cousins and approximately 60 percent were between close relatives. That the Kenuz are seen to be more conservative than the Fadija in regard to marriage conforms with our impressions of generally greater cultural conservatism among the Kenuz.

Tribal affiliation does not necessarily mean a close degree of family relationship or vice versa, as members of different tribes are often closely related while members of the same tribe may not know precisely how they are related. Still, tribal affiliation also affects marriage choice. Where the tribal affiliations of partners could be established, our sample of 105 first marriages in Kanuba yielded the counts recorded in table 6.

Although the Fadija appear to be changing more rapidly than the

*56*

TABLE 6  *Tribal affiliation in 105 first marriages*

|  | Fadija | Kenuz | Totals |
|---|---|---|---|
| Same tribe | 40 | 19 | 59 (56%) |
| Different tribe (but same ethnic group and district of origin in Nubia) | 33 | 10 | 43 (41%) |
| Egyptians (i.e., non-Nubians) | 2 | 1 | 3 (3%) |
| Totals | 75 | 30 | 105 |

Kenuz in this regard, these data confirm the persistence of Nubian conservatism in the marriage pattern. Despite the extensiveness of their urban contact, few Kanubans marry non-Nubians; neither do they intermarry with Nubians of other linguistic groups; nor have they married members of other groups in Daraw though they have lived in the near vicinity more than thirty years. Nubians are vehement in their claim that no Nubian woman would ever marry an Egyptian, and this seems to be true of first marriages though not necessarily of later ones. In addition to the three marriages to Egyptian partners reflected in table 6, Kanubans have reported six cases of primary relatives marrying non-Nubians, but four of these were second marriages and one was a third marriage. Among Kanubans, it is the first marriage that is critical insofar as it represents an attempt to ensure that the first sons of a union will be one's "own flesh and blood."

Finally, in Old Nubia, and in a muted form in Kanuba as well, the ideals of endogamy were strengthened by a belief that maintaining purity of family line would help to preserve the traditional status ranking of the contracting families. The majority of Kanubans came to the village from Old Diwan, which was adjacent to Derr, the nineteenth-century capital of Nubia; and it was at Derr that the ruling Kushaf (descendants of the Turkish and Bosnian governors of Nubia) had resided. Kanuba is often called a Kushaf village by the villagers of Daraw, even though only a few families may have legitimate claim to that status.

In Kanuba, the tribe acknowledged to have legitimate claim to Kushaf lineage is the Dawudab—descended from Dawud, one of the sons of Hassan Koosy, the first Ottoman governor of Nubia. Another tribe of almost equal historical status is the Mundolab, from the tribe of Mundol, who apparently married into the Jushaf line at an early date. That much residue of the old status-ranking system continues to influence present-day behavior is evidenced by the fact that the Kenuz, for example, are not allowed to forget that they were not Kushaf and that not one member of the non-Kushaf tribes from the village of Sisiwa in the Diwan District has married a member of either the Dawudab or Mundolab tribes—and this notwithstanding that members of the four Sisiwa tribes join with those of the dominant Mundolab tribe in controlling almost all aspects of Kanuban politics.

The fact that the greatest number of slaves brought from deep in Sudan was concentrated at Derr further complicates the already cloudy status picture. The slaves of high-ranking families often adopted their masters' names and passed them down the generations, while the masters sometimes begat progeny by their slave women. Although concubinage and multiple marriage produced many shades and degrees of relationship among them, some of the slave lines were unable to efface memories of their ignominious origins while others made claims to high status among Nubians.

Thus, in spite of the fragmentation of Nubian life caused by labor migration and other factors, the pattern of endogamous marriage has been tenaciously maintained. All groups in Egypt pursue certain norms of endogamy, however, and the persistence of this pattern among the Nubians should not be overemphasized. Because Nubians tend to occupy a low position in the general status scale of the country, the discriminatory attitudes that most non-Nubians hold toward them have undoubtedly been almost as important as in-group endogamous rules in the preservation of the pattern. From this point of view, the fact that marriages to nonrelatives occur at all might be seen as a major trend of change in traditional customs.

Although the Nubians, as Muslims, permit a man to be married to as many as four wives at once, we found only two cases of polygynous marriage in Kanuba, and these involved only two wives each. Three older men, who in their younger days had maintained households in both the village and the city before each had lost a wife through death or divorce, claimed that this had been a useful economic arrangement in the past when the cost of living in the village was negligible and when it was important to have someone there tending the fields and palm trees. Nowadays, in their view, this is too expensive, and most village men disavow any ambition to have another wife, asking, "Why double expenses and troubles?" The two cases of polygynous marriage involved a man from the Fadija section who maintained two separate households within the village and a Kenuz man who kept one wife in Kanuba and the other in New Nubia, and in both cases their first wives were financial burdens on them.

The Fadija man is one of three men in the village who has been abroad, having at one point in his service career been in the employ of a wealthy Egyptian who had traveled to Greece, Italy, and France. Proud of his sexual adventures with French women, he is also proud of being the only Fadija in the village to have two wives, though from a financial point of view his situation is unrealistic since his salary as a cook in Kom

58

Ombo is inadequate to support two wives. Sayid Ismail lives with his younger, more recent wife, visiting the house of his first wife only occasionally to see their children or to give her some money. Indeed, wife number one lives at so low a standard that she gets welfare support and must supplement her family's resources by selling poultry at the Daraw market.

The Kenuz man was about seventy-five years of age and had been widowed three times before he married his present two wives, making his total of five wives the highest in the village. The preferred younger wife lived with him in Kanuba, while the older woman saw him only on infrequent occasions when he was able to make the trip. Unlike Sayid Ismail, however, this man could afford the luxury of two wives. Having occupied a house in Old Nubia, he was able to obtain a house in the resettlement area where he had invested the savings of almost a lifetime's work in Cairo and Khartoum in some productive land. With two houses and considerable property, he is regarded among the Nubians as a relatively wealthy man.

OCCUPATIONAL PATTERNS

At the time of the 1959 census, 54 percent of the Egyptian labor force was concentrated in agriculture while the number of Kanuba men engaged in this pursuit was negligible, principally because from the 1933 resettlement until the 1940s the history of Kanuba had been largely a story of the failure of Nubian attempts to continue the farming existence they had known in Old Nubia. In spite of some nostalgia about the good old days of their grandfathers and some lingering hope of seeing the fields around Kanuba rich with grain, Kanuban men expressed little desire at the time of our study to take up farming again.

Even if the High Dam were to make water available for the irrigation of their long-dormant fields, our informants admitted that they would rather hire Sa'idis to do the farm labor. Kanuban men no longer regard farming as an appropriate means to the status goals they envision for their children—an attitude reinforced by the Nasser government's introduction of land reforms that made the traditional route to wealth and power through agriculture practically nonexistent in Egypt.

During the period of our residence, Kanubans had already made the fundamental adaptations to their initial economic problems and had lived with them for a number of years. In spite of the lack of cultivable land, the village had not been reduced to a group of women and children dependent on remittances or on summer agriculture overseen by a few old men retired from urban service jobs. In addition, the sex ratio did not reflect the great imbalance typical of Nubia as a whole; at the core of village life was a group of dynamic young men still at the productive stages of their lives. The village of Kanuba today is vitally functioning, active in organization, and high in community spirit.

Nubians have for centuries pursued service occupations in the cities of Egypt, and recent survey data show that this is still the case. In a 1967 study, Peter Geiser reported that 74 percent of the Nubian working population were engaged as waiters (26 percent), messengers (24 percent), doormen (14 percent), and cooks (10 percent).[14] Even though many Nubians persist in these service jobs, most of the younger men are now moving toward clerical and commercial occupations, and the men of Kanuba are leaders in this trend.

TABLE 7   *Employment of Kanuba males over 16 and not in school*

|  | Fadija | Kenuz | Total | Approx. % |
|---|---|---|---|---|
| Professional and semiprofessional | 4 | 0 | 4 | 5.9% |
| Supervisory | 1 | 2 | 3 | 4.5% |
| Proprietary | 5 | 0 | 5 | 7.1% |
| Clerical and sales | 16 | 2 | 18 | 26.8% |
| Skilled labor | 5 | 2 | 7 | 10.4% |
| Unskilled labor | 4 | 2 | 6 | 8.9% |
| Service | 5 | 6 | 12 | 17.6% |
| Farming | 0 | 4 | 4 | 5.9% |
| Retired | 5 | 3 | 8 | 11.9% |
| Able-bodied unemployed | 0 | 0 | 0 | 0 |
| Totals | 45 | 21 | 67 | 99.0% |

Although there are three small shopkeepers in the village, Kanubans are not predominantly tradesmen. Surprisingly, only two men from the village are employed by the nearby sugar company at Kom Ombo. Even more striking is the number of men working at clerical jobs—almost 27 percent as against 12 percent for the country as a whole and 5.3 percent for Cairo Egyptians. This high percentage would not be unusual for a city (for example, 25 percent in clerical and sales work in Cairo); but for a rural village in a rural province of an agrarian country, the distribution is anomalous and strongly reflects the urban orientation and city affiliations of the Kanuban people.

When the figures for occupations requiring literacy and education are united, the urban character of Kanuba becomes even more evident.

60

Whereas Cairo, the most urban city in Egypt, has 37.4 percent of its work force in the professional, managerial, clerical, and sales categories, almost 45 percent of Kanuban men occupy the top four categories of table 7, while Geiser's study of urban Nubians showed 11.2 percent in these types of occupations. Adding the skilled laborers from Kanuba—who, though not strictly comparable to white-collar types, nevertheless have comparable technical skills—brings the total percentage to 55 percent.

These figures show how far Kanuba has moved from both sakkia agriculture and the traditional service occupations. Although the expanding economy of Aswan Province offered many openings for service positions, the Kanubans preferred to avoid them, despite the fact that 60 percent of the men had had previous experience of this type. The service figure for Kanuba (17.6 percent) is about double that for Egypt as a whole but still contrasts greatly with the 74 percent of urban Nubians so employed.

Because a village the size of Kanuba cannot adequately accommodate such a specialized occupational pattern, the men of Kanuba are with few exceptions employed outside the village proper, occupying key clerical, supervisory, and teaching positions in Daraw, Kom Ombo, and Aswan. Overrepresented in jobs of the white-collar category, they are correspondingly underrepresented in jobs requiring unskilled manual labor. Huge construction projects, such as the High Dam, the most recent Nubian resettlement project, and even a government housing-construction project in Kanuba itself—opportunities that paid relatively high salaries and drew workers from many parts of Upper Egypt—did not attract Nubians from Kanuba, who are instead to be found in such bureaucracies as the Post Office, the Department of Education, the Department of Customs, and the Weather Bureau.

That the migration experience has decisively influenced the economic adaptation of this village is clear from the men's occupational histories. About 80 percent of the men of Kanuba had had more than two years' experience in cities; those over twenty-five years of age had had an average of fifteen years' experience in cities; and no man in the village was without extensive firsthand knowledge of cities. On the other hand, almost 71 percent had had less than one year's experience or no experience at all in farming. Those who had more than a year's experience in farming were generally older men who as youths before 1933 had worked on the land in Old Nubia.

Although Kanuban men know the city well, they have reversed the usual rural-to-urban movement and have chosen voluntarily to settle in a rural area instead. The reasons for this are both economic and social. Because of the low cost of living in Kanuba, a family of any size can be maintained with far less financial strain than in the city. In Kanuba, all but one or two families own the houses they occupy; no rent is paid; food

*61*

is cheaper, and it is easy to keep a few chickens and goats for home con-
sumption or to sell for a little extra money on market day.

In this region, too, there are many more opportunities for those
qualified to hold white-collar jobs than there are in the city, where competition for salaried positions is intense. The great rural-urban movement in Egypt today coupled with the tremendously accelerated pace of
education have created rising demands for trained personnel in nonurban
areas as well; but people possessing such skills tend to move to the cities,
leaving less competition for such jobs in provinces like Aswan.

Finally, social discrimination in the city accounts for some measure
of the return to the village. In spite of the fact that many Nubians have
moved out of the traditional service jobs, some of them even attaining
positions of eminence, there continues to exist among Egyptians a general image of them as servants or primitives from Sudan. Men whose
pride had been wounded by acts of discrimination arising from this attitude had returned to Kanuba, partly for access to relatively prestigious
occupations in which they could take pride, partly to be among their
own people, where they could speak their own language without con-
straint, rely on kinsmen whenever necessary, and enjoy the atmosphere
of greater security and protection afforded women and children than is
to be found in the city.

THE DUAL SOCIAL WORLD

In the course of an interview on the subject of religion, one of the women
of Kanuba remarked: "Most of the women will go to hell and the men
will go to heaven. The Prophet said that women have less minds." Although women outnumber men in the village, they are not only socially
subordinate but in some ways resemble a separate caste. With few exceptions, women are believed to be intellectually inferior to men, cowardly,
quarrelsome, overconcerned with trifles, uncooperative, emotional,
impulsive, and unpredictable. Paradoxically, they are also thought to
be more passive, quiescent, and obedient than men.

Above all, it is believed that women possess inordinate sexual desire
and insufficient restraint to control it. The most extreme manifestation
of this view is to be found in the female circumcision ceremony, whose
express purpose is to preserve premarital chastity. In spite of this painful
protection, it is held that a girl should be married as soon as possible to
eliminate even the possibility of a shameful premarital accident, and it
is agreed that Nubian girls have no choice in the selection of a husband
and should have none. To an outsider, sexuality appears to be obsessively
feared in Kanuba as a force destructive to both the individual and society.

In local Arabic, the colloquial term for adult members of the female sex is *marra*—a term carrying overtones of immorality in some parts of Egypt, though in Kanuba its only derogatory connotation arises from the inferiority associated with femininity in general. When applied to males, however—whose traits are less overtly verbalized and tend to be conceived in terms of contrast with the traits of women—the term is an insult. Although young boys are given much greater latitude in their behavior because they are thought to be naturally more active and mischievous, men who are cowardly, excessively gossipy and quarrelsome, who refuse to go along with group consensus, or who sit frequently with the women may be termed *marra*. A young man who burst into uncontrolled sobbing on being informed of the death of his wife during childbirth was regarded with disapproval by men and women alike, as women generally accept the prevailing view of their nature.

It is claimed in Kanuba that women participate only in decisions that pertain to the running of a household. Anything of a political, communal, or business nature is decided wholly by men without reference to women's opinions. High positions of leadership should never be in the hands of a woman because this is against Islamic law. "A woman's proper place is in the home serving men, not in public life commanding them. Their proper activities are in the things for which their minds are fitted—that is, housekeeping, crafts, and childbearing."

Although the wife-mother may play a mediating role in family affairs, the final decision rests always with the father. Quoting verses from the Koran to the effect that a man's testimony is worth twice that of a woman and that the man's inheritance is double the female share, Kanuban men regard silence as the sign of agreement in women. A man who suggested that Islam provides for the consultation of a woman was overruled by others who stated that, in practice, this rule was applied by consulting her after the decision had already been made.

In view of these attitudes, it is not surprising that the segregation of sexes begins at a very early age in Kanuba, until by the time of puberty their contact and interaction are minimal. As they grow older, girls are restrained as much as possible from contact with young unmarried men, especially nonvillage men. Women no longer work in the fields as they did in Old Nubia, and it is believed that they must be watched when they go to the regular weekly market in Daraw. When it was proposed by one of the young village leaders that the women be registered to vote in order to give more support to the Nubian candidates for the Arab Socialist Union, the idea was initially rejected on the grounds that they would have to come close to nonvillage men at the polling place.

*Sexual separation*   Men and women are seldom seen in each other's company in Kanuba. Women avert their eyes on passing a stranger, often take another path if they see men approaching, and when young, usually stand or leave the room on the appearance of a nonfamily adult male. While men wear no single differentiating color or style of clothing, outside the home all women wear a black overdress and black head scarf, which distinguishes married women and women of marriageable age while at the same time minimizing differences between them, symbolically merging the two into a single observable and equal category.

Parents normally begin directing children to associate with members of their own sex between the ages of four and six. As they grow older, boys are permitted greater freedom of movement, even outside the immediate peripheries of the village, while girls are increasingly confined to the home. At school, boys and girls are segregated on opposite sides of the classroom, and most girls are not permitted to continue their formal education after primary school. During the period of our study, only two girls from Kanuba were to be found in the upper grades of the Daraw intermediate and secondary schools. As they approach maturity, young men and women separate into still more mutually exclusive roles. The majority of men work outside the village at clerical, mechanical, or service jobs, while Kanuba women confine their economic activities almost exclusively to the household. A sketch of daily activities plainly reveals the continuing separateness of the sexes in the village.

On a typical day in Kanuba, the men, in Western-style suits, catch the highway bus to their offices, schools, or hospitals in Kom Ombo, Daraw, or Aswan. Returning to the village in the early afternoon and changing into gallabeyas, they eat and rest for an hour or two before either joining a group of men in front of a village shop to lounge about, gossip, or read the newspaper or going with the group to the mosque for the evening prayer and lesson.

Women begin their day by making tea, after which such tasks as feeding the animals, bringing water from the village tap, cleaning the house, and preparing food are allotted on the basis of the age and preferences of the women of the household. Later in the morning, visits are made to the sick, new arrivals, or friends, and visitors sharing in the tasks of the households visited—baking bread, sewing clothing, or preparing vegetables for cooking. Occasionally the village medical clinic may be visited. In the afternoon, women may prepare food for the returning husband and attend to other routine tasks, many going to the fields near the village in late afternoon to cut clover for the animals. The evening is occupied with friendly visiting or helping the sick until retirement at ten or eleven at night. The necessities of child care are attended to as they arise, and the devout make their prayers at the proper times throughout the day.

Outside the household, the only interactions between the sexes are likely to be chance meetings in the streets or conversations while making purchases from itinerant peddlers or one of the village storekeepers.

When the women go to Daraw for weekly supplies on market day, they gather in a special place and sally forth in twos and threes to make their purchases, while the men, who generally keep a sharp eye on their activities, wander freely through the market buying things and engaging in conversation with Daraw friends. Sexual separation even influences behavior within the household since contact between adult males and other family members is limited. Men customarily eat at least one of their early meals outside the house, and in most households the husband eats his evening meal alone or in the company of other males.

Although weddings, funerals, yearly feasts, Ramadan, the birthday of the Prophet, and other social and ceremonial occasions interrupt the regular routine of the village, segregation by sex is consistently maintained. At weddings, the women dance together opposite the men, eat separately, and play separate complementary roles throughout the celebration. At funerals, they sit together in the house ritually weeping and wailing while the men sit outside preparing the shroud. The body is washed by a member of the same sex as the deceased. The men carry the casket to the cemetery in an exclusively male procession, eating at the mosque for three days after the interment; women meanwhile gather to eat with the female relatives at the house of the deceased.

Ramadan is the only time of the year when women are permitted to enter the mosque for the nightly service; again, however, they stay at the rear, separated from the men by a large curtain. After the service, men go to the village club for an evening of jokes, stories, and speeches while women visit one another's houses in small groups. During the entertainment programs occasionally put on by the club, men sit on benches at one side of the courtyard while women and girls sit across from them on the ground. The skits enacted at these programs have all-male casts notwithstanding that female roles are frequently involved.

The yearly feasts are the only occasions when every man encounters every woman of the village. At these celebrations, the men make a procession to all the houses in the community, where the women of each household greet them and serve them cookies, candy, and cinnamon tea. This annual ritual seems to represent a symbolic rapprochement between the sexes, emphasizing their physical separation and dramatizing their complementary roles. After the procession, however, the customary communal meal takes place in sexually segregated neighborhood groups.

*Effects of sexual separation*   There is no question that segregation by sex impedes the flow of information in the community. Of a 40 percent random sample of the married women in the village, not one gave information that tallied exactly with that of her husband in regard to his income: 48 percent gave a figure different from that given by the husband, while 52 percent had no idea what his income was. Several women were uncertain of their husband's occupation; one did not know where her husband worked; there were also several cases in which women had no idea how much land their fathers owned.

In several other instances, information that was common knowledge among the men and of vital concern to the village did not reach the women until sometime later and even then in incomplete form. Many women, for example, were uncertain whether they would occupy the new houses that the government was building to replace old ones, although this was months after the decision to rebuild the village had been made and many of the houses were already half-completed. In another example, a village man who was running for an office in the Daraw area knew the election results immediately, although some women were still unaware that he had lost for several days afterward. Similarly, many women were still ignorant of the death of President John Kennedy two or three days after the event, though the men had previously sent a delegation to our quarters to express their condolences. Indeed, such is the lack of information flow between the sexes that a woman does not tell her husband when she is pregnant; he discovers this only by observing the physiological signs.

The effects of sexual segregation are also reflected in proficiency and choice of language. From the schoolboy to the oldest, every Kanuban male is proficient in Arabic, which (unless they are trying to conceal information from non-Nubians) men speak in their jobs outside the village and often among themselves as well. Women, on the other hand, speak Nubian almost exclusively among themselves. While no woman is entirely incapable of communicating in Arabic, our field workers rated only 25 percent of the women in our sample as excellent in Arabic, with proficiency equal to that of the men; 27 percent were rated as adequate; 28 percent had difficulty communicating; and 20 percent had such poor competence that a translator was needed to obtain information from them.

Exposure to schooling and knowledge of the outside world also exhibit a striking sex differential. Of all the adult women in Kanuba, 77 percent were totally illiterate compared with only 8 percent of the men. While 18 percent of the men had attended secondary school or higher, no adult woman had gone beyond the primary school level. Among men, too, political awareness is high, and discussions of current events are frequent and spirited. Six men in the community received newspapers daily, and these were passed around during informal social gatherings in the evening while a radio loudly broadcast news programs, political speeches, recitations of the Koran, or music.

On the other hand, only one woman in our sample reported reading parts of the newspaper daily, while 11 percent read parts of it on rare occasions. Although 26 percent of the women listen to the radio every day, or at least four times a week, the majority tune only to programs of

66

music and Koran recitations. Twelve percent occasionally listen to an educational program for housewives, called "Women's Corner," broadcast from Cairo, but only one admitted ever listening to political speeches. Not surprisingly, this limited exposure to the mass media is reflected in a lack of knowledge about the outside world. To seven questions that we asked about such topics as the location of Libya, the name of the president of the United States, and the purpose of the then just-completed Arab Summit Conference, 87 percent of the women interviewed could not answer one out of seven; 8 percent knew the answer to one question, and only 5 percent were able to answer two questions.

As might be expected from the evidence on literacy, men's knowledge of orthodox religion is far more extensive than is that of women, for whom religious participation tends to be a private, individual matter. Although no man in the community can be called a religious scholar, many keep religious books in their homes and most gather at the mosque every Friday for the weekly ritual, while a smaller group that assembles at the mosque every evening for religious reading and prayer is composed of men who enjoy arguing the fine points of doctrine to reinforce their knowledge of Koranic texts. Women, as previously mentioned, enter the mosque only during the evenings of Ramadan and in general receive no regular reinforcement of whatever religious knowledge they may have.

The only part of the Koran that is memorized by all adults is the brief opening chapter that is used in most Islamic ritual. After this, although some know the names of other chapters and are vaguely familiar with a few of the stories to be found in them, women's knowledge of the Koran diminishes to near zero. Most of the men, on the other hand, know other chapters by heart and can refer to some of the traditions about the Prophet's life in support of arguments concerning the practice of Islam. Older men, especially those who were educated in the Koranic primary schools, can quote long passages from the Koran, and most men and boys are familiar with the Sufistic chants praising the Prophet that are used for the zikrs occasionally still held in the village. Women do not participate in these chants, however, and therefore have only the most rudimentary notions of the beliefs embodied in them.

The use of charms for protection against the Evil Eye, the resort to sorcerers to make or to defend against sorcery, visits to the tombs of holy men to make vows and ask favors, requests of specialists for predictions of fortune from the spirits of the Nile—all such traditional Nubian or other folk-magic beliefs are primarily female activities, although not all women believe in or perpetuate these things. The presence of a new medical clinic, the sophisticated attitudes of many urban-oriented young men, and opposition by the conservative Ansar al-Sunna group in the village have influenced many people, men and women alike, to disavow such practices.

*Social structure*   The nuclear and compound households that are the basic social units of Kanuba are integrated at the community level by male participation in two democratically organized institutions, the village association and the village club, which have representatives of all tribes and sections on their boards of elected officers and which handle all important external and internal village affairs. Below this, the men divide on the basis of opposed religious beliefs into two voluntary, informal subgroupings—the Ansar al-Sunna, a strict reformist group, and another group inclining more toward popular Islam. Less structured are the groups of young men who frequently meet to smoke and drink together in the evenings.

The female social organization is made up of neighborhood cliques whose internal unity arises less from an overlapping of ties than from a network of dyadic reciprocal obligations among pairs of women. That is, the women of each neighborhood are formed into two or more cliques whose individual members (or households) owe obligations of visiting, service, and sometimes food or goods on the arrival, presence, or departure of relatives or guests, on occasions of illness or of need of any kind. During weddings, feasts, and funerals, every woman in the village is responsible for some service or visiting obligations, but it is the neighborhood clique groups on which the major burdens devolve, according to the importance of the occasion and of the persons involved.

Thus, although the social organization of Kanuba clearly reflects the dichotomy of sexes that characterizes all other aspects of village life, the separate male and female parts of the social structure are articulated at their base by the joint membership of men and women in the family households on which the present social organization of the community rests.

# SHATR MUHAMMAD SHALASHIL

## 4

Against the foregoing background of facts about Nubian and Kanuban history and culture, the personal document that follows not only illuminates the dynamics of Kanuban village life but causes many of the motivations and actions of an individual innovating leader to become understandable.

ALEXANDRIA

Although I was born in Diwan Nubia, my mother became pregnant in Alexandria. She moved to Diwan about a month before she delivered me. At that time my father was working in Alexandria. I have been told that my birth was not a difficult one. My grandmother, assisted by Fatma Bahr, made the delivery. According to what I heard later, I only stayed six months in Diwan. Then my mother moved back to Alexandria where I stayed for about two years before returning to Diwan again. We returned because my mother had to give birth to my brother Abdul. We stayed in Diwan only a short time and returned to Alexandria again, where we lived together with my father for two years before making another trip to Nubia for the birth of my brother Saber. After Saber's birth, my paternal grandmother took me back to Alexandria while my mother stayed on in Diwan with the other two children, Saber and Abdul.

Both of my grandfathers were great sheikhs in Diwan. They were famous holy men. My father's father's name was Muhammad Ahmed Hussein, but he was known as Sheikh Sanusi. He always used to carry the Koran in his hands, even while attending weddings and funerals. He would preach at the slightest opportunity and give lessons at any time. He was known as a scientist of religion, but he was also a farmer. His main interest was to advise people and persuade them to give up what he considered the bad Nubian traditions and habits. He wanted the women to stop braiding their hair. You know how they braid their hair with small braids? He said it was a Pharaonic habit and that the many tiny braids and the oil make the head dirty. That is against Islam, which says that the head must be clean. I had little contact with this grandfather and know him only from people's stories. He opposed my famous grandfather, Sheikh Taha Abdul Shalashil, my mother's father. Sheikh Shalashil was known for his love of popular Islam, whereas Sheikh Sanusi was orthodox. They remind me of our Wahabi*—Hag Abdullah, the imam, and Sheikh Salam El Abu Baker, who used to hold zikrs every day in Kanuba.

The grandmother on my mother's side spent her whole life in Diwan, although she visited Minya once or twice where her son was working. I always liked her, but I never knew her very well and I only remember her from my very early childhood. She is the one who took care of my other brothers when they were living in Diwan. My closest relative in my childhood was my father's mother, who took me to Alexandria so that my mother could afford to bring up my brothers.

Although I moved back and forth between Diwan and Alexandria several times, there was one period when I stayed in the village in Nubia for several years. At that time my paternal grandmother was the *nakeeba* [caretaker] of Sheikh Taha Abdul Shalashil—that is, she took care of his tomb. She must have been about 70 then, and she is still alive at 110. I remember that she always dressed in white when she went to my grandfather's shrine. She wore it because of her duty to receive the people who came to receive *baraka* [blessings] from Sheikh Shalashil. Many men and women of different ages came from everywhere to receive his *baraka*. People made vows by slaughtering animals. My family made *fatta* [bread soup] and offered it to everyone on his birthday. My grandmother always took the special part of the animal, the liver, and maybe some other part of the body as her payment from visitors to the shrine.

*A conservative reformist group in Islam that arose in the early nineteenth century and now dominates Saudi Arabia.

At that time I was also a *nakeeb*. I must have been about five or six, and I put on the *nakeeb* dress only when visitors were coming to the shrine or when it was time for the *moulid* [birthday or saint's day celebration] of the sheikh. I don't know why they selected me. It was probably because I was the grandson of the famous sheikh. I had no duties except for eating and playing; but on the special days when people saw me, they kissed my hand to receive *baraka*. They were pleased when I played with their children or entered their houses. I remember how I was dressed in a white gallabeya with a green sash, though I dressed like this only on special occasions and only in Diwan. When I was in Alexandria, I never dressed that way. Whenever I went to Diwan people liked to kiss me, to carry me on their shoulders, to be nice to me, and to feed me. I believed I actually had *baraka*. I remember that many times I offered my hand to be kissed even before being asked. But now I don't believe in such ridiculous things.

In Diwan we had a *kuttab*, a school for learning the Koran. (We didn't learn much else.) The old sheikh of the *kuttab* treated me especially kindly because I was a *nakeeb*. The slaves also treated me with deference in comparison to the other children. There was one of them whom I liked very much. I don't like to call him a slave because I dislike slavery. He (his name was Hussein Morgan) taught me how to swim. The slaves often used to take care of the children in Old Nubia. My grandmother always used to tell Hussein to teach me to swim like a crocodile, saying, "The *nakeeb* should not be drowned." Parents always encouraged their children to learn to swim because we played near the river, which was dangerous.

I still remember the Nile. It made a big impression on me. It seemed very very wide. The opposite bank was tremendously far. The sight of the girls coming to the river to fill their jars with water and returning home is still vivid to me. They used their veils to strain the mud from the water during the flood season. We always drank the water from under the *zeer*\* and used it to make tea. I especially remember the excitement of games at night during the full moon. We used to throw stones to see who could throw the farthest. Another game was called *hagala*. Children still play this game here in Kanuba. With one foot raised, you try to push the other and to avoid being pushed, but if your foot comes down you're out.

In the evening the people used to sit out in groups during Ramadan in front of their houses. They entertained themselves with stories and by drinking much *abreek*.† During the Small Feast they offered dates and cakes and everyone marched in procession to all the houses in the village to eat, giving the Nubian feast greeting, *"Korigayna alay!"*

\*Tall water jars; the water is filtered into a small jar underneath.
†A drink made from lemon or bottled syrup with finely flaked bread in it.

Dates were found everywhere in those times. Goods were exchanged for dates. There was no money. In back of our house there was a very high mountain. Once I went out with the sheep alone. A wolf came and took one of them and ran toward the hills. I shouted as loud as I could, and luckily a man was nearby. He called one of the slaves, who ran after the wolf and returned with the sheep. I also remember a fox who came to eat the chickens in our house. Hussein Morgan made a trap to catch him. In the morning we found the fox with a very bad smell. My grandfather told Hussein to throw it away. We small children trooped after him into the mountains to watch him get rid of it. Because of the awful odor we did not stay long. As soon as Hussein put down the fox he started running, and we all ran after him as fast as we could back to the village.

I still remember the tales that people told about monsters with tails coming up from the river to eat dates from the trees and taking some back to the people in the river. The monsters were called Aman Dogir and were said sometimes to eat people who tried to prevent them from taking the dates. If I walk at night and look at palm trees I still remember these stories. My grandmother told me such tales even in Alexandria, but my mother and father did not like them and never told them to us. My father told us religious stories instead.

There was a big boy called Yussef Gamal who was one of our playmates in Diwan. He was strong and tall and fat. He would stop us on our way to the *kattub* and frighten us into giving him our food. I liked to build sakkias and shadoufs out of mud and stones—tiny ones. I played with many girls, and I had two kinds of gallabeyas. At home I wore a yellow gallabeya without a collar, along with my sandals and small skullcap. Maybe I had pants underneath, I don't remember. After the prayer, people burned incense and sometimes had a zikr. That was very exciting. Anytime a visitor came from Cairo, he would bring a large box. On the second or third day of his stay, all his relatives would receive a gift from it. People always called it the box-opening day. One time one of my relatives received playing cards from one of the visitors. This seemed very curious to me.

In one game the boys caught birds in a snare. I hated that game. I was always against them and always tried to free the birds that they caught. I have no explanation why I felt that way, but I still prevent my children from hunting birds. I am known as a friend to birds—I feed them. Didn't you notice when you came to my house that there are birds living on the roof? Even if they dirty the house, I still like them. I hate to see children pulling the cat by the tail, too. I never was cruel to animals when I was small. In Diwan there were many cats and dogs and they were useful. People liked them because cats eat mice and dogs guard the houses from foxes and wolves.

I was fond of playing on the sakkia. I liked to sit behind the man as he drove the cows around and listen to the squeaking of the big wooden wheels. But my memory of Diwan is vague. It mostly consists of pictures like those I have told you and of smells and sounds. I remember Old Nubia as being a place with big mountains with the cemetery nearby. There were big houses, palm trees along the banks, and an island in the Nile. I remember quite well the sight of many many palm trees along the river. When people caught a scorpion they would pin it to the wall. I don't know why. Once after I had taken my bath and was putting on my clothes, I felt something crawling on my skin. I shouted, "Save me, Shatr is dying, it's a scorpion, save me! save me!"—but it was only a cockroach and everyone laughed.

My grandmother used to tell me that many spirits and demons were always around us. She always said that people must say "by the name of God" before they eat in order to cause the devils and spirits to go away. She explained that spirits are of two kinds, the angels and the devils. The angels lead persons toward heaven and the devils lead one toward hell. Also, we wore charms around our necks to protect us from the Evil Eye. The spirit I feared most was Aman Dogir, who was said to come out of the Nile at night. I feared it intensely. After sundown I never went near the palm trees or the river.

Something that is very vivid in my mind is the gold chain that I wore around my neck and also my white gallabeya. Children in Old Nubia had great freedom in comparison with when I lived in the city. I remember going into the kitchen from time to time to cook for myself or to look for food. I used to run freely along the Nile and climbed up on sakkias and talked to the cattle drivers. Sometimes I would even fix tea for visitors and offer it to them on the tray. This must have been when I was six years old.

I also remember the solemn spirit of the Friday prayers and how the people would hold a zikr after the prayer every week. They would sway and go "Allah hi! Allah hi!" It seems that I can recall Sheikh Musbah and his bony face leading the chanting even for those times, but perhaps this memory is from a visit I made to Diwan later at the age of ten or eleven. At any rate, the scene of the chanters swaying to the pulsing rhythm of the drums and the fragrant incense is one I will never forget. Once I remember trying to burst my way through the crowd and join the zikr circle, but I was sent away. The zikrs that I attended later when I came to Kanuba were lacking the spiritual discipline of those back in my dim childhood. People are now more interested in eating the *fatta* than in spiritual communion. This is one reason I oppose zikrs now.

I think my great fear of darkness (which you know about) began in Diwan when I was small. My grandmother would always warn me not to go out or a wolf might eat me. Whenever I wanted to go from one part of the house to another, she said, "Wait, don't go alone." Even when I was curious to see what was happening outside, she would pull me back and say, "Stay by me." I think she feared the dark as much as I did.

Whenever I went with her visiting she would always say, "Let us return before sunset. We should go back before dark." I cannot remember when I was not afraid of the dark.

My memories of Old Nubia are few and not too clear. After we moved to Alexandria (I was six), I can remember more things. In Diwan, of course, everyone spoke Nubian, and one of my most vivid experiences happened the second day after we permanently returned to Alexandria. I remember that I went out into the street and met some boys who were speaking in Arabic. I did not understand them and I began to speak in Nubian; but instead of replying, they laughed loudly and called other children to see. They started to call me *berberi*, and they sang this song: *"Ya berberi ya bun, harami el-gebna wal-zaitun"* ["Nubian, you brown one, robber of cheese and olives"]. I did not understand the meaning of this rhyme, but I liked the tune, so I actually joined in the singing. This only made them laugh more. From then I began to learn Arabic. Day by day, playing in the alleys, I learned Arabic words and phrases from the games. But my language was still not good when I joined the school. The boys always made fun of me because of my color, my kind of face, and my hair, but especially my accent. I tried to imitate the other children's accents, but they snickered and ridiculed me. I felt ashamed.

I was a naughty boy and I liked toys. When I was walking with my grandmother in the streets, I would stop in front of a toy store, point at a certain toy, and refuse to move until my grandmother bought it for me. I was very stubborn and she had to buy many toys for me.

I used to swim at Anfushi Beach near Alexandria. My father and grandmother told me not to go, and they beat me, but in vain. They even used to put red color on my thighs so they could tell if I went to the beach. But I loved to swim and used to sneak off many times. I doubt if I could swim now. Maybe I could swim for about twenty meters only, but I guess I probably could still easily float on my back. Once I stayed out of school and went to the beach instead. I played hooky because I knew I had to recite one-fourth of the whole Koran that day and I did not know it, so I preferred not to go. That was the first and last time I did that.

The first school I went to in Alexandria was a *kuttab*, and the day that I played hooky was from that school. The real reason that I stayed away was that I dreaded being thought of as stupid. This was because I really was very good at reciting the Koran. The second school I went to in Alexandria was a primary school. The boys used to insult me when I was in that school. The children used to beat me and push my fez down on my head. They called me "you *berberi*, you son of a dog." But once I put some tacks on top of the fez so that when they pushed it down it would hurt their hands. One boy pulled his hand away and shouted ow! ow! ow! I ran as quickly as I could.

My grandmother was angry at the way I was treated, and she went to the school one day to meet the headmaster. She shouted at him in Nubian. Naturally he could not understand it, and everyone laughed. Many people gathered to see what was happening. When I was a pupil in the school in Alexandria the teacher used to spank me frequently, but really I was not naughty. On the contrary, I was quiet and obedient. Each day the teacher used to assign us two pages of the Koran to be recited the next day. Even though I liked the Koran, I was unable at that time to memorize two pages every night. So every day I had to receive a spanking, and once I even played hooky as I told you. The Prophet Muhammad says, "Be gentle to your children the first seven years and the following seven be firm." My teacher knew this, of course, but he still wanted us to repeat the Koran so that he could get a gift from our fathers for making us so clever.

At that time, and about up to 1931 when we lived in Alexandria, my father worked as a clerk in a company in the city. I don't remember what company. I seldom saw my father and had no close relations with him. When I was older, my grandmother told me that my father played with me when I was an infant, that he carried me, etc., but I don't remember it. All I remember about that remote period of my life is that he was severe and unkind. Whenever he returned to the house I stopped playing or even talking. As for my mother, I did not see her very much in my early childhood because she was in Nubia, but I remember she beat me only once. My grandmother never beat me. But from my father I received many beatings.

When I was in school, in those first grades, most of the teachers liked me because I was a quiet boy. I was always at the top of the class, always good in Arabic. The teachers showed one another my work. I still have some of my grades. I still remember one of my teachers, Sheikh Muhammad Kamel. He made a great impression on me. When he first came to our school the boys gave him a hard time, as they did with all new teachers, but he was a kind man. He dressed in an Azhar uniform* that looked funny to us. The boys tried many ways of teasing him. When he turned his back to write on the blackboard, they threw chalk and screamed. I never took advantage in that way.

When Sheikh Kamel first came he gave us a lecture that made a deep impression on me. He is one of the few teachers who never raised a stick. He never punished a pupil. He was well liked by all the students, and he set an example for me. He taught me that to be popular and to get ahead, one should always treat people kindly. He used his beautiful style in the

---

*The dress of sheikhs from Al-Azhar University in Cairo, generally a long gray garment almost reaching the ground, with a maroon fez wrapped with a white turban.

Arabic language to persuade the pupils to obey. He believed in persuasion, not force.

In Alexandria we lived in Gomarek District near the waterfront. The street was very narrow and dirty, but the house was not too old when we moved in. It had five floors, and we lived on the roof in a flat of two rooms with a wide hall. The rooms were very broad and the ceiling was high. There was no electricity, so we used small lamps, but this flat did have safe drinking water. The bathroom was also wide, and the W.C. was next to it. It was fairly large, too. The street outside was paved with stones. There were no Nubians in this building, nor for that matter in the whole district. They lived mainly in two districts called Attarin and Moharram Bey. For some reason, my father preferred not to live in these districts, and, in fact, during all his life he avoided living among Nubians. He always wanted to live near a mosque, and there was one nearby wherever we lived. In Gomarek District there was a mosque called the Sheikh Mosque on the same street as our house.

I still remember this house with pleasure because there I began my life with all its troubles. The children used to call me *berberi* and make fun of me, as I told you. They used to hit me for no reason. Maybe I encouraged them, but I never defended myself. I was a coward and afraid in the beginning. Later I became friends with all the boys. I even became their leader. I remember that I always led them to the places where we went to play and enjoy ourselves. Sometimes a group of us used to go down to the docks to help sort the oranges being loaded onto the ships. The oranges were put in large heaps on the platform to be sorted before they could be exported. The man in charge used to reward us with a few oranges, which we ate—and those we couldn't eat we played with. I never told my father, mother, or grandmother about this because I knew that they would stop me from going. Many times I went to the beach with this same bunch of kids. The beach is the famous one called Anfushi. Sometimes my father discovered that we had been to the beach and he beat me. I usually tried to conceal the fact or to lie, but my father could easily tell. We swam only in our undershorts and stayed out in the sun for a long time afterward to dry them before we came home.

On the corner of the street near our building there was a small coffee shop called the Bundag, and across from it there was a Coptic church. Even now whenever I hear the London bells over the radio I think of this church. I used to stand outside and listen to the music. I remember that music so well that even while I am directing our plays and skits here in the village this music goes through my head. When I think of these things I see that small narrow street and my small self in a white gallabeya, barefoot, and being followed by the kids shouting *"ya berberi ya bun, harami el-gebna wal-zaitun."*

In that house in Alexandria I had some friends. The best ones were a

girl called Faiza and a boy nicknamed Bish-Bish. They were not
Nubians, and they were living in the same house in an apartment near us.
We always played together on the roof. My favorite game was wedding, and
I always liked to play the role of the groom with Faiza. Bish-Bish
played the father who gave me permission to marry his daughter. This is
all I remember about that game. There was also another group of
boys and girls whom I played with on the roof or in the street. I can't
remember their names, but some of them were classmates. Faiza, her
brother Bish-Bish, and I would sit together for hours looking at illustrated
magazines. Boys were always coming to the house and asking for me,
and my grandmother used to chase them away.

One day when I was about six or seven, a very surprising thing
happened to me. A very old man and a young man about twenty-five came
to the door. My father was there and he let them in. They asked me to
sit on a chair. After I had done that, they brought a pan and put it on the
ground under my legs. They raised my gallabeya and one of my uncles
raised my legs up and asked me to look up and watch a small bird. I was
curious and a bit frightened. Suddenly I looked and saw the old man with a
knife in his hand. He was cutting my penis! I was really shocked at the
sight of blood pouring into the pan and by the sudden pain. I still vividly
remember the golden chain they afterward put around my neck to prevent
the Evil Eye. No one told me that I was to be circumcised before it
happened. It was a complete surprise. It all happened in a minute. I had
heard about circumcisions when I had visited Diwan, but no one talked
about it in Alexandria. There was no ceremony or preparation as was the
tradition in Nubia. Later that day some Nubian relatives came to visit us
and offered me candy. Some of them gave my father small gifts of money.

During that period of my life my father was living in one room of the
flat, while my grandmother, grandfather, and I occupied the other
room and shared the same bed. I always used to sleep between them. It
always seemed to me that my grandmother was my real mother, and I still
feel that way. She took care of me and always treated me kindly. During
this time grandfather used to be very annoyed at me because of my nagging
for toys and my insisting on getting my own way. My father gave me half a
piaster a day, and I spent it on toys, whistles, and candy. My grandfather
did not give me any money regularly, but sometimes on feast days he
would give me a little something. I also collected coupons, and once I got
a pen for them, while another time I got a small bag of candy. I liked
my grandfather a great deal but did not feel as close to him as I did to my
grandmother. In that flat we ate on a floor table, whereas later, in
my stepmother's house, we sat on chairs around a big table. We ate with
our fingers in the Nubian way or else used spoons, never knives and forks.

I loved to visit the marketplace in Alexandria with my grandmother.
I especially enjoyed the "street of women," and I passed it every day on my

way to the *kuttab*. That street was narrow, and I remember it as always crowded. All the bright-colored goods in the merchants' stalls were attractive to me. The picture of the crowds of women with their black shawls is still in my mind. They all wore them then.

When I was about eight years old in Alexandria, a very important event happened. As I told you, my father, in his job as a representative of a company in the city, traveled around contacting many companies and stores. One day in the open market, one of his customers asked him to marry his daughter. She was very pretty, and, as my father was such a good friend to the man, he accepted the proposal. That woman that he married had a great influence on my life. My father is still alive and so is that woman, my stepmother. She is now ill, and I ask God for her speedy recovery. Even today I ask God to cure her. My father still lives with her in the Zetoun District of Cairo. He is not working now.

When my father brought home his second wife, my grandmother became so angry that she left the house and traveled to Nubia. This was the first time she did not take me with her on such a trip, and when she left I was crying. She kept telling me to listen to Daddy, and she told me a little about the "newcomer." She said, "A woman will come to live with you and your father. You should call her *nena*. She will treat you kindly, and she will behave as if she were your mother." I very seldom saw my real mother in those early days. She stayed in Nubia most of the time. I cannot remember any time that I lived with both my mother and my father. Each time that my mother came to live with my father in Alexandria, my grandmother and I would go to Nubia. I remember always being glad when I heard them talk about my mother's arrival, but when she arrived it was no more than two or three days before I left, disappointed again. Actually this happened only about four or five times during the nine years in Alexandria.

That period when I was staying with my grandparents and father was the time I had more contacts with Nubians than anytime until I recently moved to Kanuba. My grandmother never visited a Nubian family, either of relatives or nonrelatives, without me. I enjoyed those visits a great deal. It was the only opportunity to see Nubian people, especially children. All the other childrena i usually played with spoke only Arabic, but with these children I spoke Nubian when we played. However, we never spent a whole day or night at their houses. My father never asked me to go with him when I was that age. And even though he was around, I rarely saw him. Since he preferred to stay with Egyptians, he would never go with us to visit Nubians. Once, when I was about seven years old, I went to the wedding of my father's brother. The only thing I remember from that wedding is the huge number of pigeons that were served to the guests.

There were no great differences between the houses of the Nubians we visited but I noticed a big difference between their houses and those of Egyptians we knew. The picture in my mind is that the Nubians either lived down in basements or on the roofs of buildings, while the Egyptians lived in apartments. Whole Nubian families often lived in a single room, but the Egyptian families my father knew had several rooms. The furniture in those Nubian rooms was old and little, and it's strange but I don't remember any of our typical Nubian decorations.

Anyway, when my father married his non-Nubian wife he moved to a new flat. Before the wedding, nobody let me know what was happening. It was apparently a quiet wedding, not at all like our usual long Nubian ones with all the music and dancing. One day after my grandmother left I heard them talking about moving. Then one day my father and I moved to the new building in another district called Kabari, and then my grandfather also returned to Nubia. At the new flat I found a new woman sharing our living quarters. My father had first introduced her to me as his friend's wife. I did not care, but I did not understand the whole situation. Soon I found out who she was. People began to ask me, "How is your stepmother?"

We only stayed a few months in that new district. I was unhappy there. In fact, I cannot remember any happy times in that place. For some reason, I could not talk easily to the boys around there. It was strange, and the conditions and atmosphere were different. There were things that I was not used to, such as a girl servant, electricity, a big wide flat with four rooms, a large hall, a wide kitchen, and a W.C. The house was also on a public street. After a short time we went back to our old district, Gomarek, near the harbor. My father rented a flat very close to where I had lived with my grandmother. My grandfather came back at this time and used to spend most of his time in our house, eating with us and sleeping there. I was fond of toys then and had a train with a station on a circular track. I also had something known as a garden toy made from a big piece of wood on which there were some trees, cows, sheep, and plants. I even had a hobbyhorse.

It seems that my father's business was doing better at that time. After about a year my father and stepmother had a child called Showab who is still alive. He is now an officer in the army—I like him. During this time I slept with my father in one bed. My stepmother slept alone in another bed, also in the same room. That room was very big. There was also an extra bedroom which they called the guest room. The servant slept in the kitchen. Many relatives of my stepmother came and used it, but no Nubians ever visited us. This is the house where we sat on chairs around a big table to eat. I still didn't use a fork or knife but only a spoon. Once I was playing with my brother Showab in the guest room, and I was carrying him and throwing him on the bed. I was very pleased to see him jumping up and down and laughing. That bed had springs. All of a sudden he fell and began to cry loudly. My stepmother quickly ran in shouting and screaming. She accused me of trying to kill her child. My father did not try to stop her. I remember that Showab slept in the same bed with his mother.

Many boys used to come every day to play with me or ask for me. My stepmother was sick of them. She disliked them and constantly shouted "go away!" She told me to tell my friends not to come. "Shatr, Shatr, Shatr," she said, "Go and live in the street, it's better for you." I heard this many times. We usually played in the afternoons after coming back from school. We played thieves and policemen. I liked to be chief of police with a whistle in my mouth and have authority over the others. I remember in that neighborhood there was a foreign woman, *hawagaya,** a crazy one, who was our neighbor. Sometimes when the real policeman passed we would all run and scurry away. Now in Cairo the children are not even afraid of them. They don't even move if one approaches. It was different when I was a child.

In my time we all were barefoot in the streets. Now it seems that all the children have shoes. The street for me was a release because my stepmother's house was a prison. There I was neglected. In that house nobody liked me. It was very different after my grandmother began to care for me. She gave me much love. I still remember how the street merchants looked with their long sticks wrapped with toffeelike candy. I would run to grandmother and she would give me a piaster to buy sweets. All the children followed the man as he shook his small tambourine. He would give each of us a piece of candy from his stick in exchange for our two melleems.

Another memory is of the wedding processions that we used to see in the streets of Alexandria. The picture is of the big crowds of people dressed in gallabeyas, the rows of taxis, many children running around, and large groups of women, some in brightly colored clothing. In front of all of them was Sheikh Zarouh and his group of musicians. Some of them carried drums. Sheikh Zarouh balanced a long pole on his nose, sometimes with a ball on it. At night two or three people went ahead of the procession with lanterns to light the way. I often recall this whole scene and how fascinated I was with Zarouh and his interesting stick.

I associate my grandfather with the mosque because he always took me there with him, and it was he who taught me to pray. A big difference between my grandfather and my father was that my father always wore European clothes—pants, shirt, and coat—whereas my grandfather always wore a traditional gallabeya.

Anyway, we get back to the *hawagaya* who was in the neighborhood. Her name was Catherine, and she always called me "you *berberi*, son of a dog." I can see her now—very large, a woman with a fat face and very fat legs. She used to urge the boys to collect cigarette butts, and she would

*A word for foreigner.

80

pay them a little money. She didn't like me because I tried to stop the boys and to turn them against her. She became very angry with me, and that was why she called me *berberi* and black. Once my stepmother shouted at her not to call me *berberi*, and they were about to fight.

I cannot remember much about my early childhood dreams, but something I can never forget was one night when I forgot to go to the W.C. before bed. I had a dream in which I wanted to go to the toilet, and I was crying because I couldn't fnd the place to go. I met an old sheikh with a long beard who asked me what was the matter. I told the sheikh what I was looking for, and he answered, "Do it here. Do it here." So I did. I was sleeping with my father at that time, but he did not wake up. In the morning he asked me who did it, and I said, "The sheikh did it." This was the first and last time that happened, believe me! He was going to hit me, but he began to laugh. That morning my stepmother turned the mattress over. She was very angry.

CAIRO

In the early 1930s we moved to Cairo for some reason. We lived in the district called Bab el-Halk. My father rented a new flat in a new building in that district. My father, my stepmother, my half-brother, myself, and the servant, whose name was Hadra, lived there. My brothers Abdul and Saber were still living with mother in Diwan. But shortly after we moved to Cairo, one day I discovered my mother had left Nubia and was living in Maadi, which, as you know, is a district outside Cairo. I remember finding out that my father went to visit my mother in Maadi and spent the night there sometimes. When he went, I had to stay behind; I could only go to see my mother when he did not come—I don't know why, but that is what I can remember. My mother lived for about three or four years in Maadi, and while she was there my sister Fatma was born. For some reason, all of my father's Nubian family lived with my mother except me—that is, my two brothers and my sister and my grandmother. I was very sad because I could not live with my grandmother again, even though she was nearby in the same city. Maybe my father wanted me to stay in his house since I was the oldest. Soon after we were in Cairo my stepmother gave birth to a baby girl named Laila. She is now married to my father's sister's son and has a certificate in needlework.

The Egyptian women who were living in the same apartment house with us were always urging me to resist my stepmother, saying, "Do not listen to her! Fight with her! Don't let her treat you that way!" They used to ask me: "Why does she treat you so unkindly? Why does she make you sleep on the floor while she and her sons sleep on beds? You're a son of her husband, not a servant." My stepmother did her best to educate her children, but she didn't do the same for me. She treated me brutally and complained to my father whenever he came home. At one time I was spanked every night for very trifling reasons. But now it doesn't matter. In spite of all this, I still ask God for her recovery. Once I asked the servant girl to get a spoon for me. When she didn't do it, I shouted at her to get it and pushed her slightly. The girl didn't complain, but my stepmother interfered and I received the worst beating from my father that I ever got. I still remember it vividly because I thought it was for a trifling thing.

It was in 1931 that we moved to Cairo, and I remember hearing them talk about it in Alexandria. My stepmother was always complaining about her health and saying she wanted to move to Cairo. When I found out that we were moving I felt sad. I didn't want to leave that district, I loved it so much. But my father finally got a better job in Cairo and that suited my stepmother, who complained that the weather in Alexandria was bad for her health.

The house in the Bab el-Halk District was on Darb Saida Street. It was a new building, built on the European style and with good finishing. Nobody had lived in it before. Our flat was wide—four rooms with water and electricity. It had two W.C.s—a *baladi* and an *afrangi*.* My father paid two-and-a-half pounds a month for that flat. The doorkeeper was a man from Daraw named Ahmed. Probably he is dead now. There was a theater in that district called the Aragon, which I dearly loved. I used to go to it daily and sometimes even twice. It only cost one melleem. In the beginning I felt strange in the new place. Maybe that is one reason I went to the movies so often. But when I started to school I got to know some boys and made friends with many of them. Once a boy asked me, "Do you want me to teach you how to love girls?" I answered yes. I can't remember what he taught me, but I still hate this boy much. His name was Hassan Ali Ahmed. He was one of my classmates.

When I was ten, my grandmother came to visit my father and to see me. She stayed only a few months, and then she went back to Alexandria to live with my grandfather. When we moved to Cairo, we left my grandfather in Alexandria. My father's brother, who previously had worked in Khartoum for Shell Oil Company, came to Alexandria to stay with my grandfather, while my grandmother returned to Nubia. That uncle settled in Alexandria and established a grocery store there.

As a child I was always an introvert—always afraid of something, I knew not what. My schoolmates always mistreated me, insulted me, and degraded me. I was a mouse among cats. But one by one, day by day, I became their leader (I am not boasting). Finally I could control them. I will tell you how this happened. I became friends with them one by one,

---

*Baladi* refers to any items or utensils of the type used by poor people—in this case, a simple floor toilet; *afrangi* means French or European and here refers to a European-style toilet.

individually, by giving them candy and spending my daily allowance on them. They gathered around me. I made a place for myself among them. I also did my best to better my Arabic so that they wouldn't have any reason to make fun of me. At first my accent was very bad, but after awhile I was very popular with teachers. They all liked me. My Arabic teacher liked my good handwriting. It is one of my principles always to improve myself and to go on higher. "None is born a master." This is what one of my teachers always said. It was in this school, the second primary in Bab el-Halk, where the children used to beat me and push my fez down on my head and call me "you *berberi*, you son of a dog."

After awhile in the second primary school I was transferred to one called the Dawaween, a private school. I was eleven at that time. In that school I was always at the top of the class—if not first, then second. I always had the highest grades in Arabic. In the Dawaween, the school secretary once called me from my class. I went with him downstairs and found two of the school servants waiting for me. The secretary asked one of them to carry me over his shoulder, and he told the other to spank me on my seat without giving me any reason. It was one of the worst beatings I ever received. Then the secretary told me that he did this because I was second in the class when previously I had always been first. I like that man because he taught me a lesson. When one reaches the top, he must stay there. If I were to meet him now I would embrace him. But even when I was a child I was a coward, and I still am one. I never attacked anyone in my life. The children used to hit me and to tease me, but I never returned the same to them. When I complained about them to my grandmother, she advised me to be peaceful and not to hit them back. She told me to tell them: "I am not a *berberi*, I am not a slave, I am free. Stop hitting me— *ana sherif fourshi.*" This is a Nubian phrase.

Once my father wrote a recommendation for me to give to the headmaster. I put the letter in my book to deliver to the teacher the next day, but for some reason I didn't deliver it. When I returned home, my father asked me the headmaster's reaction. I told him that the teacher had read it and then told the children to stop hitting me. However, my father accidentally found the letter in my book. He asked me what a person who lies deserves. I foolishly replied, "A spank, of course." Then my father brought out a stick and said, "Then receive it." It was a very bad beating. From then on I was very careful not to lie to him. I dislike lying, and I teach my children not to lie.

My father used to hit me with a long stick on every part of my body. He did not confine his beating to any one part. Many times he spanked me because my stepmother told him to. I remember running everywhere, inside the house and out, with my father chasing me with the stick and my stepmother shouting her orders, "Enough on his hands, hit him on his back!" Then after he left home for work, I sometimes returned to finish my breakfast. I avoided him for several days before we started talking again. Lying and stealing were the two things my father disapproved of most and for which he gave me the worst beatings. When I was young I always stole biscuits. My stepmother used to make cakes and biscuits and would hide them in a locked cabinet. Whenever she left it open, I would sneak a few out so that she wouldn't notice anything missing. Do you know, now I never have my food locked away from my children? On the contrary, if one of them asks me for anything, I tell him to help himself.

Once I told a lie that caused my father much trouble. I got a bad spanking for it afterward. My father gave me a piaster to buy ice. When I went downstairs I found my half-brother Showab playing with the kids in the street. I asked myself why he could play while I had to run errands. So I told him to get the ice. I waited for a long time and he did not return. I was playing when my father came down looking for me. He asked me where Showab was, and I said I didn't know. He seemed to know what I had done and forced me to admit it. Then he made me lead him to the ice store, and with every step he hit me on the head and kicked me in the pants. I was about thirteen. But in spite of the number of beatings I received from my father, I still liked him. It was hard to communicate with him when I was young, but later I asked his advice and I always respected him. As you can see, he advised me not to marry a non-Nubian, and I followed his advice. Among all my relatives in my childhood, the only one with whom I had a close and easy relation was my grandmother. I was not afraid of her.

The teachers in the school used to beat us and hit us frequently. One particularly, a man called Ezel Din, used to hit me on my back with a long stick. He taught arithmetic. The more he hit me, the more I hated the subject. I hated him and still hate him when I think of him. My earlier Arabic teacher, Kamel, who never raised a stick, made me love the language, and I continued all my life to love it. I used to memorize all my Arabic lessons and tried to improve in order to please him.

During my early childhood I was not naughty, but when I was about eleven or twelve I began to get into much mischief and trouble. I liked to ride bicycles, and I rode for four or five hours daily for several years. I used to take picnics to different parts of Cairo—the Nile, the Citadel, Hussein District, Sayida Zeinab, etc. We often stayed out most of the day. One incident that I remember vividly happened when I was about nine years old. Our family went to visit my father's sister in Cairo. One of my cousins, a boy about nineteen years old, asked me to play with him. He said, "Let's go up to the roof and play a nice game." When we went up to the roof, he said: "Let's take down our pants. I will put my penis in your anus for awhile, and then you put yours in mine. We'll take turns. It's lots of fun." I became frightened and refused and went back to the flat and told my aunt immediately. She called him and screamed and beat him. I didn't go

84

back to that house again and actually have not seen that cousin for twenty-five years.

That flat in Cairo was well furnished. There was a bedroom, dining room, and a reception room. The servant girl slept on a mat in the kitchen. I slept alone in a small room on a small mat with a cover. My father, stepmother, and her children all slept in one room in two beds. The house was near a mosque. We stayed about three years there, and then we moved to a new house in the same district. Nobody told me anything about our moving. I was surprised one day when I heard them talking about leaving. Oh, I remember now. My stepmother disliked the other people who lived in the house. She said she felt strange there, she could not communicate with the neighbors because they were all foreigners—Armenians and Greeks. Our new place was in a district called Shalashil el-Mouz. On the same street also lived Attiya Sharard, the famous musician. He was my friend. We were in the same school.

During that time, my stepmother mistreated me a great deal. She took care of her own children and neglected me. In fact, I was treated like a servant. When we went out walking, the girl servant carried one baby and I carried the other. I always had to do menial jobs around the house, helping the servant. My father would leave the house at eight in the morning, come home for lunch around eleven, and take a nap for two hours. After that, he left the house and didn't return until ten or eleven at night. I used to get up early in the morning and go to sleep early at night. I had liked all our neighbors in the previous house. They were all kind to me. They would ask me to come in and would offer me food and candy. I really liked them and I felt sad when we left that house. I missed them.

We stayed in Shalashil el-Mouz for only one year, then we moved to a small house in el-Zetoun District. My father bought this house. As usual I had no idea about moving, and one day I found my stepmother giving instructions to pack the luggage. My mother was living in Maadi at that time with my two brothers, my sister, and grandmother. One of my father's other brothers fell sick about that time and had to remain in bed. He was paralyzed, and I was sent daily to serve him. I had to clean his house, which was in Abdin District, and to buy things from the market for him. I paid short visits to my mother in Maadi, but I never stayed long. Finally my mother had to leave Cairo to live in the village of Kanuba. She found that it was too much for my father to afford two families in Cairo. I was sad at my mother's departure even though I had not seen much of her. I was so sad I wept.

This last house to which we moved was in an isolated place. It was a small villa on only one floor. It had three wide rooms and a very wide hall. It was an old house. I lived in that place for about eleven years, from 1935 to 1946. My father still lives in that same district, but recently he moved to a new house. That house had running water and electricity, too. I was about thirteen or fourteen when we moved there. My father gave me the smallest room in the house and provided me with a mat with a cover, a pillow, and a hanger. Once my grandmother visited us and was surprised when she saw where I slept. She shouted at my father and told him to buy a bed and table for me immediately. The next day my father went out and bought a wooden bed and table. Much later, when I got a job in the British Army, I furnished the room better, with a comfortable bed, cabinet, a desk, a mirror, and a rug.

In that house I became a little closer to my father because he began to instruct me about religion. He ordered me to pray and showed me how. I had learned the basic things earlier from my grandfather, but now I learned how to do it the right way. In that period of my life I went to many different mosques to pray and to attend religious sessions and classes. My father liked to study religion and to give lessons. Sometimes he would hold classes in the house, and my stepmother's relatives came to listen. I seldom prayed publicly—only in front of him and my stepmother except when we went to the mosque.

My grandfather worked as some kind of an overseer on the estate of Prince Omar Tossen in Alexandria. He died when he was still employed there, while we were living in Cairo. My father did not inform me of his death at first but only said that he was going to Alexandria to see my grandfather. After he had left, my stepmother told me what had happened and I wept bitterly, although I had no clear idea what death was at that age. I saw many other people weeping about my grandfather, so I wept too. The only thing I understood was that I would not see him anymore. I was only twelve when my grandfather died.

Many years before, my father had worked on the same estate with my grandfather. My grandfather then helped get my father the job as clerk. In Cairo his job was still as a representative of companies, but I cannot remember the exact nature of the job. All I knew was that he was an effendi; he wore Western clothes and sat at a desk. He never wore a gallabeya in his work. His jobs became better and better, and one of them was with a private foreign company that sold tea, coffee, chocolate, soap, and stoves. In the beginning, as far as I remember, he worked as a cashier, then as a canvasser, and then as a representative of the company in Cairo. When he was a salesman and a canvasser, he traveled to markets in many places, even as far as Aswan. He sometimes was away from home for three weeks at a time during a two- or three-month period. When he finally became a representative, he liked the new position because of the stability. He didn't have to move around all the time. I never knew anything about my father's income, but we lived in a moderate neighborhood. The gossip was that he could educate his sons in the university.

We also lived in some comfort in our house in el-Zetoun District, where I lived for a long time. I never asked him how he had enough money to buy it or about his income and livelihood, but I know that even now he has enough savings to live on. I never send him money and he never sends me money either. He only sends mail, one letter every month. You might be surprised that when I receive his letter I kiss it and weep before I start reading it. I don't know why. I often reread the letter two or three times. I'll show you the last letter I received from him. He writes me regularly.

My brothers and my stepmother write me only on special occasions like the feasts. The only one of my brothers and sisters with whom I now correspond regularly is my brother Saber, who lives in Cairo where he is a teacher. He sends me gifts, sometimes of money. For the feast, he sends me at least two or three pounds, and I am grateful to him. My brother Saber is an introvert: as my father says, he is easy to guide and control; he always did what he was told (not like me!); he takes things for granted; he thinks Allah is responsible for everything in his life, but that does not mean he is a religious man. His wife controls him like a doll.

My half-brothers are very different from one another. Hamdi is a very nervous personality. Once he came here to the village and stayed for three years. He could not stand village life and failed to make any friends. He was snobbish toward Nubians and scorned Nubian customs. He only wanted electricity, clean water, and radios. He was selfish and thought only of his own comfort. The only reason Kanuba tolerated him was because of me and my mother. I was relieved when he left for Cairo. I like my other half-brother Showab, but I now feel small and inferior when I am around him. He is an army officer while I am only a clerk, and people know that there is a great social gap between us. He was always the favorite of my stepmother's family, and in comparison to me he was always favored. His skin is lighter than mine, and he actually did not know he was part Nubian until very recently. Showab's hair and that of my sister is very straight.

In 1936, because of the war between Italy and Ethiopia, the Italian company for which my father worked went out of business. He then opened a shop in Asmawi District where he sold tea, coffee, and candy. My stepmother persuaded my father to stop my schooling so that I could help in the new store. This store is across the street from the old Keika Mosque—my father and I used to go there. We prayed there because it was the nearest mosque to my father's shop. The street was a narrow one leading toward Attaba Square. Now the district is completely changed.

Before, there were no tall buildings, and the mosque towered over the tops of the shops. Now it is hard to find a man wearing a gallabeya in that street and hard to find a woman in a malaya [a wrap worn by Egyptian women], but in those days everyone wore them. Also now there

are no red faces—I mean British soldiers. The street was narrow
then, but it was never so crowded as it is now in Cairo. Nearby there was a
small restaurant where Nubians and Sudanese people went. I used
to eat my lunch there sometimes. I don't have any especially good feelings
or memories about that section of Cairo. I don't feel anything unpleasant or
sad, but somehow the recollections are not pleasant either. DKUJ I do
remember the clacking rhythm of the wooden slippers in my ears while
walking down the street. Nowadays when I visit Cairo I don't hear
that sound any longer. Next to our shop was another one owned by Hag
Akwawi, the grocer. I used to sit with him in front of the shops and
tell him of my troubles. He would listen to me and say "it doesn't matter"
or "never mind." I liked him very much. He was kind.

Across from our shop, on the other side, an Armenian and his
wife had a shop and lived on the first floor. What impressed me about this
family was their unusual activity and the fact that the wife worked
there. Whenever I went there to buy cheese or *halawa* [a sweet made of
sesame], I always found them busy doing things. This always surprised
me because it didn't happen in the other shops in the district. At this time
I did not envision spending the rest of my life there, and I was determined
to complete my studies and get away. I resented the fact that my
father made me work in the store while he sent my half-brothers to school
as my stepmother wanted.

I used to get up around six in the morning, have a bite, and then go to
the shop to open it and clean it. Most of the day I spent out in front
drinking tea and coffee. I only got sixty piasters a month and I worked
thirteen hours a day, from seven o'clock in the morning to eight in the
evening. I had a bicycle with a box in front which I rode to and from work.
When I returned home I was too tired to do anything but sleep. In a
word, life was despicable.

I remember one incident that happened during that time. A man
came to me and told me he represented a group of workmen who
were ready to buy tea, and he asked for some samples. I gave him a good
amount of tea, but he never came back to pay, and I found out later he
was a fraud—that I had been tricked. A few days later, when my father
found out, he blamed me and told me never to trust people. He said,
"Always examine a man before giving him anything." Another time I was
in a shop alone when a man came in and asked for chalk made from
marble. I told him no, but he said he thought I would find a large quantity
of it and that he would buy all I had if I could find it. "If your father
brings some of this, save ten boxes for me and I will pay one pound for
each," he said. About an hour later another man passed the shop selling
chalk. He had twenty-five boxes, and I eagerly bought them all for
fifty piasters each, thinking I was making a shrewd bargain. The other man

88

never returned to buy the chalk, and we had a large quantity on our hands for a long time. When I told my father the story, he became very angry and said, "One box is worth only fifteen milleems!" He called me stupid and good-for-nothing.

During this time I always wore a gallabeya, and during the winter I wore a coat and a scarf. Many Nubians came to the shop to buy tea and coffee, but I had no closer relationship with them than selling; I did not make any close friends among them. I had to take the train back and forth from Zetoun District to Ramsees and walk the rest of the way to save money. I used my extra money to buy leftovers from Gropis' pastry and candy shops.

Sometime during that period of my life I made two trips to large *moulids* in other parts of Egypt. One of them was the *moulid* of Desouk. My stepmother and my paternal grandmother went to spend a few days. I don't remember much about it except for the train ride. Another *moulid* we attended was that of Sayed el-Bedawi in Tanta [the largest celebration of a saint's birthday in Egypt]. I think I was around twelve, and I went with my father. What I remember most was a discussion about *baraka* among my father and some other men. It involved getting the *baraka* and paying silver coins in the collection box. I also remember the large crowds and the train that took us there. We passed canals, and I noticed trucks and cars on the way. Trains were very different in those days. Today one sits in a comfortable chair and everything is orderly. People are not sitting everywhere with luggage all over the floor, in the seats, above you, and in the aisles. Now people don't sleep in the luggage racks, and you don't find people in the aisles selling eggs, *tameya* [a food made of fried beans and many other ingredients], sesame bread, and everything else. Everyone now sits in his own place with his own bag. In those days there was much more confusion.

One thing I remember about the Sayed el-Bedawi *moulid* and some other ones in Cairo, too, was my father buying me sweets and getting candy and dolls to distribute among the others when we returned home. My favorite doll was a horse. Whenever I think of *moulids*, I think of the ferris wheels. I used to stand and watch them for a long time, but I seldom rode on one. I also remember the Sufi brotherhoods doing zikrs and the sound of the drumming on the tambourines and how they swayed back and forth. It seems like there were many more zikrs in the *moulids* in those days than there are now.

My father was neither poor nor rich, but I guess our standards were higher than most people's because we were living in a European-style house. We had two W.C.s, the European one and the *baladi* one. Even though my father had a hard time after the Italian company went out of business, we still stayed in that house. He was able to support us from the small store for several years, but after the war he returned to the Italian company.

When I was about thirteen I was tired of that work, and I asked my father to look for a different job for me. I told him I wished to work as a mechanic. Through one of my Nubian relatives, I got a job in the repair shop for British Army equipment. In that job I earned ten piasters a day. Oh, first it was seven piasters and later it was raised to ten. I'll tell you the story of how it was raised. I went to the house of the director, who was a pasha, and I asked the doorkeeper if they had a cook. He said yes, so I asked if he was an Egyptian. The doorkeeper said, "No, he is *berberi*." So I asked where he was from. The doorkeeper didn't know but only knew that he spoke Nubian. So I waited for the cook to return, and when he came up I greeted him in our language. He greeted me in return, invited me in to eat, and even offered to wash and iron my laundry.

This cook liked me, and later he introduced me to the pasha as one of his relatives. I spoke to the pasha and applied for the cook's job. He gave me a card and told me to meet someone the next day. When I met the man, I lied. I told him my father was working at the pasha's house. This official, who was in charge of the garage where I was working, raised my salary and became friendly with me because he thought my father could do something for him. That experience taught me a lesson. If I had not done those things I would still have been making seven piasters a day.

I always had a very good relationship with my half-brother Showab. When he was very young I used to carry him and play with him, and he always liked me a great deal. He preferred to eat with me more than with his mother or anyone else. She did not like that. I remember that as soon as I was at home, he would be with me until I went to bed. I played camelback with him. As to Hamdi, my other half-brother, I also used to play and entertain him, but Laila, who was born later, was too young. I did not play with her as much as with my two brothers. I don't think I slept with any of them.

My mother never visited my stepmother. In fact, they avoided each other. My stepmother looked down on Nubians and avoided them. In fact, my mother and stepmother never even saw each other. I remember distinctly that my mother never once inquired about my stepmother. She always felt sympathy for my father. She was very kind and had a very good heart. She was unselfish to an extreme. When she lived in Maadi, she found out that it was too much for my father to afford two houses, so she decided to move to Kanuba to reduce his expenses. She also did not want to interfere with my father's life in Cairo. I do not know how much my father sent her monthly, but I am sure that my stepmother's family received more of his income. My mother always said that marriage is a matter of fate. "God doesn't want him to live with me," she said, referring to my father. Our Nubian relatives used to blame my father and reprimand him. "What happened to you, Muhammad, what's wrong with your wife?" My father's reply was always, "This is fate," but many times he did not reply at all.

When my mother was in Maadi, my father and I were the only ones who went to see her, but we never went together. My half-brothers never went there or mixed with my brothers. I remember the first time Saber saw Showab was in 1943 in our house in Zetoun. Now I am closer to my two real brothers, Saber and Abdul, than to my half-brothers, whom I hardly ever see. But when I come to Cairo I still visit them.

I was seldom sick in my life, especially as a child, but once I remember I was poisoned when we were living in Zetoun. And I don't remember why, but then I went to Maadi to stay with my real mother. I vomited and had diarrhea for four hours, and I thought I was going to die. I did not know the cause of the poison. My mother took care of me. My stepmother never cared as much about me as for her own children, and she neglected me. Just a few years ago, in 1958, a nurse here in the Daraw hospital pretended she fell in love with me. I was about to be deceived, and she asked me to marry her. But I refused because I remember what it meant to have a stepmother. That's why I am doing my best here in the village to stop anyone from taking a second wife. One is enough!

When I was thirteen or fourteen and still working as a mechanic's assistant in the mechanic shop in Cairo, I began to find out about sex. One night I woke up and found something strange coming out of my penis. It surprised me. It got the bedclothes all wet. I thought I had urinated in my sleep. I went to the W.C. and took off my shorts and washed them out, wrung them out, and put them under the mattress. Since I didn't know what it was, I did not tell my father about it. The next day I asked one of the boys who worked in the shop with me about it. He laughed and put his hand on my shoulder. "Congratulations, Shatr, now you have become a man." I asked increduously, "What is the relationship between this stuff and manhood?" He replied that now I could have intercourse with any woman. I asked another boy and he told me the same thing. He also told me how to masturbate. I began to notice that I wanted to look at girls and to touch them.

A few days later my stepmother said, "What happened to you, Shatr? Your voice is becoming loud and deep. Are you *balaghat?*" I found out later that this meant passing into adulthood and puberty. That affected me, and I felt nervous after that whenever I had to speak. I did not know what she meant, but the way she said it made me think something was wrong. I began to listen more to the boys' talk about sex, and I liked to talk about it too. These boys talked about the feeling of

*91*

masturbation, and they advised me to do it, too, so as not to feel bad about not sleeping with girls. I thought and dreamed of that. At first I didn't do it much, but then I found myself doing it while I was in the bath. The boys said to buy pictures of actresses to look at while doing it so that it would give more pleasure.

One day I was sitting with my father when I found myself asking him about that stuff and masturbation. He looked at me intently and said: "I advise you to stop it. Prophet Muhammad said that those who have intercourse with their palm 100 times will go to hell, and he who has intercourse with his palm is considered to have intercourse with his mother." This shocked me. He continued by warning me that this bad habit will cause sinful desires. He told me to participate in sports and not look at nude pictures. "Work hard and sleep directly. Masturbation is forbidden by religion and bad for the health," he said. But I didn't stop, and in fact I did it more. I felt guilty about it and played sports often and worked hard all day. I tried to stop looking at nude pictures, but I couldn't give up the habit for some reason. Once about a year later a group of my fellow workers of my own age brought a woman to a flat. They were all having intercourse with her and they asked me to join them; but I was afraid, and I went to a nearby coffee shop and waited for them.

Several times in this period of my life I went to the out-of-bounds district in Cairo called Clot Bey, but I had no courage to go to any of the prostitution shops. Yet I enjoyed walking in the area and seeing the naked women standing around trying to attract attention. I was always afraid to enter because of my fear of "the disease." I knew that many of my fellow workers and friends had gonorrhea and it made them miserable. Once my father called me aside and told me that in a dream he had seen me in Clot Bey. He had seen some boys urging me into a house, but I had refused. He asked me if that was true. I was astounded and I admitted it. After that, I seldom went to that area because I was afraid my father would see me in a dream. I think that youth corrupts youth. If one's group is bad, the boy will be bad. That is why I intend, if God gives me life, to make my children marry young, perhaps fifteen or sixteen. The father is the driver of the house.

Now I don't have intercourse much with my wife. I don't even have it on the regular time as most people do here in Kanuba—that is, on Monday and Tuesday and perhaps Thursday. They say that Prophet Muhammad preferred Monday or Tuesday, but that is nonsense. I am sure that is a woman's invention to guarantee intercourse at least twice a week. Now I am forty-two years old, and I don't think much about it. Most of the time I go to sleep directly. Sometimes I listen to the radio and then pretend to doze off so that my wife will not expect anything from me. Usually a man's desire and capacity increase up to the age of forty, and then it begins to go downhill. I am past that age now. I never take any of those things that people use here to prolong the pleasure, like *helba* [a tonic made from yellowish grain], hashish, etc., but there are people in this village who do use such things. I won't mention their names.

During my childhood I always felt like a stranger. I did not mix with the Nubians in Alexandria or Cairo. My stepmother was responsible for this, and she took my father away from many of his close relatives and friends. In my lifetime my father did not join any Nubian club, nor did he ever visit one that I know of. My stepmother was white and very pretty. She looked like an actress named Hoda Sultan. My father also was not too dark, but my stepmother was an Egyptian and, of course, you know the Egyptian idea of Nubians. They always degrade them. She always wanted my father to avoid his Nubian background and to behave like an Egyptian.

I don't remember any specific disputes and quarrels between my stepmother and father. I think they had small arguments, but they were nothing out of the ordinary. However, my father was weak in front of her. The picture I still have in my mind is my father as a religious man who always prayed at the prescribed time, reading the Koran daily, going to the mosque, and not mixing much with other people. My stepmother was the boss of the house. If they had any dispute, I always got out and tried to avoid having any involvement in it. As I got older I tried to spend my time more and more away from the house; that's one reason I couldn't observe their relationship too much. I never saw my father compliment my stepmother in front of me.

When I was in primary school, no one helped me with schoolwork. My father simply told me to study my lessons and to keep up my school duties. Later, when I was older, he helped me a great deal in understanding religion, but he never helped me with my academic work. He was very religious and had plenty of "yellow books"* about Islam. Every week he used to gather up my stepmother, my half-brother, my relatives, and men and gave a speech. He used to explain technical things about Islam to them. When my father beat me, he never shouted or accompanied it with any words or explanation. He only beat me severely! I remember the pain, but what made me feel worse was the feeling of rejection I had. There were even times when I hated him for a long period, and then we would somehow get on good terms again. He beat me so many times during my childhood, but my stepmother was the one who always urged him to beat me for small, trifling matters.

When I was working in a repair shop for a couple of years as a helper to the mechanics, I always wished to be in a better position, to raise my salary, so I looked for another job. When I was about seventeen, I went by myself to the railway department; that was one time when I had no

---

*Old religious books printed on inferior paper.

one to help me. I applied for a job there and had to take an examination. I passed it successfully and was appointed a welder. At that time I used to give my father about one pound a month, even though he did not need it. The rest of my salary, which was about six pounds, I spent on clothes and recreation.

Actually, this was about the same time that my mother decided to leave Maadi, where she had lived about four years, and to move to Kanuba. My grandmother went back to Old Nubia, Diwan. They both left the same day. My mother took my two full brothers, Saber and Abdul, with my sister, Faiza, to Kanuba. There the cost of living was much less than in Cairo. She felt that she could not live adequately there on the little money my father gave her. I felt lost and left alone. I did not know why my mother or grandmother did not want to take me. How I wished that I knew, but it's funny that it doesn't interest me now.

*British Army period*  I had that job as a welder at the railway for several months, but then I found that the British Army had higher pay for the same type of work, so I applied for a job. I passed another exam and was hired as a welder for nine pounds a month. This was better—nine pounds a month in those days was very good. I was very pleased and felt that I could afford anything I wanted—clothes, food, and recreation. My father knew little about me at that time or what I was doing even though I was living with him. I had a small separate room with a bed, a table, a hanger, and a small mirror. I used to spend the whole day away from home and return late at night just to sleep. I rarely ate with my stepmother's family, although sometimes I included my half-brothers in my fun.

My experience with the British Army was very important in my life. The British care a great deal about the people who work for them. If one gets sick or doesn't come to work, they don't fire him for that reason. Once I was sick for several days. My boss came to visit me and permitted me to return to work when I got well. The British are very punctual. They are well-organized people. They like and take care of those who are devoted to their work. This is my general impression. One of the good things I liked in them is their tolerance. If someone makes a mistake, even if it's intentional, they always give him another chance. They also give a person confidence. They always discuss with the workmen before beginning a task, even if they permit him to do what he wants to do. I think I learned this from them. There are many other things that could be mentioned about the British. They are smart. One feels that while working for them he has a value. They encourage one and they pay well, and they appreciate good work. One of the things that I got from the British is the way to treat people—that is, as human beings.

Once I was a boss, a chief of a small division. This was sometime in the period between 1940 and 1944. I was about nineteen or twenty. There were three Christians of the Coptic sect working with me, and I trusted them and treated them as colleagues and equals. I did not have anything against them, but these three Copts tried to make a *mahalab* against me [an attempt by a third party to separate two people who are friends]. These three Copts told the other workmen that I had refused to recommend them for their yearly increment. These Copts urged the other workmen against me and tried to create a bad feeling. However, the other workmen didn't believe what they said. The workmen refused to make this *mahalab*.

The British are polite. Now I remember! I was a boss of eleven Muslims and three Copts at that time. Actually, all the workmen were demonstrating and asking for increments. The British director was passing by and wanted to know what this trouble was about. The three Copts told the director that the workmen were making a demonstration because they didn't like me! They convinced the director of that, and he wrote an order to prevent me from entering the section the next day. When I came to work in the morning the doorkeeper prevented me from coming in. I still remember that doorman's name, Am Said. He told me that I was transferred to another section. But I asked him to let me enter to meet the director and talk with him.

When the director told me what the three Copts had said, I suggested that he call in the workmen and ask them what happened and how they felt about me. He did that while I stayed out and waited for his report. I was very nervous and almost wept. But then I heard them cheering and heard them say, "We want Shatr, we want Shatr." Then I really did weep. After that I asked the director to fire those Copts, but he transferred them to another department, the same one where he was going to send me. I felt that day as if it were a feast. I had won the battle. But this incident taught me to be very careful of Copts. I was stung by the Copts.

I remember another incident that illustrates why I like the British and the way in which they don't hesitate giving one a hand if he is in trouble. Once I was riding on tram 8. I had in my hand the Cairo newspaper, *El-Ahram*, and I was very glad to read that Nahas Pasha had returned to the government. Near Tawfik Palace in Shobra the tram stopped, and British soldiers took all the passengers to police head-quarters. I had on a coat and scarf. This helped me much and protected me from the police sticks. The British soldiers were looking for members of the Muslim Brotherhood. At the station I persuaded one of the soldiers to let me use the telephone to call my father. But instead I called my boss and told the general director what had happened. After about fifteen minutes the general director himself appeared at the police station in full uniform, and he took those of us who worked with the British

Army in a truck. That officer spoke both Arabic and English, and he was very impressive.

My relation with my British boss was very good. I liked him, and he would invite me often into his office to drink tea. Drinking tea and smoking cigarettes were my favorite pastimes, although, as you know, now I don't smoke and I drink very little tea. Sometimes my boss gave me tickets for the theater or parties that he couldn't use. No, they were not exactly parties but were admittance tickets to a garden where things were sold and proceeds went to the poor. But it seemed like a party, and I liked the atmosphere there. I did him some personal services, too, such as fixing his cigarette lighters. That is a trifling thing, but it shows my relationship to him. I went to his house only once. I was not invited, but I went there to sign some important papers. I entered through the servants' entrance and talked to the Nubian cook who showed me the way. That was the only time I went there. The British are very nationalistic people. I remember that some of them didn't like Churchill at that time, but all of them loved their country and the royal family. Their love for their country is beyond description. Another thing I like about the British is that they give a person a chance to do things in his own way—that is, as long as the results are all right.

Once an officer called Boski called me to his office and accused me of being a spy. He accused me of stealing some secret plans from his office. At that time I could speak and understand English much better than I can now, but most of the Britishers I dealt with spoke both Arabic and English. When he called me, I trembled and the thought went through my head that they would hang me. I knew that even though I had not stolen anything I could not prove it. My immediate boss helped me prove my innocence. He gave me a chance to search for the drawings, which were for machines (not really very secret). He tried to prove that I did not take them out of the camp. Finally we found them, and Boski was so happy that he gave me a raise of ten piasters a day.

I'll never forget that even when I was a small workman they did not fire me, although once I was absent for forty-five days. That time I was ill and my boss came to visit me. When I came back to work, he gave me a job that wouldn't tire me. During that illness I thought I had TB because I coughed up blood, and the doctor diagnosed it as TB. He told me to stay in bed and not to move. However, my father took me to a sheikh called Muhammad Shakr who used folk remedies and charms. He told me I had nothing, and he was right. I soon got well. Anyway the British paid me for the forty-five days plus overtime. I never will forget that.

During my years with the British I went to many Christmas parties. The workmen were allowed to participate, and once I was in charge of a masquerade party for the workers. I came dressed as an Azhar sheikh.

96

There were some Englishwomen in the camp who worked as secretaries. They came in the British Army uniform with coats like men. I heard many stories about them from the workmen. We all thought that they were there to entertain the soldiers at night besides their secretarial jobs in the daytime. I avoided them at the parties, although many Egyptians had relations with them. Even though I avoided them, I dreamed of them many times.

Among the British people I remember most is a man called Birdley who lived in the camp. He was one of my bosses, and he usually discussed any raise in pay with us before giving it to us. He gave me several raises and encouraged me. He was very generous to me. My contact with the British was only during work hours or connected with my work. I never became close friends with any of them. I never invited them home. They liked to discuss all kinds of political affairs with me, and, in general, they showed more preference for Nubians and Sudanese than for Egyptians. They called the Egyptians "rubbish." Maybe because it was our honesty. However, the British did like Mustapha el-Nahas [a political leader in the 1930s]. One incident I remember was when I led a group in protest against the fact that we were not allowed to pray during working hours. We made quite a disturbance, and I was their leader. However, the British are reasonable, and they extended the time for prayer after that.

During most of the British Army period I was an active member of the Muslim Brotherhood. The group of brethren of which I was a member had a room in which to pray by the canal. Our working hours were from 6:30 in the morning to 1:00, then we would have a break for one hour and then work from 2:00 until 7:00 in the evening. We had a tea break at 10:00 besides our lunch at 1:00. On Friday we had a break of three hours in order to attend the prayer outside of camp. The distance from my home to the camp was very far. I took the train from Zetoun to Ramsees Square, then I would take tram 8 to the end of Shobra; after that I had to walk half a kilometer. Every Tuesday after I got out of work I attended religious lessons at 7:00 in the evening at the Muslim Brotherhood prayer room.

On many other days I went either to our shop or to the sporting club. I also used to ride my bicycle in the afternoons to do some business. That was on my days off. One day I was riding my bicycle near the Abassiya Bridge very fast, and a policeman on some sort of motorcycle saw me and tried to catch me. It just happened that a train was coming and the guard was lowering the bar to stop the people from crossing. I quickly went under the bar and crossed while the train passed, stopping the policeman. I had just enough time to escape up a nearby street. After that incident I didn't ride a bike for a month, and I bought a hat to disguise myself. I brought that bicycle with me to Kanuba. In fact, I was the first one to ride a bicycle down here in Daraw.

The British were not intimate with me and I had no good friends among them, but there was one British engineer to whom I felt fairly close. He told me that he had a big farm with lots of land, many cows and sheep. He always expressed sorrow at having to leave his farm. Whenever we talked our favorite discussion was about that farm. He used to tell about the dairy products from the cows. He also told me about packaging vegetables and taking them to market. I would like someday to do this. I had little contact with the British soldiers personally. I avoided them. My only close relationships were among the technicians and laborers, the British as well as the Egyptians. The soldiers were in charge of guarding the camp. There were many air raids at that time. What frightened me was the bomb shelters, which were always dark and gloomy. Often I asked some friends to take me to the bomb shelter and stay with me.

I learned something from Birdley which I use now. He never faced a problem. He always put people in front of him to face the difficulty, whatever it might be. He always stayed out of the limelight. This is what I do here in Kanuba.

Before working with the British Army I had a very bad impression of the English. In my observations of their behavior in Cairo, I always saw them drunk, aggressive to passers-by, and fighting and quarreling. They teased and made fun of everyone who met them. In spite of this bad image I went to work for them, and there are some things that I still do not like about them. Once a man stole a very small and insignificant thing, and I saw how he was severely beaten. Another man broke a soldier's eyeglass, and he was beaten until he died. His name was Said— I still remember him. After he had the fight with the soldier, he came running to hide in my place. The soldiers caught him and took him and beat him until he fainted. They threw water on him to revive him and then beat him again. He died a few days later. This upset me so much that I wept. I hated them for these incidents, and it was then that I really saw how people use power wrongly and I understood the idea of imperialism. That man who was being beaten looked so pitiful, I couldn't stand it. Whenever I hit my children I remember that incident. That's why I always try to refrain from hitting them or hit them lightly. That's why I let Hussein handle the other boys, and I tell them the reason is because he is the teacher. But really it is the memory of this incident that prevents me from hitting them, even when they do bad things.

Another bad thing that used to upset me about the British is that they were often suspicious of their workmen. Whenever something was missing, they would line us all up and search us. They didn't distinguish between who had a high position and who had a low one. We were all lined up regardless. Sometimes even now, when I open the display room here in the village for visitors, I warn some of our boys to keep an eye on them. Even when Yehia Darawish came to the village, I told them to keep a close check. When they asked me why, I said why not? They don't make any distinction between high and low in the British Army.

Once, when I was the head of that group of workmen that I told you about before, I was asked to make five thousand fenders, half for the left and the other half for the right. For some reason I made five thousand for the right side only. When I discovered that, I was terrified and I planned to escape. But where would I go, and how would I get out of the camp? After being distraught for several hours, I finally decided to go to the directors and tell them what had happened before they came to inspect my work. I found one of the high directors, and I asked him to forgive me for this mistake or to let me go in peace—that is, to fire me. What surprised me was that the man gave me another chance. If he were Egyptian he would not have done that.

I was always interested in religion because of my father, and during the early part of my work with the British Army I was a member of a group that followed the teachings of a famous sheikh called Muhammad Shasli. For almost a year I went almost every day to attend his service. There was a large group that came to see him perform every night. I was one of the most regular, and the sheikh noticed that and asked me to be one of his favorites. I was thrilled that he had selected me. Every day after work I went immediately to him and spent the rest of the afternoon and part of the night in his service.

Shasli used to hold zikrs every Sunday. He sat on a high seat in front of us wearing the Al-Azhar uniform. People sat below him on rugs in the mosque. Those who were in his special service, like myself, held incense burners, and we also passed among the audience putting perfume on people's hands during the service. The sheikh began in a low voice and slow rhythm: "Hoo, Hoo, Hoo" [referring to God]. The chanting slowly got louder and faster, and the people kept repeating after him for several hours. After the people became very excited from the incense, the chanting and swaying, all of a sudden the sheikh stood up. All the people followed, and he began saying "Hi! Hi! Hi!" ["Alive! Alive! Alive!" meaning "He is alive"]. After maybe an hour of this he would stop, and the attendants would offer tea. At this time the sick would come to be healed, and those who had problems they could not solve introduced themselves to the sheikh and asked for advice. He usually prescribed vegetables and some kind of herbs and sometimes honey for the sick, which is a remedy given in the Koran.

Before or after the service, I carried a water jug for him or prepared his table. I was closer to him than most of the officers who served him. He showed a great interest in me, and I advised him a great deal. He was such a powerful personality that for a long time I did not notice many of the strange things he did. I did not wonder about them at first. But after a while I noticed that the sheikh did not pray at the regular times. I wondered why he did not pray, whereas all his followers prayed all the time. I noticed that people would ask him to lead them in prayer, but he would excuse himself. "I never pray with you because my soul leaves my body and goes to Mecca and comes back. My soul does not like to pray in Cairo." It's funny but everybody accepted that and we believed him. I never suspected him because many famous people came for his advice. Government ministers and many educated men came to receive his blessings and to hear what he had to say about their problems. He had a male and a female secretary, and he received thousands of letters from different parts of the Middle East and other parts of the world. I noticed that he read hardly any of the letters that he received.

One woman came every night and cried and begged the sheikh to spit in her blind left eye as she said he had cured her right eye before. But the sheikh said: "No, God does not want your left eye to be cured. He forbade me to spit in it!" I was one of his favorites, and he allowed me to go directly to his room without going first to get permission from the secretary. Gradually all these things that he did aroused my suspicions about him. I found out that many of the letters that he received were written by his own secretaries who addressed them to him. Some of the people who came to sit in the crowd and talk about the sheikh's blessings and claimed to be cured actually received money from the secretary. Also, I began to wonder why the sheikh never recited the Koran.

Sometimes when attractive women came to ask his advice, he would take them into his private room for a long period of time. When he did that, he would light a red lamp above his door so that no one would disturb him. He told us that the reason for these activities behind closed doors was that he was trying to find a practical solution for very serious problems. I began to argue with him. I was disillusioned and began to disobey him. Finally I lost confidence in him and left. A little while later he was put in prison because other people found out he was a charlatan and took money under false pretenses.

*Muslim Brotherhood*    It was shortly after that time, I guess when I was twenty, that I joined the Muslim Brotherhood. A man called Anwar, with a small beard, was working with us as a mechanic. I used to ride every morning with him on the train. I had to take the train from Zetoun to Bab el-Hadeed on Ramsees Square, and so I would see him every morning. He always carried religious books and read them on the train. He even preached to the passengers. It turned out that he was the chief of a small unit of the Muslim Brotherhood. After I knew him for some time, he once told me that I looked religious, like I had a good heart.

He said I should join the Muslim Brotherhood, which was a group of truly religious men. I liked him and was flattered. I agreed, and he took me to the general office in Helmia, where I filled out a form and became a general member.

The main reason I joined was because I admired him personally, though I did want to learn more about religion. Members of the Brotherhood gathered there on Tuesday to listen to a preacher. On that Tuesday he introduced me to many people high up in the organization. There I saw Hassan el-Benneh [founder of the Muslim Brotherhood] for the first time. I began to attend regularly, and Anwar became my guide. I took him as an example. I wanted to be like him someday, to have people seek me for advice and to understand the Koran and traditions as well as he did. Actually the man taught me a great deal. He gave me many religious books to read, and I read them avidly. I was still a youth at that time, and one day some friends asked me to join the Scouts. But I was too fat to be able to do the things that Scouts do. Walking and camping were too much for me. One day Anwar asked me to join a secret association within the Brotherhood to learn the use of guns, but I refused.

When they started a newspaper, I bought a share for four Egyptian pounds, and I used to contribute articles from time to time praising the Brotherhood. I was an active member and became well known. When I bought a founder's share in the Brotherhood for four pounds I thought they were going to build a mosque in Shobra, near where I was working. This was an area inhabited mostly by workers. I wanted to be a leader and to convert these workers' attention to religious matters. We thought we would use the mosque not only for the purpose of daily prayers but also as a center for a school to spread the religious movement and an awareness of religion. We wanted to teach people the true Islam—I mean the religion preached by the Prophet, that religion which is well described and explained in the Koran. In a word, I was very active against popular Islam at that time. I am still against it and lean toward Hag Abdullah's group here in the village, although I am now not so active and I am now more tolerant.

I don't know why but since my youth I have had a great interest in religion. I always wanted to increase my knowledge and understanding of Islam, and that is why I joined Sheikh Shasli's group. I thought that I would learn much from him, but later I discovered that he was an ignorant impostor, a humbug. Once, my uncle, Sheikh Salama, went to Cairo especially to see Sheikh Shasli, who was very famous. He knew that I was associated with him, so he wanted me to take him to the sheikh's house, but I refused. When he asked me why, I told him about my suspicions; but he did not believe me, so he went to visit the sheikh alone. I don't think he was convinced until Sheikh Shasli was imprisoned.

Sheikh Shasli gave me a good lesson about the falsity of most sheikh cults. After that experience I have scorned all those who pretend to have any kind of *baraka*.

I did not join the Muslim Brotherhood for political purposes but only to learn religion. During my membership in that association I had the opportunity to listen to many religious lessons and teachings, to read books, and to learn a great deal from Anwar, my guide to the true Islam. I became very active. Since at my job with the British Army I was a boss of quite a large group of men and knew many others, I organized a group, an association with about five hundred men. Actually, before that, I had organized many of these men as a sort of welfare group. At first it was not religious. Everyone had to pay two piasters a month, and we were collecting about ten pounds a month. We had oral laws, and we used the money to help needy members and gave gifts to people who were getting married. But if someone was marrying a second wife, we did not give him anything and excluded him from the group. I even used my influence as boss to stop increments for anyone who married another. I refused to keep the money we collected but gave it to someone who was known for his honesty. I always wanted to keep clear of suspicion in case anything should go wrong. I used to take large groups from our association to visit the shrines of famous sheikhs in Cairo and to attend lessons given in the famous mosques.

After I joined the Muslim Brotherhood I transferred the whole association as a unit into the Brotherhood. I knew Hassan el-Benneh, the leader of the Brotherhood personally, and I attended his lessons regularly. But even though I was a loyal member and got many members for the group, I always disliked their aggressive attitude. Once the main office of the Muslim Brotherhood distributed forms to be filled out. One of the questions was, "What is the position you would like to occupy if the war starts?" My answer was, "To be in a canteen to sell food to the soldiers." It is a funny answer, but it shows you that I don't like violence. I dislike war, disputes, quarrels, and fights.

When I came to Kanuba I organized a unit of the Muslim Brotherhood. Sheikh Salama was against me. He had a lot of foresight, and he did his best to ruin that unit. He said that the group was primarily aggressive and political with no purely religious aims and predicted that one day they would use force to promote themselves and would be conquered. This dispute with him didn't last because Hassan el-Benneh was killed that same month and the government imprisoned his followers. The next day I collected all the books that I had from the Muslim Brotherhood and burned them. From that night I severed all relations with the Brotherhood, and no one has contacted me since, thanks to God.

*102*

*Theater group*    I like to laugh and to make people laugh. I joke about everything, and people think of me as being a clown. All the people with whom I mix like me. In Cairo there was a group of actors called the Ansat el-Aneil. I filled out a form to join that group. The first thing they asked me to do was to learn to play the *oud* [an instrument ancestral to the lute, larger but similar in shape]. I took lessons for about two months and practiced daily, but I discovered that I had no talent for music and that I preferred acting. I asked them to give me a chance as an actor, to test me. I passed the test and was selected to play the role of a servant.

I stayed some time with that acting group and always had the role of a servant because I was dark and a Nubian. I remember that when I appeared on stage, the people laughed loudly at me because I was very fat and it was hard for me to move around. When I laughed, my whole body shook. When I pronounced Egyptian or European words, my accent would make them laugh. Instead of saying "telephone," I would say "tefelone" or something like that. I would always garble my speech purposely.

One of the plays I liked best was a story of a man who married another woman in addition to his first wife. His second wife was a dancer who upset his wife, maltreated his children, etc. When he married this woman he thought he would live in paradise, but instead he discovered he was living in hell. This play was *The Miserable People*, a story about a rich man who had some children before he married his second wife. This wife was fooling him. She was a loose woman working as a dancer. She married him only for his money, which she took and spent with other men. I played a servant in the house whom the children liked and trusted a great deal. In the play, I saved money from my earnings and bought things for them. Finally the rich man became bankrupt and the second wife left him, but when he needed money to eat, I, the Nubian servant, gave him the money I had saved. He appreciated that and rewarded me.

In my theater period I was very ambitious. I had high hopes, and I liked the applause. I still daydream about that time and hear the applause in my imagination. Discrimination stopped me from achieving my ambition of becoming a famous actor. It was because I was a Nubian that I could not get any other part beside that of a servant.

I liked Muhammad Sayed, the director of our troupe, very much. He had a sense of humor, and he was a strong personality. What I liked most about him was his combination of seriousness and sense of humor. He had good judgment and gave everyone his due. I admit that I imitate this man now. When I direct a party or when I try to get some benefit for Kanuba, I imagine him and try to act as he would act. Sometimes I used to go with Muhammad Sayed to picnics at the dam at Helwan, and I attended his acting class in Shobra. After I left Cairo for Kanuba, I corresponded with him for several years but finally stopped, and I do not know anything about him now. I would like to see him.

Our acting troupe had no theater of its own. We moved from one place to another, and we used to play for large crowds, but usually they were people of the lower classes. For instance, we played in the Rahani and Basfar theaters. During this time I had so many activities— the Muslim Brotherhood, the theater, as well as my work—that I was going from morning until night and I neglected my prayers. My father became very upset and said it was a sign that I was starting the loose life. He was sure I was getting into bad company, although he did not know exactly what I was doing in the theater. He considered acting to be a low activity, and my stepmother continually caused lots of trouble between me and my father. She ridiculed me and told him sarcastically, "Go and see what your son does."

Once, when we were playing *The Miserable People*, I invited my father and stepmother to come. I purposely wanted to show him what a stepmother means to children and how it upsets the family. After the play my father was very very angry, and he advised me not to act again. I quit the theater shortly after that, partly because of my father and wanting to avoid quarrels and troubles with him, but it was more than that. I was afraid I would fall into a wrong way of life. The other members of the theater didn't want me to leave and they tried to persuade me, but I refused. Actually, one of the main reasons I quit was because of discrimination against me.

I was noted among the group as an enemy of women. I didn't mix with them or join in their activities. I never invited a girl for a glass of wine or took one to movies. I never spent a melleem on them! This is why I was not a favorite among the actresses. They called me "you *berberi*" and viewed me as a servant whether I was on the stage or off. Some of them wanted me to take them out and to become friends with them. They wanted me to offer them drinks and take them to picnics. I refused because I was poor, but I also feared having sexual contact with them. I never tasted liquor in my life. Liquor kept the distance between me and women. They always wanted a man to take them by car after the play and buy them drinks. I am not that type, and besides I felt out of place because of my color. I also feared my father. He would soon have discovered if I went to those bars, because Nubians worked in all of them and those Nubians remember a face!

I dreamed many times of making love with some of those women, but I was always afraid to try it. One time one of them became angry with me and shouted, "You are a servant out of the play as well as in it!" I felt that most of the workers at the theater looked down on me, although they acted friendly enough. I had no real friends among them.

You know I am light-skinned, and when I played my part I had to blacken my face. After playing my role I'd quickly wash my face and escape through the side door, though traces of the make-up stayed on my face and lips for a long time.

I did have some friends among the clerks and smaller employees. I hoped to be another Ali el-Kasr, the famous Sudanese comic actor. I liked Negib el-Rehani very much also, he was my ideal. Oh, another reason why my father wanted me to quit was because I was showing Nubians in a bad light, making them appear ludicrous and funny. He said, "Shame, you are insulting your people." So I left the theater, although I liked it very much. I am very fond of acting. During that time I used to memorize the roles of the other actors, and sometimes I would even help the director. My salary was only twenty-five piasters a month for the first year, but after that I was raised to twenty piasters for each performance. My usual time on stage was only from fifteen to thirty minutes. Sometimes I assisted the make-up man. I was in that troupe for four years, from 1941 to 1945.

Besides acting, I was also fond of sports. Although before I had liked swimming, I especially like gymnastics. But I was very fat when I was in Cairo, and when I became too fat to walk I decided to join the sporting club known as the Muktar Club. Actually I was not fat before 1941, but after that I seemed to eat much. I guess the opportunity I had with the British Army was what enabled me to eat so much. I had things there that I had never had before, and they sold things cheaply. A can of cocoa, for example. I used to eat it rather than drink it with milk. I was so fat that I had to ask a doctor for advice. His recommendation was not to laugh so much and to eat less. He also gave me some drops to reduce my appetite and advised me to take up a sport. That's why I joined the sporting club.

Sometimes after I finished my work in the theater I went to the club, where I took off all my clothes except my shorts and joined a group of fat people to run three kilometers every night. We started after 9:00 when the streets were fairly empty. I always took my place in the rear. The trainer was in front, and I had an agreement with a restaurant owner to let me enter his restaurant dressed only in my undershorts so that I could have something to eat or drink on the way while the group continued on without me. Then when they returned that way, I would take my place in the back of the line. This worked until the trainer found out, and from then on I was put in front of the line.

During this whole time of the war and the British Army I was very active. Once I started a small workshop in Shobra. I wanted to find out what the people wanted, the goods that they would need during a shortage. Once I heard that there would be a shortage of stove cleaners, so I bought many empty tins to make cleaners and sold them cheaper than the regular price. Once I also made thumbtacks. I had to stop this because of the high taxes. I had some laborers working for me and an assistant who took care of the shop. My father didn't know anything about it. After I quit going to the Sunday zikrs of Sheikh Shasli, I spent about an hour or two there every day and sometimes my whole Sundays. I figured that the British forces would one day evacuate, and I wanted to be prepared in case they did move. I did not want to be without a job. I also had the idea of making matches, but I was unable to because it required a raw material from abroad. My business didn't last long, and I lost my investment.

You may remember that I left school to work during my third year of intermediate school. I had been forced to leave because my stepmother didn't want me to continue. But I always wanted to better myself, and I began studying to finish the second primary school and get a certificate. I made friends with the neighbors so they would lend me their books and explain things to me. I studied with a keen interest. These people were all Egyptians, and after a year of doing this I got my second primary school certificate from the Eh Tabi School in Zetoun. After this I joined a private secondary school, but I couldn't continue because I had no time.

I also thought of joining another institute where attendance was not compulsory every night. My father gave me so much work that I had to stop my education for awhile. When I worked in the British Army and began to earn good money, I thought of my education again because I wanted to improve my position. That was when I joined the British Institute in Cairo to study engineering. The courses were given in English, so I had to join the English class in order to understand the instruction. My main hope was to get a certificate in welding engineering, which would push me to a good position, that is, to be a boss. I wanted to earn more money, and I hoped to go abroad for higher education. I hoped the British would send me to England, and I attended the English class regularly for two years. My enthusiasm for education began to slow down. I felt I was not getting ahead with it, and my attendance began to be irregular. Finally I stopped completely.

During this time, between 1940 and 1944, I also took many trips around Cairo with my friends. I especially went with one of my theater friends called Muhammad Sabet. I had a small camera and took many pictures. You have seen them. I went to the pyramids and the museum and to Helwan to swim, and I often went to the dam. I was just like a tourist. I also went to many weddings of Egyptians but not of Nubians. I remember the processions with the bride and groom; sometimes there were twenty-five taxis following blowing their horns. Most of the weddings I went to were those of my companions at work in the British camp. Sometimes I did it to establish good relations with the Egyptian workers.

During the period I worked in Cairo I had many friends, and among the closest of them were Christians, like Lewis, Seleem, Marco, and Maurice. They worked with me, and I established very warm relationships with them. Some of us used to spend most of our spare time together. Actually, I had no Nubian friends then. We usually went to the movie house once or twice monthly. My Christian friends liked American films, whereas I liked Arabic comedies. We never discussed religion, and we were good friends in spite of our different beliefs and rituals. The one I liked best was Marco, who was shy and polite. He was a Greek orphan. The group used to make fun of him, but I never did. He finally left Egypt to join the Greek Army. He sent me many letters, but about ten years ago he stopped, and I don't know what happened to him. Lewis was a Catholic, but Maurice was Orthodox. The only time I visited Christian churches was when I attended the marriages of Maurice and Lewis.

One of the things I regret most about leaving Cairo was leaving those friends with whom I had a very happy time. We went to movies, exchanged visits, and made picnics at various parks in Cairo and at the dam. We were always laughing and joking. Probably the time of my friendship with the Christians lasted about five years. I never associated with Nubians during that time, and I never went to Nubian associations or clubs in Cairo or Alexandria. I guess it was because my father tried to avoid them, and perhaps I was trying to escape the fact that I am Nubian.

Around 1944 or 1945 some British Army forces were moving to Palestine. They asked me to go with them, but I refused. I dislike fights and aggression. I dislike being around it. I was always well liked by people I worked with. Once my boss recommended me for a job with Shell Oil. I passed an exam, but at the last moment I did not take that job. Another time some of my fellow workers wanted me to join them financially in a theater in Shobra, but at the last minute we had a disagreement and I left them.

I used to give my father two pounds for room and board each month during my work with the British Army. I also asked him to keep some of my other money for me. He has never given me money since I was a child, except twice. When I moved back to Kanuba in 1946 or 1947 he gave me about 150 pounds, and he also gave me some money when my irrigation project failed. I needed it to pay my debts. I never wrote my father for money, but sometimes he used to send me a little cash for the feasts, especially for Ramadan.

In 1944 I had an accident. You know how the trams in Cairo don't stop. Once I was trying to grab the pole to get on the tram, but I slipped under it. I had many wounds, a broken nose, and my brains were shaken slightly. The ambulance came for me and took me to the hospital, where I stayed for twenty-one days. I vividly remember the day my father came to the hospital. Suddenly he called to me and asked for my hand. While he held it he read some verses from the Koran, and when he finished he said, "Go to your work and God will guard you." Those verses from the Koran had their influence because I got well. Some other people who came to visit me were surprised when he offered them Coca Cola because, according to him, nothing could happen to me. He sincerely believed that God would help me. Another accident happened to me in Maadi a couple of years before. I tried to sit on a chair like I am sitting in now [folding chair], and I broke my leg while trying to sit. I did not go to the doctor, but my mother's aunt (whom we Nubians consider to be an expert bonesetter) treated me and it healed.

After I quit the British Army when they were moving to Palestine, I went to Suez looking for a job. For about three days I looked around, and especially I was interviewed at Shell Oil. I thought I could get a job as a welder there with good pay. This was in 1945 near the end of the year. As I was walking the streets of Suez I met a dark man who I thought was a Nubian, and I asked him to direct me to the oil company. I told him I was a stranger, and I asked him if he could help me since we were of the same color. The man showed me the way and invited me to his place after I had finished my business. When I visited him I discovered that he was the owner of a milk store. He told me that when he came to Suez he was like me—looking for work. He had dreamed of having a dairy and selling milk. He had started with one cow and gradually, through hard work, he came up. Now he owns one of the three largest dairies in Suez. During the three days I spent in that city I visited him three times. I was amazed at his success.

The man told me that living in Suez was expensive and that it was not easy to find a job with the oil company. He suggested that I work for him, but I refused because I was already thinking of moving to Kanuba. I wanted to carry out my own projects since I had some money saved and my father had been pressing me to go back to Kanuba. However, it it is still one of my dreams to have a dairy like that man had in Suez. For me, the best places have water and are green. In my daydreams I see our village here green and full of palm trees. I make the analogy of green and paradise. I want Kanuba to be green.

My father kept trying to persuade me that it would be good to go back to Kanuba and invest the money I had saved cultivating the family land. He thought that I would do better there than in Cairo. He felt that I was being corrupted by my friends and activities. I came back to Kanuba in 1946 full of dreams and willing to struggle. I tried hard, but all my trials were in vain. I lost all my money in my pumping scheme.

108

After that failure, I had to look for a job to earn a living. Finally I found the position in the hospital which I now have.

*Marriage in Kanuba*    During my childhood I always felt motherless. Even though my grandmother acted like a mother to me, I still felt motherless. I remember very little about my actual relationship with my mother up until 1944. I can say that the tram accident was the starting point of my new relationship between me and my mother. As soon as she heard about that accident, she immediately sent a note to my father asking him to choose one of two things—either to send me to her or to let her come and see me. My father, who did not want her to come to Cairo, asked me to go to Kanuba to see her as soon as I was well.

I went within a few days of recovering. Meeting with her was truly strange. All the way on the train I tried hard to picture her. I finally got to the village, and I recognized her immediately and rushed toward her eagerly, but she refused to shake hands with me. It was because I was an adult, but I did not know this. Incredulous, I said, "I am your child, I am not a stranger!" She then covered her hand with part of her dress and shook hands with me through the cloth. I was so amazed and shocked that I felt suddenly sick, and I told her: "Don't treat me as a stranger! I came to be with you. You're my mother. It doesn't matter if I share your room or even your bed!" After this upsetting meeting, I stayed with her in the same house, and we talked the whole night, mainly about marriage. She pressed me to marry soon and gave me thirty names to choose from.

My stepmother had been urging me for some time to marry her brother's daughter. The girl used to come frequently to our house in Cairo. She joked with me, knitted pullovers, and even made shirts for me. She showed a special interest in me and I had no objection to marrying her, especially since she was trying to please me in many ways. However, when I talked to my mother about her, she became angry at the idea of marrying a non-Nubian. My mother was not the only one with these feelings; my father privately was of the same opinion. Of course, all my friends wanted me to marry an Egyptian. They thought the lighter Egyptians were more beautiful, and they all wanted to marry one of them. But I followed my parents' advice and I refused. I did not want to repeat my father's story. Many of the people, even my relatives, were expecting me to marry an Egyptian as my father had done. One of them commented, "You, Shatr, we even excluded you from the Nubian list because we thought you would marry an Egyptian!"

My uncle, Sheikh Salama, then sent me a letter telling me that he had chosen his wife's sister as a bride for me. The girl was one my mother favored because she always liked my Uncle Salama. My father also agreed, so I consented to marry. At first I concealed this decision from my stepmother and only told my father. I also sent my answer to Sheikh Salama, who then sent a letter to my father instructing him to write officially to the bride's father. When my future mother-in-law came to Cairo (she was also my distant aunt), I visited her with gifts. I did not discuss the marriage with her at all, but after that I sent my uncle, Sheikh Salama, a necklace and a ring to present to my bride. I had no idea what she looked like. My mother blessed the marriage and commented that since my bride spoke Nubian she was acceptable.

After I had made all the arrangements, I finally told my stepmother about the marriage. She was angry and so was her brother's daughter, who was planning to marry me. The girl had been making a pullover for me, and when she heard about my engagement she threw it into my face. The second time that I came to Kanuba was to finish my arrangements through mother and to try to see my bride. I stayed only three days and I failed to see her. They hid her, according to the Nubian tradition, and I returned to Cairo greatly disappointed.

When I finally came back to Kanuba I was very nervous as I approached Daraw on the train. I did not know what my new life would hold. I think even though my brother Saber had gotten on the train with me at Idfu, it made me even more nervous because I really did not know him. Anyway, when the train arrived at the station, I found a group of men, women, and children welcoming me. I had never had such a reception before. Each tried to show me a special welcome. Women were giving joy cries, and suddenly I felt my anxiety gone. For the first time I felt that I was among my own people, my relatives. The road to Aswan was not paved then, and they put me on a donkey to take me three kilometers from the station to the village. This was my first experience on a donkey and I was frightened. I found the village looking like the mountains to me—that is, it was desolate with no fields around it. It was much more desolate than I had remembered Old Nubia as being.

One of the things that struck me in the first days spent in Kanuba was the great amount of attention that everyone lavished on me. All day, every day, small groups of the villagers came to my house to talk with me, visit, entertain me, and sometimes to have supper with me. Each family in the village invited me to eat at their house. The picture I have in mind of my early days in the village is of crowds of people visiting and of food. I was impressed by the Nubian habit of sending trays of food to visitors. This generosity was not like anything I had experienced in Cairo.

At first I had no gallabeya gowns, and I felt like a stranger when I wore my pajamas. In Cairo after work, men always used to wear pajamas in the streets. But this custom was strange to the village; everyone wore a gallabeya. Also I remember I was very formal when I went to visit or to have lunch or supper. I always felt that I had to wear a suit and tie like the effendis [officials and middle class] in Cairo. You can see how this has changed now. One thing that puzzled me when I first came was what to answer to questions from the villagers about our relatives in Cairo. I was too embarrassed to admit that I had hardly ever visited them while living there. But I liked to be away from the confusion and noise of the city with its taxis, crowds, and horns. This peacefulness was attractive to me at that time. It still is.

One experience that sticks in my mind is how on the second morning of my arrival I was awakened by cold water being poured on my face. What a shock! I suddenly heard my grandmother telling me to get up and pray the dawn prayer. This was something completely new. I didn't expect it. "What would people say if you don't go and pray?" my grandmother asked me. At that time in the village, when all the old men were alive, it was the custom for most men to go and pray in the mosque at dawn. Praying in the mosque was then much more of a "must" here in Kanuba, although praying the dawn prayer is actually only a "should" in religion.

One thing that looked very different to me in those first days was the food they offered me, the *shaddi* and *shamsi* bread, etc. I did not remember these foods from Old Nubia, but it is very different from the *baladi* bread we have in Cairo.* At first I didn't like the different ways of cooking that the Nubians have. But in spite of that, I remember the first three or four days of my visit as being a time in which I was over-whelmed by generosity and friendship, and I immediately developed a great affection for the village. I was also impressed by the custom of everyone accompanying a traveler to the train station in Daraw.

My wedding took place in January 1946 on a Thursday here in Kanuba. I arrived three days before the wedding, and I returned to Cairo three days after it. I think it was the last really traditional Nubian one here in Kanuba, but I certainly was not familiar with Nubian customs. For instance, during the night procession they gave me a cross made out of dry palm leaves that had henna and perfume on it. I was instructed to walk to the bride's room carrying this cross. I did not know the purpose of it, but I carried it. Most probably it is a Pharaonic custom.

Also during the procession a woman carried a large metal washtub with a smaller tub in it. In the smaller one was a water pitcher and an incense pot. Sheikh Salama was in charge of organizing the procession. It started from my mother's house with two lines of Boy Scouts with drums followed by a man with a large drum. After that, I and my friends came with the musicians. We were followed by the crowd of women in the back of the procession. As we approached the bride's house, the

*Shaddi* is the typical flat Nubian bread of millet; *shamsi* is a popular bread of Upper Egyptian style; *baladi* is the common simple bread of Cairo and the cities.

singing stopped and a zikr was started by Sheikh Salama.

I was married in my father-in-law's house. I spent my wedding night in that house in a separate room with the young men. I gave the bride's father a marriage payment of twenty-five pounds, but he gave me back five and told me that it was too much and that I would need it. The procession was from 11:00 P.M. to 2:00 A.M. in the morning because we stopped to dance every few yards. The *barkeed* ceremony started at 8:00 A.M. and lasted till 11:00 A.M. After that they left me to do the things that I had to do.

During the *barkeed* is when small gifts [*nokout*] are given to the groom, but I refused to take them from anyone because I had heard, especially from my grandmother, that many disputes take place between families because of this *nokout*. An example, not from my wedding but which occurred later, is when a woman in Diwan sent a letter asking to get three piasters from another woman living in Kanuba, because she had given three piasters *nokout* earlier and this was not returned, even when her children got married. What was funny was that the woman sent the letter registered, costing her three and one-half piasters besides the piaster stamp on the letter. There are several disputes right now here in the village between women because of this *nokout* money. I have done my best to get rid of this troublesome custom.

When the procession was finally over and we came to the bride's father's house, a man was standing by the door to prevent anyone from entering. I was allowed in with a special guide, and the bride was sitting on a mat on the floor surrounded by young girls of her age. She was covered with a cloth. The only thing I could see were her eyes, and I noticed the golden ornaments strung across her forehead. As I was standing there, a girl came up to me and gave me some kernels of millet and asked me to throw them on her. This is the symbol of life. Another girl gave me a glass of milk, which I was told to offer to the bride. She drank some and I drank some too. I was eager to discover more about her body and what she looked like, but I could only see her two eyes. Anyway, my impression was good. Then I was escorted out of the room. Later I found out the milk symbolized the hope that our lives would be pure and clear like milk. I was led away to another room in the bride's house where a group of young men were waiting. We didn't sleep a moment. They joked, played, and danced the whole night.

Early in the morning, my bride and I were taken separately to watch the sunrise. We stayed for awhile and then came back. This is a Pharaonic custom, because in ancient times people worshiped the sun. After this we had the *barkeed*. I have forgotten the details of this except the *nokout* gifts. I let all my friends know indirectly that I would not accept any *nokout* because I had enough money at that time saved from my British Army work. Finally, about 11:00 A.M. the people left me to my destiny.

I was taken to the bride's room, and the only people with me were the bride and the *mashta* [a slave woman]. It was the first time in my life to be alone with a woman and to see her body. I asked the *mashta*, "What are you going to do with us?" She replied, "Aren't you a man?" I said with a humble voice, "Yes, but tell me first what I'm supposed to do and what you're supposed to do." This conversation took place outside the bride's room, and she could not hear it. The *mashta* said, "I will hold her for you." And she gave me a white handkerchief and told me to put it over my first two fingers and put it into the vagina of the girl while she was holding her. I said, "Haven't you invented a better way than this? This is brutal." She said, "Yes, we can use a razor." But I said: "No, no, no! You stay outside and I'll do it my own way! If I need you, I'll call you."

I then entered the room and closed the door behind me. I put out my hand and said *"Sallamu Aleykum"* [traditional Islamic greeting meaning "peace be unto you"]. She seemed surprised and did not take my hand or answer. I was wondering how sexual intercourse takes place. I had no idea how to go about it. I did not even know what a vagina looked like or where to find it. Believe me, I'm not exaggerating. Then suddenly I thought I remembered some of the discussions on sex I'd overheard among the laborers and young men. They talked about using their penis and that a woman had to lie on her back and raise her legs. They said that before having intercourse you should warm the woman up by kissing her and playing with her breasts; so I decided to try that.

Just as I was considering how to begin, I heard the *mashta* knocking at the door and asking what was happening. In a shaking voice I said, "I beg you, in the name of the Prophet, wait a little and leave me alone!" Then I said again to my bride, *"Sallamu Aleykum!"* She had been sitting on the bed all this time with her back toward me. I approached and clumsily grabbed her and kissed her. I told her to lie down and raise her legs, but she resisted. I said, "I will use my penis instead of my fingers," but she still kept her back to me.

The *mashta* was still outside shouting and asking to come in, so finally I opened the door for her. "I will use my penis. I only want you to hold her for me," I told her. I was bashful and went to the corner to take off my clothes while the *mashta*, who was a very strong woman, pulled the bride's dress up and held her legs. She said, "Come on, Shatr, come." The girl was still rigid and resisting. I was so frightened that my penis refused to become erect. I had no choice. I had to use my fingers. When she groaned I closed my eyes. It is a bloody, brutal action! The pounding of drums outside prevented anyone from hearing what was going on, thank God! After this I felt strange and did not know what to do. I wanted to leave. The *mashta* told me to go into the other room while she took the handkerchief to the bride's family.

Later in the afternoon I was sitting with friends when a desire for my bride began to flame in me. I did my best to get rid of the boys, but they frustrated me. They did not want to leave and hung around until after sunset. As soon as they left, I went in to her and really had intercourse. She was still rigid and afraid. It was painful for her, but I wanted to discover what was inside. Then I did it again at midnight, and this time she wanted it and enjoyed it. The next day I did it once every two hours. I knew I was leaving for Cairo, and I wanted to have intercourse as much as possible before leaving.

When my friends came to visit me that afternoon I was in a bad mental state. I could not help thinking of the troubles I had had in the last few hours with my bride and the *mashta*. I was upset by the disgust and pain but remembering also the intense pleasure. I was very anxious lest I should waste all my time receiving young men and visitors. I especially disliked receiving people I didn't know. Things are different now. Now I like friends to come, and I don't worry if I do not have intercourse for a week, two weeks, or even for a month. The dancing went on continuously for three days and three nights, and I had to play my groom's role outside the house, but all my thoughts were on sex. Finally it was over and I had to leave for Cairo, but when I got there I could only think of returning to my bride and my new life. I quickly finished up my business in a few months and came back to Kanuba to stay with my wife for good.

After I came to settle in Kanuba, I made a secret campaign against the practice of having a *mashta* on the wedding night. I avoided discussing this with the old men, who like to keep the Nubian tradition, and only made my remarks to young men, especially to those who were about to marry. Of course, young men are eager to have intercourse the first night, so I knew they would be receptive to my ideas. I vividly described my unfortunate experiences, urged them to eliminate the *mashta* and to use their penis instead of their fingers. I also urged them to insist on meeting the bride before their marriage. I said, "How can a man have intercourse with a woman to whom he has not spoken even one word? Islam is against that."

Sometimes when young men were about to get married I would take them secretly to see their bride before the wedding so they could see her first and be familiar with her face. For example, I took Muhammad Taha, my brother Saber, and Gamal; that's why Gamal is such a good friend of mine. At first I couldn't make much headway against this custom of the *mashta*—young men give in to their parents—but I worked against it secretly.

114

You know, the wedding procession takes a very long time, about three or four hours usually, so sometimes I went to the groom during the first confusion and said, "Come with me." I would then take him aside and say, "The *mashta* will do this and that, and your penis will not become erect, etc. etc." They would become frightened, and then I would take them secretly to the bride. I can get in to any house through my friends. I would take the groom in and let him take the bride's virginity privately. Then I would quickly return to the procession. It would only take about a half-hour, while the procession takes three or four hours. Then later, when the *mashta* came and knocked on the door, he would say, "I have finished. Here is the handkerchief. I don't need you."

This first step was important because the *mashta* was prevented from entering the room and interfering. I could have tried to take the groom to the bride before the wedding night, but I chose that time for several reasons. First, the procession is a time of confusion when no one would notice such things. Also, at such a time I did not want to give the groom time to think or discuss this with others because the idea went against tradition and custom. People would turn against me if they knew what I was trying to do.

## KANUBA

Even when I was in Cairo I was always interested in farming, and even when I was a child I used to grow small plants in a plot next to our house in Zetoun. This is how interested I was in agriculture. Since I had saved some money, was interested in farming, and had such energy and interest, my father encouraged me to move to Kanuba. I also wanted to be with my mother, as I told you, and to live with her since I had never lived with her for any length of time before. I quit the company where I had been working for a few months and moved to Kanuba. I had not seen my mother, except briefly, for many years, and I hardly knew my brothers and sisters. Abdul, the brother born after me, had once come to Cairo; so when I saw him at the Minya station during the time the train stopped there, I recognized him right away. He was in Minya because many of our relatives lived and worked there.

When I got to Kanuba, my brother Saber and my sister Fatma were waiting for me along with my mother and many relatives and friends. Actually, Saber was waiting for me at the Idfu station, which is about fifty miles before Daraw. He got on the train there and accompanied me to Kanuba. At that time we had not seen each other for ten years. In the Idfu station I saw a Nubian standing in front of me, staring at me. He paced back and forth on the platform, looking at me strangely each time he passed. He frightened me, so I asked him if he wanted anything.

*115*

He said, "I am looking for Shatr Shalashil." We embraced and we both wept.

I had not seen Fatma since she was a child, and when we saw each other she refused to shake hands with me and hid herself. She treated me as a stranger, even worse than a stranger—she acted terrified. I called to her while I wept and said, "Come, I am your brother, we both have the same father and mother!" Since that time in 1946 a deep relationship has developed among my mother, my sister, my two brothers, and me. My father came to Kanuba only twice. The first time, he came to the wedding and stayed a couple of weeks with my mother in her house. Then he came again in 1958 when my mother was very ill.

When my mother left Maadi to come to Kanuba she never again returned to Cairo. She stayed in the village till her death this year. She believed that marriage was a matter of fate. She said that my father married another and neglected her because that was her destiny in life. In spite of that second marriage. she always welcomed my half-brothers. Once Hamdi, my half-brother, came to work in Aswan and found it difficult to live there. I asked him to move here, and he stayed with us for three years. I did my best to please him, even to the extent of cooking the kind of Egyptian food to which he was accustomed instead of serving him Nubian food. But he could not get used to our life here and after three years returned to Cairo.

When I first came back to Kanuba I lived at Sheikh Salama's house, where I occupied one room. I stayed there about four years because my mother had no room in her house. I paid my own expenses. I had decided to have a house of my own, and I started to build it soon after I arrived here. I spent those four years building it. Many days I even worked on it myself. Salah Muhammad, the famous Kenuz builder who lives here in the Kenuz part of the village, built the domes for me.* Some other builder from Daraw built the other parts of the house.

I cannot remember the cost exactly, but I bought four kirats of land [a kirat usually equals $1/24$ of a feddan] from Hag Omar and his father for 20 pounds. I divided the property into three parts; one for me, one for Saber, and one for my other brother Abdul. My brothers did not pay anything and I did not ask them for money, but Saber helped me a lot in building that house. He was working in Sudan earning a great deal, and he sent me money for two or three years. I can't remember how much exactly but he must have sent around 100 pounds.

I fenced the land first and planned to build a big house for all three of us. I discovered that this was a very bad idea because many disputes and fights would take place, if not among us then among our wives; so we decided that each should build his own. We tossed a coin

---

*Shatr's house is the only one in the Fadija section of the village with Kenuz-style vaulted roofs.

to determine who would have which third of the land. After everything was settled, I prayed thanking God. I put the pump in the courtyard myself. I wanted to build a house similar to those in Cairo, but my mother refused. By this I mean that I wanted tiles, pipes, water taps, glass windows, doors like in city houses, a dining room, and a sleeping room. My mother told me to build my own house as I wanted but not to build Saber's in the European style. Saber didn't agree with my mother and wrote to me to build his house in the European style. But I replied, "Listen to mother because she will be angry, and we don't want a nice house and an unhappy mother." I greatly enjoyed participating in building the house. Sometimes I cut bricks, and usually I worked on the house after my work at the hospital. Many people helped me work, Sheikh Abdullah and his children, also Hussein Gamal and his children, etc. Most of these children have grown up and are not here in Kanuba now. As you can see, I even put in pipes to make it easier for my wife so that she could always have running water.

When I first came here, just before the beginning of 1947, I started to work enthusiastically. I had some money saved up, and I wanted to develop the area and become rich. Many people here welcomed my attempt. They encouraged and helped me by giving me money without receipts. Also the people did not hesitate to help me when I was in hard times after the first failure.

My failure was due mainly to the water. The men who installed the pump deceived me by putting it only twenty-one meters down when it should have been about thirty-five. After my failure, the people tried to gather enough money to buy the pump from me to build a mill; but I refused because I was afraid it might not work, and I sold it to some other people outside the village for a loss. I had a hard time. During that period, I had only one gallabeya, and I washed it at night so that I could wear it the next day. Sometimes I had no money to feed my family because I spent all the money in trying to work the land and develop it. I encouraged the people to start cultivating the land. I had ten feddans, and I cultivated the whole ten. I also tried to irrigate the land of Hanafi Baba, Salah Halil, and Abdu Mahmoud. They paid me eighty piasters an hour, and each feddan took four hours to irrigate. I had great hopes. I wanted to emphasize horticulture and palm trees because that is very profitable. I also had the intention to plant fruits and clover and to have a farm with animals in order to provide the village with meat and milk. This would have given me a stable income.

I planted a palm tree every six meters. I also planted many trees among my own ten feddans in order to protect the crops from sand and wind. There are one or two of those trees still alive out there, though they are stunted. Most of them are dead now. I used all my resources, but nature conquered me. But that's all in the past. In spite of my failure

I still have hopes of continuing in agriculture when we get some water from the High Dam. Someday I will realize my dreams. You always hear me saying I want Kanuba to be a paradise.

*Popular versus Orthodox Islam*    When I came to Kanuba at the beginning of 1947, Hag Abdullah was the imam of the mosque. Actually, he has been the imam since the village settled in 1933. When I came, I found the two extremes in religious practice. The popular Islamic group was headed by Sheikh Salama. The majority of the village followed him. Sheikh Muhammad was one of his followers, and now, since Salama left, he leads the popular Islamic group. People liked to listen to Sheikh Salama. He is a very persuasive speaker, and he makes people enjoy themselves and laugh. He liked to laugh and sit with people on the *mastaba* [outdoor stone bench usually built into the side of a house]. At the time, he was dynamic and persuasive. His agruments were strong, and he knew how to give evidence and be logical. Sheikh Salama is wise, an *afreet kibir.** He is a modern sheikh. That is why people of all ages like him. Even though he jokes and smiles and sings songs, he is a good Muslim.

When Sheikh Salama was here, he used to give a zikr in the mosque or outside several times a week. He comes from a family of zikr givers. Even now in new Diwan his brother also leads the zikrs. Actually Sheikh Salama is in harmony with the Old Nubian tradition of Islam. When I first came here, zikrs were very strong in the village and very popular. When Sheikh Salama made a zikr, he even invited the people from Daraw and they came. He was a dynamo. He organized many things and kept the custom of the zikr going. When he held the zikr, he lined the men up in two rows with the chanter at the head of the first row. They would begin a rhythmic motion with their head and body and repeat one word such as "Allah!" We don't have them very much any more. When Sheikh Salama left, the zikrs declined, especially because the imam is against them.

When I came here, Hag Abdullah's group, which is sometimes called the Wahabis by the others, was in the minority. We had few followers in comparison to Sheikh Salama. But Hag Abdullah wants to force religion on the people as if he were spoon-feeding medicine. He is always talking about what Islam prohibits, whereas Sheikh Salama always talked about what Islam permits. That is why the people preferred to listen to him. People like to enjoy themselves.

I can remember many disputes between these two groups in those early days. On the *mastaba*, in the mosque, and in the houses, arguments

*Literally, "big jinn or spirit"—a colloquial term meaning a person who likes to joke and has an exceptionally animated personality.

*118*

always took place whenever Sheikh Salama and Hag Abdullah came together for any reason. They always drew crowds around them. As I said, Sheikh Salama's arguments were strong. Hag Abdullah is an extremist. He likes to impress people with his dignity. He never jokes, and he doesn't listen to music or allow dancing. However, he has a weak personality and is not intelligent. He would have had no chance to promote his ideas if Abdul, my brother, had not come to the village to help me with the farming at the same time that I came in 1947. When Abdul came, Hag Abdullah saw this as an opportunity to promote his ideas, because Abdul is a fanatic Wahabi and a strong speaker. Actually, Abdul and I believe the same things, but our methods are different; he is a fanatic, but I am flexible.

Hag Abdullah and Abdul formed an Ansar al-Sunna group, which believes only in the Koran and traditions of the Prophet. They believe that they should only do what the Prophet Muhammad did. Hag Abdullah and some other men in the village learned about this doctrine when they had worked in Cairo. Disputes always arose between the two groups because the Ansar al-Sunna are always trying to stop the Old Nubian Islamic traditions. Hag Abdullah wanted to stop the visiting of saints' tombs, to stop the women from attending zars, and even to stop the *moulid* of the Prophet in the village. Of course he was against the zikrs that Sheikh Salama was always leading.

The dispute became so severe that finally Sheikh Salama wrote a complaint against Hag Abdullah's group and asked the government to send someone to settle the matter. After awhile the government sent an inspector from Al-Azhar who said that Sheikh Salama's attitude was not harmful to Islam and that both groups should be permitted to worship in their own way. I remember one Friday before that when most people in the village prayed twice—once with Hag Abdullah and another time with Sheikh Salama.

During Sheikh Salama's period of dominance in the village, religion was very active. He used to give zikrs at least every two days and sometimes two on the same night, one after the other. He might hold them in a house, in the mosque after the prayer, or in front of Sheikh Muhammad's store on the square. He was really fond of zikrs, and his dynamic lessons in the mosque were always crowded. Even though he was not the imam, he often gave the Friday sermon because he is known as a holy man. Sometimes in the evenings he gave religious lessons. He even held special sessions for women on the weekdays so that they could become educated in religion. People came from all the villages around when Sheikh Salama lectured.

I do not agree with him in everything concerning religion. I am a moderate, but now I lean more toward the teachings of the Ansar al-Sunna and Hag Abdullah. At the time that Sheikh Salama was in the village, I used to follow him, although not too strongly, because I was disillusioned with that sheikh in Cairo. But, as I said, I am a moderate. I know that many people here go to the cemetery although we tell them not to go. They still go secretly. I do not reprimand them because I know that change needs time. It's enough for the present to know that fewer and fewer women go. But Hag Abdullah is stiff. He always wants to raise the stick.

I am more like Sheikh Maher, the great Nubian politician who came to speak in our mosque. I try to apply his method. I hold the stick in the middle, as the saying goes, even though I now tend more toward Hag Abdullah's group in my beliefs. What I mean is that I believe, like them, that Islamic religion should be purified of impurities or innovations. All these things like zars and zikrs are religious innovations, which I think have grown up after the Prophet Muhammad. They are not really true Islam. Unfortunately, the Nubians were influenced long ago by Sufism and still have many such innovations, and they have many pagan practices from their Pharaonic days.

But, anyhow, I still do not completely differ with Sheikh Salama. I know that he is a good man. I remember once I had a strange dream; that was in 1950. In it Sheikh Abu Shalashil, my uncle, the great sheikh from Diwan whom I never met personally, came and introduced himself to me. I was very frightened and I could not understand why he said to me, "I advise you to grab Sheikh Salama by the hair." As soon as he said that, he disappeared. I remember that he was dressed like a Bedouin Arab from the desert. He had a cane and spoke in Nubian. I never understood the meaning of this dream. Actually, I only differ with Sheikh Salama on some principles, but my bad experience with Sheikh Shasli in Cairo stopped me from believing in sheikhs and in Sufism.

Of course, Sheikh Salama believes strongly in the power of dead sheikhs, and he says he will bring the coffin of our grandfather, Sheikh Shalashil, to New Nubia. He will build a new shrine. As I told you, I admire Sheikh Salama very much. When he was a leader here in the village, I was one of his helpers and I learned much from him in spite of the fact that I do not believe exactly as he does. I told you how he disliked the Muslim Brotherhood and how he convinced me to leave it. He predicted their fate while Hag Abdullah was neutral and had no comprehension of the danger.

*Village rural association*   In 1947, when I came to Kanuba, the rural association of the village was already in existence. It had been founded the year before, in 1946, and I joined it immediately when I arrived. Sheikh Muhammad, in addition to being head man of the village, was also working as a servant in the school, and someone sent in a complaint to the government against him because it is against the law to have two jobs at the same time. We never found out who wrote that complaint. Sheikh Muhammad is loved by everyone in the village. Maybe it was somebody from Daraw. Anyhow, Sheikh Muhammad had to choose only one job, and he asked our advice.

The leaders of the village held a meeting which I attended; Sheikh Muhammad was also there. They discussed the problem and decided that Sheikh Muhammad should maintain his job in the school and give up the job as village sheikh. The janitor job in the school gives a steady income which he badly needed, at that time about seven pounds monthly. He now makes fourteen pounds a month. The villagers were poor and they could not compensate him to be only their sheikh. At that meeting we chose Kamel effendi as sheikh to replace Muhammad. He was also the association's chief of the board at that time. Everyone knew that he would be selected, but we had to go according to our laws, so we had to nominate two other persons. Ezat effendi and I were also formally nominated, but it was unanimous for Kamel effendi. The requirements we set for a nominee are that he should own at least ten feddans, live permanently in the village, and have no incomes from governmental or other work. Sheikh Salama was the secretary, and the board consisted of eleven old men.

The association was founded to give support to the poor and needy and to hold celebrations on religious holidays, for example, on the *moulid* of the Prophet. At that time the board held their meetings only once or twice a year. The whole association met occasionally in the mosque, but the board met at the chairman's house. Most of their dealings were secret. They did not have discussions in the open as we do now. Most of the people in the village did not approve of the way the board carried on their business. I talked with many of the villagers individually and urged them against the board's way of dealing with matters.

When Kamel effendi died, the village elected Ezat effendi. After two years Ezat died, and Sheikh Hassan Salah took his place. All this time I began to talk to people to convince them that the meetings should be open and that everyone should attend the board meeting and take part in the discussion period. I said that everyone should take part in offering suggestions, but my efforts were in vain. Salah didn't change anything. After his death I made a *haraka** to separate the positions of sheikh and chairman of the board. I was successful, and we elected Sheikh Salama to be chairman of the board, although he was not sheikh of the village.

All those sheikhs, Kamel, Ezat, and Salah, died a short time after their elections. People began to relate their deaths to the fact that they had been elected as sheikh, and the village went without a sheikh for a whole year after Salah died. No one wanted to risk death. Then one day while a group of men were talking in Gamal Abdul's house, the problem of the

*A term meaning "movement"; here it has the special meaning of creating a favorable climate of opinion to accomplish one's goals.

*121*

sheikh was raised for discussion, and I suggested that we nominate Sheikh Osman. I said, "He is retired, honest, and has a good reputation." I also pointed out that the sheikhship should not be concentrated in one tribe and that other tribes should be given a share in the responsibility of village control.

The idea was well received, especially since nobody really wanted the job as sheikh. Sheikh Osman's wife opposed the idea and said that I wanted to kill her husband. Sheikh Osman himself hesitated but he finally accepted. Suliman Ahmed and I were formally nominated along with him because we were among the few who had ten feddans. Since it is considered by the people as a neutral place, the election took place in the mosque. People were officially sent by the government to supervise it. Sheikh Osman was elected and has remained the sheikh until now, although he does not have much influence.

We began to invite all the people to the general meetings of the association. We also sent invitations to the people who were members but who were living in Cairo, Alexandria, and Diwan. A committee of four was formed to organize the election process, and we were able to apply a new way for the first time. A blackboard was posted, and anyone who wanted to run would write his name down. About twenty wrote their names. For the election, we had people write their choice from the names on a piece of paper. These were put in a closed box, and after that the votes were sorted and counted. After the board was selected, they met and chose their chairman and secretary. Before the meeting I made a successful *haraka* among the elected members to elect Sheikh Salama to be their chairman. Sheikh Muhammad has been the treasurer since the beginning of the association. He is known as being honest and trustworthy, and everyone has faith in him.

It was Sheikh Salama and I who began a new policy in the club for the purpose of widening its aims and for developing a better relationship between the board and the village. After that election, he and I began to change many things about the organization and activities of the club. We moved from the mosque to an empty house next to Sheikh Muhammad. I formed committees to give an opportunity to young men who are not on the board to participate in the club and to prepare them for future positions of responsibility. We organized a committee for sports, health, and one for support of the needy.

I suggested that it would be a good idea to light the village streets. The board agreed, and I used some of our funds to buy thirty-five lamps which we put up at various places in the village. A non-Nubian farmer called Abu El-Hassan, who had lived for a long time in the Tongala area of Old Nubia and whom we trust, was in charge of lighting the lamps every night. We put them up at various places on the house front to light the street. Besides the lamps, we put a common pump in every street. I was always thinking of changes that could be done to the village. Many of these changes did not have much effect, because now look, we only have about three of the lamps left and the pumps no longer work. Nevertheless, one day the village will be as I see it in my dreams.

Once I was walking in a funeral of a dead woman. She was being carried on an *angareeb* bed [made of twisted palm strings over a wooden frame] covered with a sheet and then raised onto the shoulders of the men. The feminine shape of the woman was clear to be seen by everyone. I didn't like that. Another time I was walking in the funeral of a dead man who was sick before his death. His stomach was bloated out, and it was a ludicrous sight and many people were laughing. Then I had an idea of how we could change the method of carrying the dead. I began to talk to people about building a box especially for the purpose of carrying bodies to the cemetery. People did not like the idea and ridiculed it. But I went ahead and had a box made in Daraw. I made one similar to those used in Cairo. A week later a woman died, and I took the box early in the morning to the house. Her family refused and insisted on using the *angareeb* bed according to the Nubian tradition.

I had a great deal of opposition from the people. Sheikh Hassan Salah asked me about the box, so I asked him to try to see how comfortable it was. This was in front of Sheikh Muhammad's *mastaba*, and many people were present. Hassan Salah jokingly agreed to lie down in the box and covered himself with the sheet. He then asked some of the men to carry him to see if it was better than the bed. The strange thing was that a week later Sheikh Salah was hit by a train, and he was carried in that same box. It was a terrible misfortune to all the village. Nevertheless, since that time, whenever a person dies I have always delivered the box to the front door of the bereaved family to remind them that the body should be carried in that way.

When Sheikh Salama left Kanuba in 1960 a new election took place. I made a *haraka*, especially among the young men, for the purpose of convincing them not to select the old men as leaders. This was because we had such a difficult time with the old men the last time. I wanted to have my ideas about change in leadership approved, and I knew I would receive the most opposition from the old men.

Besides this, I made another *haraka*. Abbass had always been a troublemaker, and he was always one of the stupidest of those who opposed me. He thinks much of himself, although he is ignorant. I found that the only thing to do was to elect him to the board and to get him on our side in order to rid myself of his opposition. I was elected chairman of the board, and Gamal was elected secretary. I asked all the people to attend the meetings, and I told them that no secret discussions or meetings would take place. In order to get my ideas across, I usually talk to members of the board individually to get their opinions. If one agrees,

*123*

okay. If he doesn't agree, I leave him for awhile and send one who agrees with me to talk to him. Then I wait until things look favorable to have a meeting. When we do have one, there is no fighting among us; the village praises the way in which we handle our business. I don't deny the existence of opposition, but we don't fight.

I now have a group of good young assistants whom I call the "executive board." That is not an official title, and they are not all actually members of the board of the association. It is a group of six. This group is a dynamic force in the club. There are many other young men who are members of the association, but they don't have any influence. When we don't like a person or the way he behaves in the village, the group of six agrees to avoid him and to show him that he is really a zero. We don't declare this openly, and everyone spreads the idea in his own area. If the person comes to the *mastaba* in the evening, we are not friendly with him. If he attends the meeting, we don't listen to what he says. If he visits any one of us, we don't offer him anything to eat or drink.

Another case is Abu Hanafi. He is known as a smoker of hashish, a drunkard, a liar, and a troublemaker. He was very bad in this way several years ago, and we applied this method to him. He had to change his ways. But Abbass is the worst troublemaker we have. Some years ago, after Sheikh Salama left, Abbass actually had some leadership in the village because of his strong personality. He pretends that he is benefiting Kanuba, but actually he is doing many bad things. The majority of the young men here are working with me for the same goals. We want to get our village ahead. We usually say *"we* did it," but Abbass always say *"I* did it." There is a group of people in Kanuba working in silence, but Abbass only wants to strut. The way he talks and walks is obnoxious. He struts.

Last year two soldiers from the Camel Corps came walking through the village, and they asked for some water. They were from the camp, which is near the cemetery. Abbass quarreled with them and warned them not to walk through the village again. Then he sent a telegram to the governorate asking the officials to order the Camel Corps not to walk through the village. He wrote a stupid telegram in which he said: "Are we occupied by the Camel Police? Is Kanuba an Israeli village?" What is ridiculous is that he signed this on behalf of the people of Kanuba. Actually, no one in the village agreed with him. We were all angry because he signed for all of us without telling us anything.

Our way is always to discuss and to vote if we want to send telegrams, even to bereaved people or for congratulations. Abbass likes to make a show, but we understand him. Recently he caused trouble with the laborers who were excavating the gravel in order to build the new village. He warned them to stop taking the gravel away and threatened to kill them with his gun. He is also the only one who opposed the building of the clinic on his family's land. Actually, he doesn't own any land himself, but he always talks as if he were a large landowner. He was in Alexandria when we gave the governorate the land on which to build the clinic. When he returned he declared loudly, "If I were present at that time, I would have prevented Shatr from taking my land." But nobody listens to him.

*Some troublemakers* One of the worst scandals that has taken place in the village was when Abbass hit his mother with a stick. It was the talk of the village for weeks. Nubians in particular respect their mothers highly and think of them as having *baraka*. How could one dare to beat his mother when Allah says, "Be nice to her and love her. Talk nicely to your mother. Never express dissatisfaction to your mother. Never shout at your mother, etc." So what about beating them? Abbass already had many black marks against him, but this incident caused him to be called "the one who beats his mother."

Abbass is a rude man, and that is why his wife left him. He has a suit in the court to try to get her back, but he will not succeed. Everyone is against him, and her father ordered her not to go back. By the way, he will be transferred to Assuit. This is not due to one of my *harakas* but to a report from the police. It came because he abused his membership in the Arab Socialist Union. I solved a part of a problem by creating another. I wanted Abbass out of Kanuba, so I persuaded Muhammad, his brother, to move from Diwan to Kanuba—that is, actually, I persuaded him not to move to New Diwan from Alexandria as he had planned but to come to Kanuba instead. These two cannot stand each other, and their mother prefers Muhammad above Abbass.

Abbass then found his authority in the family here lost to Muhammad, and he began to stay away more and more in Kom Ombo rather than returning to the village at night. However, I found that Muhammad is also a troublemaker and his children are a bad influence on the other children in the village. That's the way it goes sometimes, God wills it!

You would not guess it now, but after Sheikh Salama left the village Abbass actually appeared to inherit his authority. I wanted to take the place of Sheikh Salama, but Abbass is very strong, both physically and in personality, but he was first to succeed in collecting the young people around him. Sheikh Muhammad was afraid to oppose him, and I feared him too. You know he threatens people with his gun. He is very unpredictable and wild and physically very strong. His deep voice and arrogant manner are very commanding. My plan was to get rid of him indirectly, and I never opposed him face to face. Though my main reason for trying to get rid of him was to further myself as a leader, it was not only for my own aims. I thought that Abbass's ideas were dangerous and harmful to the village.

At first Abbass was strongly supported by the whole Sisiwa section of the village and by some of those, such as Rahman, who do not have strong tribes and who associate with and support the Sisiwa people. Not only those from the Mundolab tribe but even many of those from Sisiwa also dislike Abbass as much as I did, but they seemed too weak to do anything. One bad thing that Abbass did when he had authority was greatly to widen the gulf between us and the Kenuz; but I succeeded gradually in getting the leadership away from him, and now he is hardly even a member of the village.

Last month he was caught by the police in Kom Ombo when he hit a man over the head with a stick. He was let out on a bail of ten pounds, which he did not have. The Sisiwa group went around collecting money to free him, and they suggested at the club that the whole village should contribute. They claimed that it was not Abbass that they cared for but the good name of the village, but the rest of the village did not accept that. They said it was the Sisiwa name which concerned them and not that of the village.

This is one example of how tribes and local groupings from Old Nubia continue to influence our life despite our attempts to create a unified community. Hussein, Ahmed Khalil, Sherif, and Hag Ibrahim Bahrem of the Sisiwa group each contributed one pound. They then went to the Diwan people, the Dungulab, and others to ask for contributions. I found myself in a very critical position. I felt this was a test of village unity. At the same time I am against Abbass, and I felt that he had done wrong and should be punished. I was glad that this had happened to him and hoped that it would be a lesson to him about his aggressiveness. Anyway, I tried to help in finding contributions and to talk people into a unified response. Finally, I myself paid a pound and I got other Mundolabs like Sheikh Muhammad, Hag Abdulla, Aziz Kalam, and Gamal as well as Mahmoud Muhammad to contribute one pound each.

This is only one of many difficulties and crises that Abbass has caused for the village. You know his problem with his wife who has divorced him. Recently I went to his mother to ask her about getting him a new bride. I think that getting married might be good for his personality and calm down some of his aggressive tendencies. However, she picked up dust and put it on my head. Dust represents shame when people put it on their heads during a funeral, and that action was an attempt to humiliate me. It meant that my suggestion was like dirt and was received like dirt!

Abbass is the greatest obstacle to my leadership in the village, but Idris, the village watchman, is another one who is disliked by people. People don't "give him face." They usually exclude him from conversations. This is the way I encourage the village to act toward people whose behavior is not acceptable. We don't approve of Idris's lack of responsibility for his sister Fahima. But I also tell the villagers not to be violent, only to avoid him and not to give him face. Fahima is known in the village for her bad behavior. Idris never protects his sister. He hasn't taken any positive action to stop her or even to blame those who have affairs with her. It's getting so now that her contacts are more and more with non-Nubians. Her work in the clinic gives her every opportunity for this. I have never discussed her behavior with her, but I have urged others like Haroun and Gamal to tell Idris to keep an eye on his sister and to get her married again as soon as possible.

Idris is known in the village as being stupid and fat. He just eats and talks nonsense. This is why he is excluded from any activities of the village. He is supposed to be the village guard, but any criminals could attack us. He would not know the difference. Sometimes the young men describe him as "the man who forgot how to fire." What is funny is that he comes to the *mastaba* and chatters while his sister is having an affair at the house. Often people know this is going on while he is sitting there. When you people first came, I told the women not to tell Samiha [one of the members of the research team] anything about such behavior and to treat Fahima as if she were like anyone else. I reminded the women that they are all Nubians and that no matter what happens they will remain Nubians. I told them that they should suggest and remind but not to quarrel. If they quarrel there would be a big scandal in the village, and in the end it will hurt the name of Nubians.

This is a technique I acquired from Sheikh Salama when he was faced with a problem woman called Terima. This was an old woman who tried to look young, and she was always sexually entertaining the Camel Police or anyone else who wanted to come. Hussein was her favorite, and several years ago he was often seen returning from her house at night. Sheikh Salama used to talk to her and warn her. He would explain to her that adultery was a sin according to the Koran, but it did little good. In his Ramadan lessons to the women in the mosque and on other occasions he referred indirectly to the severe prohibitions of adultery in Islam; yet he always told the women to give Terima "face" regardless of what she did. I remember Sheikh Salama saying, "I don't want a scandal and the people of Daraw pointing to us saying 'Look how the Nubians act!'"

However, there is now a general voice in the village that calls for action, especially now that Kanuba has just been joined in this region by all the rest of the Nubians. Most Nubians look to Kanuba as a pioneer. But I am afraid that more positive action might lead to a killing. Idris is selfish and thinks only of himself. His sister is having affairs while he is busy looking for a bride. What makes Fahima's case less serious is that she is divorced and is unmarried now. This does not mean that she has a right always to have adulterous affairs though. Not only Islam but Nubian custom is against that.

We have another serious situation in the village—Sheikh Muhammad's son Mahmoud. Even though he has just been married, he still has a favorite woman in the village, Sultan's wife. She is married and has two daughters, one of them fifteen years old. This affair has been going on for many years. Several times it has caused trouble in the village, and some people have even tried to take violent action. Once Mahmoud and Rahman, the brother of Sultan, actually fought with knives. What makes it difficult is that the woman's husband works in Idfu and stays away the whole week. Sometimes he only returns once in two weeks or once a month. He works at the railway station there, and it is very far from the village. This has been one of the scandals in the village, and it is still one of its main problems.

What complicates it more is the passive role of our two "elders." Of course, Sheikh Muhammad is Mahmoud's father, and the villagers don't want to hurt him. They all respect him and like him. Hag Abdullah is a close relative of Sheikh Muhammad and actually a distant uncle of Mahmoud, but he also is weak and vacillating. We all thought that the natural solution was marriage, but the unexpected happened. You attended Mahmoud's marriage a few months ago, but he still hasn't stopped his affair. We also calculated that when he got the job at the weather station, he would move to Aswan where his work is, but he stayed in the village. I am sure he stayed because of his infatuation with this woman.

Mahmoud is a boy of bad manners and reputation. The people of the village generally treat him formally and try to avoid him if possible. They are cautious in dealing with him and only treat him decently because they respect his father. He is really alone and has no intimate friends. His relations with other people are always superficial. His father well knows all these things, but he can do nothing for him. He himself is ashamed and dislikes the way his son behaves, but he can't control him. Sheikh Muhammad is a prudent man, but he fears his son. Mahmoud is a devil in the body of a man. He has abused his father's position and status. He is a bad seducer. When he first began committing adultery with Rahman's brother's wife, Rahman quarreled with him and attacked him with a knife. He tried to kill him. I and several others calmed him down and prevented murder. That was about five years ago.

Nobody trusts Mahmoud to come into his house, and a group of young men in the village wanted to beat him up, but I prevented them from doing that. I wanted to solve the problem in a peaceful way. Nobody talked with Sultan about the matter, and he didn't find out until recently. Once I advised him (before he knew about Mahmoud) to take his family to live with him in Isna. I explained to him that his family needs him and that he can save money and effort if he moved. He agreed and took his family to live there, but Mahmoud, the dog, went to Isna once a week to have intercourse with the woman. After a few months she came back to the village to stay.

Then some of the young men sent a letter to the husband informing him about the relationship, but, strangely, the man paid no attention to what people said. He is an odd person, and he is also a fool and stupid. For example, remember how in the Small Feast he argued with Hag Abdullah that he should not have allowed Dr. Kennedy to come into the mosque? He was very angry because he recorded the prayer. He foolishly considers such activities to be against religion. But of course they record prayers all over the Islamic world, and nobody in the village paid him any attention. My general principle is to avoid problems. Let them do what they want to do! Abbass always creates problems by loudly calling attention to any situation, but I know that problems exist and the best way to solve most of them is to work quietly.

I'll tell you about another quarrel we had recently. You know there was one of the Camel Police living in Hag Abdullah's house. He rented a room for one pound a month. He's about thirty-two years old, is married, and his wife is far away in Lower Egypt. His room faced on the courtyard, and he had to pass the family's living quarters to get in and out. Kamel's sister Fatma was sitting beside the street door one day, and Kamel noticed that the man kept going back and forth every few minutes through that door in front of her. Kamel suspected that he wanted to attract the attention of his sister and became angry at this.

I happened to be going to Hag Abdullah's store when I heard shouts. I ran quickly into the courtyard, and there I found a group of women trying to pull the camel soldier away from Kamel. He had a stick in his hand and was ready to beat him. I took the soldier by the arm out into the street so that he could calm himself. He was very excited and said that Kamel had insulted him. I was afraid that he would bring his gun and kill Kamel, so I took Kamel aside and talked to him. Finally he came over and said he did not mean to insult the soldier but he only wanted to tell him that he should respect the privacy of his family.

Hag Abdullah was in the mosque during this time and did not know about the matter until later. I resolved that dispute, and Kamel kissed the soldier's head and apologized. Actually, the kinds of problems we have in this village are not serious. You notice that we never take any of our problems to the police or the authorities in Daraw. The police did not even know about us until once there was a robbery here of a house on the outskirts of the village. Oh, I forgot, there was another incident.

Ten years ago a man from Daraw tried to rape Sadeya when she was passing the mosque at night. You know how quiet it is there when no service is in session. She screamed, but before the people from the nearest houses could reach there the man escaped. This incident caused great consternation and fear in the village. Women and girls stopped going to the market for several years. The people were so upset that they feared to hide their problems from the authorities as they always had. They informed the police, and I am sure this is the first time the Daraw police were aware of the existence of Kanuba.

*My children*　My first child was a boy who died seven days after he was born. I selected the name Muhammad for him. As you know, it is our custom to slaughter a small sheep or goat on the seventh day after a birth, which we called the Sebua. We invited the neighbors to eat bread soup (*fatta*). Even though my son died on the day of his Sebua, I did not inform the neighbors, and I let them go on with the preparations. Even my wife did not know. She was busy cooking. After the noon prayer, people came to my house to eat and to celebrate. I pretended that nothing had happened, and after lunch and tea I said, "Let us go to the grave and bury my son." I did this because I knew it was destiny for my son. I knew people were planning to come, so why should I spoil it with news of his death. In a matter of this type I was influenced by the sheikhs of the Muslim Brotherhood, who taught us that we should accept death with full satisfaction.

But as soon as I gave this news, chaos reigned. My wife screamed and the women began putting mud on their heads. All the Nubian death customs were revived, and it was out of my control. One thing that made the grief more severe was that it was a male child who died. I don't believe in the superiority of males, but the villagers, and especially the women, still maintain this idea. Even now, people joke with me and call me "you father of girls." A man who can only father girls is regarded as inferior. People pity him. This is because girls cause great trouble. A man likes to have his male line carried on. Girls are a burden. They are attached to their home from birth until marriage, and actually their father is responsible for them as long as they live. When they marry they go to the home of their in-laws, but if divorce occurs they have to come back to their father's house and he is again solely responsible for them. Male children are a good means of support for their parents as long as they live. They keep the line alive and they keep the house of their father open.

For all of my children, I am the only one who usually names the child, and my wife accepts. But I never force my will if she disagrees. I usually select names from the Koran or take the names of famous religious figures. The way I selected the name of my last daughter, Marium, was by opening the Koran randomly and picking a suitable name from that page.

When I had my first child I had not been here in the village too long, and I noticed that the customs here were much different from what I used to see in Cairo. Here I found all the people coming to congratulate me, and all the women came to help and share with preparations according to their ability. Also, the people who came to congratulate were not satisfied with only having one soft drink and dates; they wanted to eat. The midwife was a Kenuz called Mabruka Galeya.

*130*

My second child was Tama. She is still alive, and she is the older of the two girls. My third was Hadeega. She died of dysentery after two years. Her death caused me a lot of pain. I loved her a great deal and felt very sorry for the pain she suffered. After that came Emma and Zeinab, twins. All the villagers considered this to be a misfortune. It is not only because they were twins, but it was doubly unfortunate because they were both girls. My wife was very disappointed. People who came to congratulate according to our custom appeared as if they were attending a funeral. Although I was sorry at the time, if it happened again I would not be sorry at all. Now I believe girls and boys are equal, and I do not believe in those old superstitions. I am trying to promote this idea among the villagers, and some people now agree with it.

After three months these twins died. I remember being very sorry and weeping violently. After that, came Sofia, Abdul, Mahmoud, and finally Marium. I think this number of children is enough for me because these last four all survived and my income is low. Actually, I am considered a poor man in the village. I encourage the idea of birth control, and I agree with it. I would like to convince the villagers that it is a good idea. I myself practice it by reading the Koran before going to bed and asking God to prevent the conception of more children. Marium is four now. God seems to have answered my appeals.

I have no permanent favorites among my children. There is a wise saying of the Prophet that one prefers the sick until he recovers, the young until he's grown up, and the distant one till he's returned. My oldest daughter Fatma is quiet and mature. Sofia is intelligent, and Mahmoud is a kind boy. He has a good memory. I am planning to send him to Al-Azhar because he has such a good memory. Fatma may be married very soon to Sheikh Salama's son Taufik. If nobody comes to marry Sofia, I will send her to the Islamic Institute after preparatory school. But if someone wants to marry her, I will stop her schooling. I believe that girls should be educated, but it costs much and it is more important that they get married.

Actually, education is more important for boys. When I gave my second boy the name of Abdul, I wanted him to be like my brother Abdul, religious, wise, and active; but unfortunately he is naughty and stupid, and I am afraid he will not have a good career. Mahmoud is different. He is obedient and not a troublemaker at all. He is like my other brother Saber. He always says "hadr" ["ready"].

I don't think other people in the village treat their children the way I do. I make the kind of food my children like to eat rather than just cooking and dishing them whatever I want. I try to fulfill their wishes. I also ask them the kind of clothes they like to wear. I use the same methods with my children as I do with members of the club. I ask their opinion before going ahead. I always discuss with my wife about the treatment of the children,

*131*

and I believe that hitting and insulting children is detrimental to their growing up properly.

Once my wife told me some trouble that Abdul was making. He was standing on our roof and watching people in their courtyard. This snooping is considered very bad by the Nubians. I spanked Abdul and his mother interfered, saying that it would be the last time that he would do such a thing, but I told her that I wanted the boy to say it himself. I rarely spank any of the others, but sometimes Abdul is difficult. Once I spanked Fatma because she refused to take an injection that I wanted to give her, but I regretted it later because I was excited and she was really terrified of taking the injection. Actually, I myself am afraid of shots. Sometimes I hit my children if they do something wrong, but it usually has to be something serious, not just anything. When they play with fire or climb on a sakkia (and might fall into the well), if they climb a tree or go near a well or into the desert.

If they do something very very serious, I have another method. My wife tells me, "Your son did such and such. I warned him but he did not listen." I say, "Get me the rope." I tie his wrists and ankles and leave him on the ground, pretending to look for a stick while he has time to repent. I let him pass through a period of fright while he says, "No, this is the last time I will do it, etc." Then I start to hit him, but my wife stops me and says, "Don't hit the child anymore. This is the last time he will do it." I let her stop me and pretend that I am angry but that I am reluctantly bowing to her wishes. I have used this method several times with Abdul and Mahmoud but never with the girls. My wife disciplines the girls.

I want my children to be clean and neat. This is how my grandparents taught me. It is the Nubian way. I warn them about dangerous things. Usually I warn them rather than hit them, and in fact I haven't used a stick in two years. I think the boys are in a new stage now, and I do not want to be a violent father who punishes them. But I want them to have more of a friendly give-and-take relationship with me. None of my children was ever seriously sick except the ones who died. They only had ordinary childhood diseases and colds.

All my children are circumcised except Marium. Circumcision is important in indicating a change in stages of a person's life. It is a necessary thing, and it gives health. I attended the circumcisions of both my sons, Abdul and Mahmoud, but not those of my daughters. I asked the barber the day before to come early in the morning, and I did not tell the boys about it. Actually, Kamel Mizu helped the barber to hold the boys while I stayed outside in the street. He didn't take long, and after he finished I came in to talk to them and told them "congratulations." I said: "If God wills, you'll be all right after this. You will always be healthy. Now you are starting to be men. After this no *sous* [insects that eat dried lentils, rice, and beans] will be in your penis." We try to impress on them that it

132

moves them from childhood to manhood. Besides, it is the first step in the preparation for marriage, because in Islam it is prohibited to marry unless one is circumcised.

For my girls I asked a woman, an Ababda from Daraw, to perform the operation. I asked her not to remove all the parts as they do in Nubia but to cut only a small piece, the extra piece. I did not talk to the girls on this matter. Their mother talked to them. I only congratulated them after the operation. We had no music and drumming as the Kenuz do. Actually, circumcision in Nubia is very bad. They used to cut out all the sensitive parts, and then they would tie the two legs together to heal. Then when the girl got married, they had to cut it open with a razor. This gave the family a feeling of security because they knew the girl would remain a virgin until marriage. Here in Kanuba many of us think that it is not good to remove everything—just the extra part. We try to guard ourselves by the Prophet Muhammad's saying when he was addressing a woman who was circumcising her daughters: "Cut a part but not all."

Actually, the behavior of children and their discipline is very important to the village as a whole. The fights between children can cause great trouble between their parents. Once a boy named Ali Elzildine fought another boy, Ahmed Kourda. His mother came to the club to complain, so I got all the children who were there to hear the story. I found out that it was not only Ali who beat Ahmed but a whole group of boys who had done it. I suggested that all the boys be spanked until they found out who beat Ahmed. But I do not like to strike children myself, so I asked Ahmed Khalil to do the beating. I like to keep the children's faith, and if I beat them I know I would lose it.

Last month some boys tore down the posters we had put up in the club. I asked all the men to come to a meeting, and then I asked each one to reprimand his own children. Another time Muhammad, Gaber Ismail's son, formed a gang to break all the lamps in the village and to throw stones at the people passing on the highway. I asked Hussein and Ahmed Khalil to inform Gaber Ismail about his son's doings. Gaber brought the child to Sheikh Muhammad's *mastaba* and spanked him in front of a group of men. He warned him that he would kick him out of the house and would not be his father anymore if he did it again. This seemed to impress the boy a great deal, and he has been much better since then.

There are two methods we use to solve these problems caused by the children: indirect guidance and punishment. You know by now that I prefer the indirect method, and we use it in such ways as our skits and plays which we put on to illustrate morals and the proper way to do things. However, direct punishment relieves the tension of people who are greatly agitated. If that woman who came to the club and asked who beat her son was told that we would put on a play involving boys and encouraging them to play nicely together, this would not satisfy her mood

*133*

at that time. She wanted to see that boy spanked. Another method I often suggest is that when a boy does something bad, we exclude him from some community function that everyone enjoys, like a party or a wedding, etc. However, Ahmed Khalil has the opinion that this will make the child more aggressive by agitating him. He is a social worker, and maybe he has a point there.

Generally speaking, the Kenuz children are more peaceful than ours. Maybe it's because there are fewer of them. Sometimes a fight occurs between a Kenuz and a Fadija child. I am aware of these fights and try to settle it right away because there is enough bad feelings without agitating it with the kids fighting. When such fights occur I gather the children and call Ali Gebril from the Kenuz, and I say, "This is what happened. We are all Nubians, and *khalas*" ["that's all!" or "it's finished"]. He says the same thing to the Kenuz children. I also gave instructions to all the men in our village never to spank any of the Kenuz kids because this might be misinterpreted by them.

I like to tell my children religious stories. I know that my wife tells them Old Nubian stories, but I dislike that. I know that such stories cause complexes in children. All our Old Nubian tales concern ghosts and river spirits, good and bad. I think it is better to tell them stories of heroes, and that is what I do. My relationship with my children is based on friendship and understanding. I don't tell them any stories when they are young because they are only interested in playing and eating. That's why I only discuss playing and eating with them until the age of ten. I know that my wife tells them monster and ghost stories despite my ideas on the subject.

I take that back. Sometimes I do tell them religious stories and stories concerning the miracles of their grandfather, Sheikh Shalashil from Diwan. One of these is about a branch of dates which the sheikh threw into the Nile while at the same time repeating aloud the address of some people in Cairo where he wanted the branch to go. A few months later the people in Cairo said they received that bunch of dates.

Another time there was a zikr in Diwan. In the last row were two men, one of whom whispered that he was tired and wished the sheikh would stop. He only said this to another man very quietly, but Sheikh Shalashil somehow knew this in spite of the loud chanting, and he stopped the zikr. He told the man exactly what he had said, reprimanded him for sacrilegious behavior, and ousted him from the house. You might be surprised to know that Sheikh Shalashil actually predicted the resettlement, even though it was in the last century. He said, "The water will rise and cover our lands, and all the Nubians will have to move one day." These are some of the miracles of my grandfather. The children like to hear about them.

Sheikh Shalashil tried hard to spread Islam and to stop the old Christian and old Pharaonic traditions that still remain among the people.

For example, on many Nubian doorways there is a cross in mud relief. Sometimes there is a cross on the mud storage containers for grains. In the wedding Sebua, one of the rituals is to tap the brass pestle against the mortar like a bell. Also in weddings, the groom used to carry a cross made of twisted palm fibers in the procession. These are the kinds of Christian things that Sheikh Shalashil tried to stamp out. I enjoy telling my children stories about our great sheikh.

*Rebuilding the village*    In 1947, men were few in the village, and there were more women than men. Almost all the men were working in the cities, and the village was silent. There were few activities, and, actually, it was dead. Sometimes in the winter we would gather at Kamel's home in the afternoon to entertain ourselves. In summer we usually sat on the sand next to Salah Kolo's house. Kolo was popular and a wonderful entertainer. He could recount tales and stories, and everyone used to sit and listen to him for hours at a time.

When Kamel found it impossible to continue earning his living here and had to leave the village, we moved the gatherings to my house. I leveled the ground in front of my house and put new sand to make it soft. But in 1950 the association bought a portable radio, and Sheikh Muhammad kept it in the guest room of his house. I don't know why he had a right to do that, but people began to move there in the evenings and listen to the radio on his *mastaba*.

Ten years ago there was a large group of worshipers in the mosque every evening. Hag Abdullah was always the first man there, but many people went for the evening lesson and prayer. This was mainly due to the great number of old men who were alive in the village at that time. Now the young men are too lazy to go to the mosque, and they prefer to pray at Sheikh Muhammad's *mastaba* where they can entertain each other and joke and gossip until they are ready to sleep.

When I came to the village, Hag Abdullah and Ali Amin had the responsibility for distribution of the government rations, that is, flour and oil, among the villagers. At that time Sheikh Muhammad did not have his store, but Ali Amin had one as well as Hag Abdullah. The people in the village became dissatisifed with the way these men distributed the food. It was found that they raised prices. Everyone became angry and acted against them. A large meeting was held, and Ahmed Ali, who was living in the village at that time, suggested that distribution of the rations be put in the hands of Sheikh Muhammad. Everyone approved, and so it was given to him in a peaceful way. At that time the ration was sugar, oil, tea, and cloth. Now it is only sugar and oil. Sheikh Muhammad opened his store in 1951. This was about the time that he took over distribution of the rations from the government. Since he was janitor of the school, he registered the store in the name of Mahmoud, his son. For some time now, I have been wanting to advise him to change the license to some other name because his son is now employed outside the village, but I am hesitating. I am afraid that he would be angry, and if anyone reported him to the government he might think it was me.

Once a short time after I came to the village some young men formed a cooperative association for the purpose of buying things like slippers, watches, perfume, and small gifts. It lasted for only about six months because most of the members were transferred to jobs outside the area. A man called Ali Khallil from Kanuba also opened a grocery store in the Daraw market, but he failed. Another called Nuri Clood opened a butcher shop there, but he failed too. Both of them had little capital, and their experience was limited.

In the first part of the history of our village our women never went to the market in Daraw, but when men had to leave the village looking for work in the cities, gradually more and more women began going to the market to get the food they needed. The young men were against their going, and Sheikh Salama also opposed it. But they had to go, for there was no other way to bring goods to the village. One of my present ideas is to provide the village with the things they need. We could open a small market here where women would find their needs. Not just a store but a marketplace. My dairy idea is another way to supply the village with food.

I want Kanuba to be known not only in Egypt but also internationally, like California and Washington. Not only do I love Kanuba as a village, but I love even its smallest stones. I want to see the best for these people because they have suffered much in the past. I am willing to make any sacrifice for their sakes. In order to realize my plans for the village I often use the method of *haraka*. What I mean by *haraka* is the creation of a positive communal attitude toward some new activity or thing. I always make *harakas* when some important, responsible foreign visitors come to visit the village. The *haraka* makes a good impression on the visitors, and it usually gets good results.

I do not know where I got the idea of making *harakas*, but I probably learned it while working with the British Army. However, I did not learn it from the British but from the Egyptians who were working there. For example, Churchill visited Egypt and he passed through the factory where I worked. What impressed me as strange was that the British did not do anything special for his visit. Everything went on as usual. He talked to the workers, and I saw him very close. He was short, fat, and smoked a cigar. The difference is that if an official makes a visit to an Egyptian government building or place of work, a great reception would be organized. There would be cheering and clapping. Wherever King Farouk went, a group went before him to prepare the way, to clean walls, to repair the roads, and to hide the slums. I have used this Egyptian technique of *haraka*, and it has had its results.

*136*

I found that the only way of attracting responsible people to the village was by making *harakas*. If an important official goes to the sheikh of the Kenuz in Daraw and says, "We want to tear down the houses and rebuild your village," that sheikh will raise a stick to him. But the powerful official will never listen to the sheikh. He will only visit him again. The sheikh and the village will lose more than they will gain. This is what actually happened in Daraw. However, if the official is received warmly and is given close attention, he will like the people in the village and will at least listen to what they have to say. I don't like the exaggeration that comes with the *haraka*, and, besides, I have to do many of the things myself, but it is necessary. Most of the people are apathetic. They pretend to participate, but actually they don't lift a finger unless they have to. I would like to get them all to participate in things themselves. Then maybe we wouldn't need any *harakas*.

We made some *harakas* for your group when you first came to the village, when you first visited, and then when you left the first time. You remember how we made a big party with the cakes. When you left the last time after you found out about our *harakas* and learned all about our village, the people still wanted to make them every time you left. I objected because I knew you would interpret it as being something false.

The first big *haraka* I made in Kanuba was to persuade the people to pave the mosque floor with flagstones. It had only mats on the ground. I wanted to do that as soon as I arrived in the village in 1947, but I was faced with great opposition. Some said that paving would cause rheumatic pains to the worshipers. I also wanted to build the *mastaba* in the interior part of the mosque for people to sit on before and after the prayer. Many people said that a *mastaba* and pavement in the mosque would encourage people to go there for entertainment and recreation, and that would be against Islam. No one worries about that now, and everyone is happy with the results. The purpose of *haraka* is to show one's best nature. It is display. Its purpose is to impress, its result is gain.

When I came to Kanuba to live I found the architecture greatly to my liking. The houses were wide, there were enough rooms, large courtyards, and the whole structure was well organized. In Nubian houses everything has a place. The animals are separated from the living quarters, and everything is clean. This is different from the city. It is also different from the Sa'idi villagers around here.

The only thing I did not like was the termites. You know how they ruin the wood ceilings, doors, windows, beds, everything. We use different methods in trying to get rid of them, but in vain. We tried dirty kerosene, all kinds of poisons, powders, etc., but none worked. When I built my own house, I started using vaulted roofs like the Kenuz have, from bricks and mud. I had our Kenuz builder, Salah Muhammad, build them for me. I suggested to other people that they all build vaults, but they rejected the idea. The women especially were violently against it and even attacked me for doing such a thing in my own house. Aisha Muhammad screamed and shouted at me. "How could we live and sleep under vaults! You, Shatr, do you want us to behave like *Kenuz?*" They thought the arches would fall, and they said, "Even though the Kenuz are accustomed to them, we are not!"

Although one or two people listened to me, the majority didn't. Because of their attitude and pressure on me, I only built vaulted roofs on my sitting and dining rooms but not on the bedrooms. I thought this was a foolish attitude because, in fact, the houses were about to fall on the people. The termite problem was the talk of the village. Many things were proposed every night on the *mastaba*, in the club, and anywhere we met. People wanted to improve the roofs and the ceilings, to spray DDT, etc., but none of these was a good solution.

I had another idea which was not clear in my mind. At that time there were many magazine articles concerned with rebuilding new villages near Ibis, outside of Alexandria. There were villages being resettled by the government to that area from other parts of Egypt where there was overpopulation. This was a joint project between the American and Egyptian governments. I allowed the people to discuss all these things without much comment, but most of their ideas were confused. I had a different point of view. I wanted to improve our village, to develop it. I felt that to realize this, a change must come from the roots. It should not simply be a matter of small repairs.

One of my ideas was to write the Americans about our problem and discuss the idea of rebuilding our village. I began to talk to people individually. First I went to some of the young men, and a few of them were enthusiastic about the idea, but they were not in favor of doing it through the Americans or through any foreigners. When I found that most of them were of this opinion, I suggested the idea of contacting our governorate. I felt that conditions were suitable, the Egyptian revolution was new, and the government was ready to help any underdeveloped villages. I began to write complaints to the officials. To sum it up, at the time most of the village was thinking of repairs and small alterations, I was thinking of tearing down the whole village and building a new one.

This time of discussion and thinking lasted more than two years. During this time, I clarified my ideas a great deal, but I received much opposition, especially from the old people. Hag Abdullah was the leader of those opposing me, but I gradually gained supporters. Those old men couldn't accept the idea of changing the old way much. "How can one leave a large comfortable house of several rooms and wide courtyard to live in a tin?" said Sheikh Muhammad. "Such small houses as the government would build would be funny and ridiculous!" Rahman said.

Sheikh Osman was on our side because his son Hussein influenced him. Hag Abdullah's suggestion was to change the roofs to cement ones and to leave the houses as they are, but, as you know, these would be too heavy, and the idea is ridiculous. Then a government man came with Hassan Fathi, the architect, and suggested my old idea—that we build vaults in the Kenuz way. The whole village refused this completely. However, no serious conflicts occurred, only discussions. Some other places in Daraw, like Sheikh Ibrahim and parts of Naga el-Kenuz, also have termites, but the people there made no attempt to do anything about the problem, whereas we are getting new buildings from the government. Without much effort we would get no help either.

At that time I had the idea to bring all the Nubians living in Daraw, regardless of their origin, into one place—around our own village here. But this was rejected by the Kenuz in Daraw as well as by our own people. They don't want progress, and, as you know, there is still a lot of antagonism between the Kenuz and Fadija. I wanted to make a large all-Nubian city, a model one. It would be clean, with electricity and water, with transportation, schools, institutions, and hospitals. I thought that by consolidating all the Nubians, we would be a more powerful group with a distinct identity and a powerful political influence in Daraw. In this way we would have a larger population so that we would have a claim for an intermediate school, a hospital, a train station, etc.

I talked to many Kenuz—for example, to Hag Mahmoud and Anwar—and I sounded out many people individually to get their feelings. Some of the Kenuz were in agreement with me and encouraged my ideas. They advised me to speak first to Hag Issa, the sheikh of the Kenuz in Daraw. One day Sheikh Issa came to visit the Kenuz in our village, and he dropped by the house of Sheikh Muhammad to visit. We viewed it as an opportunity and took him to the club. All of the village association and some other people came together, and we offered him lunch. We took this chance to discuss the idea with him. But when I started to talk, he didn't give me a chance to continue but stood up and shouted at me. He shouted at anyone who tried to calm him. He refused the idea completely. "You are Fadija and I am Kenuz. That's all there is to it." He rejected any idea of change in the houses or of rebuilding them. Since that time most of the Kenuz in Daraw are not on good terms with us, even though at that time some of them wanted to change his mind.

I have had many ideas about improving our village. I am willing to make any sacrifice for these people. One idea was to meet the Begum Aga Khan who lives in Aswan for part of the year, but the villagers opposed the idea completely. I wanted to get money from her to repair the mosque since she is rich and encourages Islam. People asked me, "How can you get money to repair a mosque from a non-Muslim?" I replied, "Since she is a non-Muslim, I can use the money to repair the W.C."

Another idea of mine was to have a train station here in the village so that the train would stop here and people would not have to go all the way to Daraw. I sent in requests to the governorate but they refused since the rule is to have stations at least three kilometers apart, and Kanuba is not quite three kilometers from the Daraw station. I think in the future, since Kanuba is extending south, we will be able to make a station south of where the clinic is now, and it will be more than the required three kilometers.

For many years things went along like that—with nothing happening about the houses. Plans but no results. Finally, about 1959, we had our opportunity when the plans were announced for the High Dam at Aswan, and Egyptians at least began to take an interest in the Nubians. Many officials came to Aswan to make plans and to explain to the people about the resettlement. In the newspapers it was announced how new villages would be built for the Nubians because they had to migrate from their old lands where the water would drown their houses.

During Ramadan that year, many of these officials were in Aswan making speeches and holding conferences. I knew it was the time for us to make our grievances known. I got a group from the village, and we went to Aswan to attend one of the conferences on housing for New Nubia. Through my friends in the various offices in the governorate of Aswan I got an audience with the director of construction. The group of us went in to see him one morning, and we told him the story of the termites. We told him we were Nubians and described how we had been mistreated by the government before the revolution. We didn't tell him anying more but invited him to break his fast in Kanuba.

For the occasion we prepared a big meal followed by a program of skits. We invited other officials from Aswan and several of them came, including that director of building. After we put the program on for them, we took them into the club and had a discussion of our problems. He told us there would be a big meeting and rally in Kom Ombo in a few days, and that the vice president of the UAR was coming as well as the minister of social affairs and many other important officials from Cairo. He said he could do nothing more for us immediately but that he could provide us with some transportation to this big rally. I asked him if he could provide us with a loud-speaker as well as some buses and trucks. I did not tell him what I really wanted to do.

On the day of the big rally two big buses came to Kanuba, and one of them was equipped with a loud-speaker. I was thankful to the director for remembering us. All the young men and boys went to Silsila, where the reception took place. We left the women and children back in the village. My main plan was to attract attention to us and the village of Kanuba. All along the way we sang Nubian songs over the loud-speaker, and every two minutes we shouted, "Nubians from Kanuba, those who left their home and land for the welfare of the whole of Eygpt, are coming today to receive

Vice President Hussein Shafi, whom President Nasser has sent us to realize our goals!"

Finally, when we got to the reception, there were thousands of people, many Upper Egyptians besides Nubians. I pushed my way through the crowds to get to the vice president. When I got to him, I told him: "Your excellency, our village is completely destroyed by termites. The termites are about to eat our children." The minister laughed and asked if termites ate human beings. I said: "Yes, we have evidence. If you visit our destroyed village, you will know that I'm not exaggerating." The vice president said that he could do nothing now, but he invited me to the gathering that night at the Cinema Kom Ombo. I forgot to tell you that we took the Boy Scouts from Kanuba dressed up in their uniforms, too. A group of them marched forward with drums in very good style and made quite an impression.

After the reception, we all returned to Kom Ombo and had sandwiches for lunch. I had enough time to plan for that night, so I divided our men into two groups. The plan was for half of them to be scattered among the crowd and the other half of them to be concentrated in one place. The ones who scattered would respond to my signal by loud clapping, and this would infect the whole crowd. The other half would form a cheering section close to the platform to shout "Kanuba, Kanuba, Kanuba." Also, if I saw that I wasn't being given a chance to speak, our people could create a big disturbance and shout my name to indicate that I was backed by many many people.

The vice president, the governor, the minister of social affairs, the vice ministers and officials were seated on the stage. During the proceedings I tried to climb onto the stage, but the guard prevented me; so I pointed and shouted to the vice president, "Ask him if he didn't invite me to come and talk!" I told the guard that he had no right to stop me because it was a Nubian session and I was a representative of a Nubian delegation. He finally searched me and let me move toward the platform. I climbed up onto the stage and got in front of the loud-speaker. I said: "By the name of God, peace on you people. I am Shatr Shalashil, a Nubian from Kanuba. Kanuba is honored by the vice president's visit to our governor, to the minister, and to all the officials. Our poor village migrated in 1933 after the second raising of the Aswan Dam. We migrated for the sake of the whole of Egypt. Our fields and palm trees were drowned. But ever since we moved we have had a hard life. We have no water to irrigate our land. We complained to the old government, but in vain. We used all the ways we knew to get rid of the termites that are ruining our houses, but in vain. They ate our houses and destroyed our village. Then where is our solution?"

I tried to keep the speech as short as possible and to the point. I knew that the vice minister and the vice president were waiting to speak, but I had to focus their attention on Kanuba. The vice president answered, "Insha Allah, we shall build new houses for you." I quickly answered: "Thank you your excellency, but we still have another question. The people in the village own about one thousand uncultivated feddans. This is so because we lack water. Since the government is digging a new canal to irrigate the lands of New Nubia, which runs near our village, could I ask you to order the officials to provide our village with water from that canal? We are Nubians and deserve to be treated like the other Nubians, especially since we were cheated before." The minister of agriculture replied, "Insha Allah, we will provide your village with water after we finish the resettlement." But again I quickly said: "I ask you a third question. What will be the life of the Nubians after the migration? Will their lot be as difficult as ours has been?" The vice president's answer was, "Their life will be a life of welfare and happiness."

These answers obviously pleased the crowd, so I shook the hand of the vice president and I talked to him in Nubian. The Nubians present all laughed loudly because they could understand and he couldn't. He smiled and asked me what I had said. I told him, "I asked God to give you health and wealth, and I ask you to fulfill your promise because God doesn't give health and welath to those who don't fulfill their promises." Then the vice president told the governor, "Give them 50,000 pounds to rebuild their village!" He didn't say this too loud, but I heard him. I shook hands again with the vice president, and I slipped him two other written complaints which I had been keeping in my pocket. One concerned the irrigation and the other was to put the mosque under the Ministry of Wakf.* I didn't want him to forget the name Kanuba. My plan was successful. Every time I said something, our two groups did what they were supposed to do. The whole crowd incited, so that the governor and the vice president could not help but hear the name of Kanuba everywhere. During the rest of the evening we shouted the name of the village many times, and everyone was aware of the problems of Kanuba.

After that we waited a whole year. No action was taken, but one day I heard the vice president would come to Aswan Province to lay the cornerstones of the first buildings of Nasser City in New Nubia. I decided that I would meet him no matter what. Nothing would stop me. Some of the villagers said we should meet him in Nasser City, but I suggested another idea. When his car passed the village, we would stop him because he could come by only one road. I was ready to sacrifice myself in front of the car in order to stop it. Ahmed Khalil adamantly refused this idea, still preferring to go to Nasser City to give him the complaint; so I resolved the dispute by suggesting to do both things.

*The Ministry of Wakf is concerned with the supervision of estates in mortmain and with certain charitable endowments as well.

We had a pretty good idea of the time of the car's arrival because we asked friends in other villages farther up the Nile to signal us by telegraph. As you know, Hag Omar is a telegraph operator in Daraw. About an hour before he was to arrive, we gathered all the people of Kanuba, including the women, and lined both sides of the road by the train station in Daraw with our flags and signs. When we saw the procession of cars coming, we all stood in the street and blocked their way. The cars had to stop. All the people shouted, "Up with Nasser, up with Hussein Shafi, long live Hussein Shafi, long live Nasser!" There were many armed guards and officers in the car, but they were surprised when they found themselves surrounded on all sides so that they could not move.

I knew it was dangerous, but I went directly to the vice president's car, which was easy to spot. I was very excited, and I put my hand right through the window and shouted: "Where is the revolution you are talking about? The mosque where we try to keep and maintain the revolution that Nasser and his group started, and also you, too, is about to fall on the worshipers because of the termites. We came to greet you and also to remind you of your promises that you gave us in Kom Ombo. The governorate didn't do anything. And here is the governor. You can ask him!" The vice president looked at the governor and said, "Take care of these people. I don't like all this disturbance." I was holding some gifts made by our Kanuba girls, which I handed to him. Lowa Safwat, the vice minister of social affairs was present, too. Then I saw that they were getting excited and that the guards were clearing the people out of the way, so I stepped back.

That plan was successful because after a month an architect came to examine the soil and to plan for the new village. There was a division of opinion as to how it should be built. Some of the old men still didn't want new houses. The majority wanted to build the new village toward the south. Azia Kalam was the spokesman for this group. The other group, which I headed, wanted to build on the same site as the present village is located. Sheikh Muhammad agreed with me, and Hag Abdullah had no opinion. There was another idea, too; that was to build the new village in New Diwan so that we would rejoin our relatives there. Ahmed Kahlil was the main opponent of this plan, and he asked me not to discuss it with the people. I agreed with him, and I told the people that New Diwan would be isolated in comparison to us from transportation, the market, and our work. I told them it would be a long way to Kom Ombo just to get tomatoes. I said Kanuba is a suitable place to build the village since it is close to shops. We are seeking progress. We shouldn't live in an isolated area.

There was even a fourth idea: the architect himself suggested that we build the houses where the mosque is. I vetoed this idea because I was afraid of the water and salt seepage in that area which have ruined the houses near there now. I figured it probably would ruin the new houses too. The governorate brought up the idea again of building the new houses with vaults, just as Hassan Fathi and I had previously suggested. But again everyone firmly refused such a plan. The ones who were against building any new houses at all were people like Ramadan Kareem and Rahman. I think this was because they have such large and wide houses already. Anyhow, you know the result. The houses are being built on the same site, and the old houses are being torn down one section at a time.

As far as the Kenuz people go, we welcome them in the new village. Those who own one house now will take one new house. Those who have more than one house will take the amount they own. However, the Kenuz do not want to leave their houses. I have not talked to many of them about that matter. I think it is still too early to discuss this with them. They are resistant, but as soon as the new village is built they may change and I will talk to them further.

Actually, many people who have lived for years in Cairo and Alexandria are now asking for houses. For example, the laundryman wanted to take one of the first houses even though he has not lived in the village for many years. The rest of the people protested, and he left the village feeling dissatisfied and hostile. In another few weeks there will be a conference in the Cultural Center in Aswan. I have prepared ten girls of the village to present the lady minister, Hekmet Abu Zeid, ten copies of the request for the new houses to be completed. I am teaching Fatma Abdullah how to give a speech and how to greet the lady minister.*

*The clinic*    During my work at the hospital in Daraw, I noticed that the people from Kanuba found it a hardship to come to the hospital, especially the old men and women. Although I always help them by bringing them medicine and advice, sometimes it was necessary for them to come to the Daraw hospital to receive treatment. It was actually Sheikh Salama's idea to have a small medical unit in the village, and everyone welcomed the idea. We tried to do it on our own by buying the basic medicines to keep in the club's cabinet. But people always demanded more medicines than our finances could afford, and our treatment was not professional or adequate. This small effort soon died out.

I used to follow the news about the Ministry of Health in Aswan Province and once read a newspaper article about their plan to build several clinics in the province. This was about 1961. It struck me that this was the opportune time to get a small clinic in Kanuba. The next day I discussed the idea at the village club and suggested sending in a request to

---

*This conference took place, and, as planned, Fatma, leading her group, gave a talk about Kanuba's accomplishments and needs.

the governorate. I can't remember any person who opposed the plan at that time. On the contrary, everyone welcomed the idea. I immediately wrote the request and the next Friday after the prayer at the mosque got everyone's signatures. I sent copies to the governor, the minister of health, and the general director of the medical department of Aswan.

After that, nothing happened even though I sent in several more requests. One day I raised the issue again, and we decided to form a delegation to see the governor. I can't remember who came with me that time. Forgive my memory; it is bad, especially since that accident with the tram in Cairo. Anyhow, we visited the governor in Aswan, and he was very rude to us. In fact, we were not even able to discuss the plan for providing the village with a clinic but only to discuss pure water (another of our requests) before he cut us off. Four days later our Nubian friends in Aswan informed us that the governor was going to visit Daraw to have a meeting regarding a new intermediate school. I was reluctant to attend this meeting because I thought the governor was very silly.

That night I found by chance that Sheikh Maher was giving a religious lesson in Daraw, so I decided to go. When I reached Daraw I heard a loud-speaker blaring. The governor was giving a speech. I could recognize his voice easily. I was surprised when I heard him repeating the name Kanuba. I found myself running toward the gathering. It was very crowded, so crowded that I could not get through. Some guards prevented me from entering, so I went around the school trying to find a way to get in. The back of the school was unlighted, and I was able to climb the fence and jump over. I stumbled my way through the darkness to where the activity was. That time I forgot my fear of the dark. I made my way directly to the microphone.

I told the man in charge that I was a representative of Kanuba and wanted to thank the governor for his speech. Before he could say anything, I grabbed the microphone and started shouting: "Shatr Shalashil of Kanuba thanks the governor for granting us our request for pure water. Sir governor, as I know that you are so kind, I have still another request. We need a clinic in our village. The distance to Daraw is too great for our old people and the very young." The governor took out his notebook, wrote the request down, and said "Insha Allah." That was all I was able to say before others took over the microphone.

I left before the session was over. I went directly to the telegraph office and sent a telegram to the governor at his Aswan address. I told him we were grateful for providing us with pure water and for accepting our request for a new clinic. After that we also worked through my brother Abdul in the housing office in Aswan and other Nubians from Diwan in order to keep the matter in the attention of the governor. Finally, several weeks later, to our surprise, an official from the governorate came to solicit my advice as to where was a good area on which to build the clinic. At first they selected the land of Ahmed Taha Hassan. However, Ahmed refused to sell his land to us, so we chose land belonging to Abdul's family on the other side. If the village had not offered the land to the governorate immediately, we would have lost out on the clinic. I had to send telegrams to the owners in Cairo to ask permission. I remember that night. I was very anxious to get an answer, and I couldn't even eat my dinner. I was asking God every moment to help us. The next day I received the answer to go ahead. It's hard to imagine how pleased everyone was.

We immediately took the telegram to the other representatives of Abdul's family in the village and had them sign their approval. My idea was to get other people in the village also to give a small part of their unused land to the family in order to compensate them for their loss in donating it to the clinic. I took around a list and got signatures of people who would donate a little land, and many people signed it. The next day, early in the morning, I went to the housing department and visited the architect. I also went to the medical department in Aswan in order to give them the deed to the land on which they could build the clinic. They officially approved and began the proceedings by sending the architect to draw up the plans.

This was a time of touch and go because the nearby communities of Sheikh Ibrahim and Ghabba wanted the clinic in their areas—but we managed to get it. When the people of Sheikh Ibrahim found out that the governorate wanted them to donate the land on which to build a clinic, they said they were not only ready to donate their land but to provide free labor. They tried to compete with us, but they lost. Actually, their offer came in after I already had the governor's signature. As soon as we got the approval for building the clinic, and when they actually started building, I was already planning the next step. This was to staff the clinic with Nubians only and people from Kanuba. I knew this would be difficult to achieve but that I could gradually do it since we had several of our relatives who were already working in medical clinics and hospitals, and they could be transferred.

However, we needed Nubian girls to work as nurses and assistants, and one of the main problems was how to get our girls to work. You know how most families here object to girls and women working. They are afraid they will come into contact with strange men, and they are very conservative in this matter. Secretly, through my group, I spread my idea that many girls would be needed to work, that they would get good wages in the clinic, and that it would be better if they were Nubians. Actually, I am not authorized to make these types of announcements, but I knew girls would be needed. There was an immediate outcry against girls working. All the old men and women and also some of the young men and girls were against the idea. Even the most educated men in the village, Hussein the teacher and Ahmed Khalil the social worker, opposed the idea.

*Kanuba girls dressed as nurses.*

I stopped talking about it and listened to their opinions. Then I quietly talked to some of the more needy girls individually. On purpose, I selected those who were very poor. I also selected those who had spent part of their lives in cities and who are used to more modern things. One of these was Fahima. Several of the girls consented on the condition that I get their fathers' approval. I was also looking for girls who could read and talk to people. I wanted those who are a little bit "citified."

When I talked to Hag Abdullah about his daughter Fatma, he shouted at me and said "nonsense." I left him and went to Abu Hanafi. Even though he is in great need of money and is liberal on many things, for some reason he also refused. So finally I selected Fahima. I talked to her and she welcomed the idea because she had just been divorced and the income in her family was very small. The whole family was in hard times. I talked to Idris, her brother, the guard. Since he needed the money, he immediately said, "I don't find anything to be ashamed of; I give my approval." I immediately filled out an application for her, and she got the job. At first I was afraid the officials would send her to another village to work since the clinic here had not opened yet, so I used our Nubian influence in Aswan to get her approved for a training course here in Daraw in the hospital where I worked. This was so that she wouldn't be sent far away and change her mind about working.

I wanted to find a Nubian doctor, also, for our clinic. But this is very difficult because, well, you know, there is Hassan, the Kenuz doctor who works across the river, but there are very few Nubian doctors. We have one lady doctor who is from Diwan. But she is in Cairo and is not quite finished with her internship, and, in any case, I knew it might be very difficult to get her to come to our village. Once when a group of doctors came to Daraw hospital to "break in" before going out to the various clinics in the area, I closely observed them in order to find the best. Through my friends, I was able to get Dr. Fikri transferred to our clinic. One of the main things that concerned me was the moral character of the doctor. I did not want a good doctor with bad morals. I have seen many of these during my time at the hospital.

Dr. Fikri is very good; but even so, the old men and women have no faith in the clinic so far. I think this is mainly due to two things. First, they believe in folk medicine more than in modern medicine. Second, they don't have any faith in a young doctor. Besides, he treats everything. He is not a specialist. But gradually they will become accustomed to it, and

*Kanuba leaders at opening of clinic.*

148

actually the younger people have started to go. Some of the older ones, too. Now the Nubian girl, my uncle's daughter, is about to be graduated from the faculty of medicine in Cairo University. When I met her last year, I told her, "Your place must be in Kanuba!"

*Toward greater unity*　I am very concerned about the change of governors that has just taken place. I had a good relationship with the old governor, but the new governor is a military officer. He believes in strength more than in thinking, as do most military men. When he arrived in Aswan, some people in the village wanted to go and meet him, but I advised them not to do this since their effort, money, and time would probably have little effect on such a man. He doesn't know Aswan, the people, or anything here. There's no use in sending telegrams now because there are probably so many from all over the province that he would not remember the name of Kanuba. My plan is to wait and see what he is like. When I found out that he is strict and is an officer, I decided to wait and to bring the name of Kanuba to him directly through our people in Aswan. The name of Kanuba will be well known to him before we approach him with our problems. We will surround him with Nubians who will inform him, test his ideas, and feed him details about Kanuba and about the Nubians in general. After we find out how he reacts to the problems of the Nubians, we will inform him about the needs of Kanuba in the proper way at the right time.

I will then appear and meet him with a *haraka* about our specific problems. If I appear now, at the beginning of his term, I would probably be dismissed without even seeing him. One way we will indirectly approach him is through his wife, with our girls, who are now well trained. I will catch him by the tail—his wife! The girls have just recently sent her a telegram inviting her to the village. She has responded and says that she will visit us as soon as possible. Of course, you know what will follow. We will make a big *haraka* when she comes. Every village in this area has received a form letter from the government asking them to form a committee to meet with the governor to discuss their projects. We will see what the first few delegations do and what the reaction of the governor to their problems is before we formulate our plans and decide how to influence him.

One of my great hopes now is for our village to join administratively with New Nubia. We have always felt like strangers in Daraw and that we are apart administratively. Now that the government is taking care of all the Nubians, especially in their new homes, I feel it is a good time for Kanuba to join the other Nubians and to secede from Daraw. Now that they have organized Nasser City, we can join.

One of the main problems that we face here is that the young leave the village and they don't return until they are old. This was always a

*Welcoming the governor.*

problem in Old Nubia, too, and though it is not as bad here, it is still a problem. The young men go to Cairo and Alexandria to study, and then they prefer to live there and probably won't come back unless they retire or fail. Dahab and Muhammad Siliman are good examples. One came to die and the other to retire. One problem is that the village in its development does not need these types of men. It needs youth and young intelligent men. I am planning now to make the youth want to stay in the village by providing recreation and entertainment. I think this is one of the main reasons they go to the cities. Another condition that drives them away is that Hag Abdullah always tells everyone that everything is forbidden by religion. He makes things so strict that everyone wants to leave. Also, when they get to Alexandria and they see the beach and the girls in bathing suits, they don't want to return. I can't offer them naked girls, but I would like to make a swimming pool for them in the village.

I tried to impress on the young that they are really a part of Nasser City, among friends and relatives, the Nubians, who are not like the strangers of Cairo and Alexandria. We will profit a great deal by becoming a part of Nasser City. The people of Daraw still discriminate against us and call us barbarians. The thousands of migrant Nubians will give us strength and help us stand. Also, we will help them to have a Nubian identity in this area. We will get advantages from being a part of the program. For example, when the government offers a prepared lunch to the children in the New Nubian schools, our village will also get this benefit.

We also now have a greater responsibility of reclaiming the land than we had before, since we are becoming a part of New Nubia. We will be able to deal with Nubian officials and administrators rather than non-Nubians. We will have strength in elections because the Nubians will vote together. Since the resettlement we have had unusual activity. We are reestablishing old relationships and friendships. There is much movement back and forth and getting to know one another. This gives fathers husbands for their marriageable daughters. It also gives widows and divorcees chances to remarry. Of course, marriage is a difficult problem for our village because there are not enough men to equal the number of girls. The problem is made greater by the Nubian custom that daughters are not allowed to marry distant relatives or nonrelatives.

Tribal feeling and pride is one of the most sensitive problems in the village. I am against tribal organization and feeling. When I first came, tribal arrogance was very strong, and people divided into groups on the basis of their tribe. Each individual was excessively proud of his tribe. People from the Kushaf, especially, acted proud and arrogant toward members of other tribes. Even now, there are some who have such haughtiness. The Kushaf always considered themselves the best people in Old Nubia. They were the rulers, and they considered their origin to be pure. They said they came from Turkey, and they even called themselves Turks to show their origin and to demonstrate the purity of their race. They still consider themselves an upper class. The Mundolab tribe, on the other hand, consider themselves to be the original inhabitants of the Diwan area. They also claim to be rulers, and they say they were rulers before the Kushaf came. They consider themselves to be even better than the Kushaf because of this. You know I am from the Mundolab.

Recently I have stressed the idea that the unity of all tribes and families will help the village to realize their hopes for development and change. I do not deny that there are many who like to rank all the people in the village, but our young group spreads the ideas of equality and of belonging only to Kanuba. I especially have tried to stress this among the children, who represent the new generation. There has been much friction in the village due to tribal distinctions. I hope we can exterminate these beliefs. It is a bad tradition. But I know it takes time because it is something written in their minds. It now seems that tribal arrogance is becoming less and less, and the new concepts of the socialist society have helped in uniting the peoples from the different tribes.

Another idea supporting unity which I always remind people of is that the Koran advises people to come together to form a good life. I always stress the idea that reform of the village and accomplishment of our goals will never happen unless people come together, unify, and cooperate. It will not happen unless they forget all about these obsolete tribes and remember only the village, Kanuba. This represents their life, the life they struggled for since they emigrated. At any rate, those who still think and talk the most about tribes and are the most arrogant are the ones farthest from being active in village affairs. These are the ones who think they are Kushaf and who claim to be better than other people. Actually, they have less influence than anyone. When we write a request or complaint to the government, we always use the phrase "we the people of Kanuba." We never say "the Kushaf" or "the Mundolab." This is the new prevailing spirit of unity.

The idea of tribes is still important in regard to marriage. When a young man is ready to be married, his parents offer him a list of names they have prepared from which to choose his bride. It is selected from close relatives of both the maternal and paternal sides, although the paternal is preferred. It is preferable that a person be from the same tribe and even from the same big city. Some people marry from different tribes, but they are usually two tribes that have lived near each other in Nubia for many years and have a tradition of intermarrying with each other. For example, Abbass, though his tribe is Sifikal, married from Kordufan. We have several cases of intermarriage between those two tribes.

Actually, the Nubians are mostly ugly in comparison with other Egyptians; but if you compare them with African Negroes, they look much better. Many of the Nubians have some Negro features due to the contact of the people from Sudan and Middle Africa with the ancient Nubians. The girls from Kanuba all tend to look alike. Some are distinctive and outstanding because of their nice personalities and gay ways rather than because of good looks. Women and girls of marriage age often talk about handsomeness of the young men, but I always tell the girls to pay attention to their own looks. I gave them the example of chocolate. I tell them that almost all kinds of chocolate are the same color, but they are different in taste and so are girls. I encourage them to beautify themselves.

I want to solve the problem of marriage for our girls. They outnumber the men. The solution is to attract men from outside the village, but they must be other Nubians. Some of our young men nowadays marry non-Nubians, and this makes it even more difficult for the girls to marry, since according to our traditions Nubian girls may never marry non-Nubians. This new trend will be bad for them; so my idea is that the Kanuba girl should attract the attention of youths from all parts of Nubia (except Kenuz). They will have a better chance now that the rest of the Nubians have moved and are near us. They should exploit their beauty in addition to the usual considerations in marriage based on kinship and character.

One of the problems we have always had is with our ethnic groups who look down on Nubians. When I was small, I felt lost among the other children in Alexandria and felt like a stranger. Even now in Daraw I feel that the Nubians are still strangers, though we have lived with the Upper Egyptians here for many years. Once while I was working at my desk in the hospital in Daraw, the head of the district of Ragaba came in. He looked at me and turned to the other people standing there, "Oh, how funny, a *berberi* sitting at a desk!" That ridicule hurt me deeply. The *berberi* complex affects the dignity of the Nubians. In the recent election when Hussein was running for office, I heard the people of Daraw saying to one another: "Do we vote for a *berberi?* How ridiculous." That is why Hussein lost this time and Sheikh Salama several years before him in another election.

The people of Daraw never call us Nubians. They always refer to us as *berberi*. We tried to mix with them when we first came, but it was no use. Even so, they still admire Kanuba and our advancement. Once I heard one of the Ga'afra speaking to a group. He was scolding them and encouraging them to develop their life. "Look at the *berberi*, the humble people. Look how they are developing their life! More than any of you people do."

Once a Coptic inspector came to the hospital to check my work. When he entered, he asked me to give him a chair and a desk. I stood up and gave him my seat. He looked at me arrogantly, asked my name, and asked, "To what race do you belong?" I said, "I'm a Nubian." He asked me, "Why do you dress like this? You are very careless in your dress." I replied, "I'm a poor person. Please sit down." He checked my books and found that I had been careless in registering some of the births for the last month. He put the book aside and started to check other books; but while he was doing that I succeeded in slipping the book away and had it filled in correctly by one of my assistants. After about an hour of abusing me, the man called my boss and told him how careless I was and that I should be penalized for failing to keep up my books correctly. I then said humbly, "What did I do?" The inspector very ceremoniously opened the book to prove my failure to my boss, but he found nothing. Everything was correct. He began to shout and insult me, but I did not answer at all. I merely ignored him. This incident always reminds me to keep the record of the village club complete, as well as my work at the hospital. I am never able to do it, but I dislike Coptic inspectors intensely.

Another time an important man from the town of Bin Ban across the Nile came up to the hospital in Daraw where I work. He looked like a sheikh because he wore a black cloak, carried a white umbrella, and rode a donkey. He came into my office, set some papers on my desk, and in a commanding tone said, "Sign these!" I said, "I'm sorry but I have some important business to attend to. Would you please wait a few moments?"

The man shouted: "You *berberi*, you tell *me* to wait? How dare you speak to your master like this! Is it because you are a clerk and have a desk? You are still a *berberi!*" I was extremely upset but I said nothing except "God forgive you." That incident was another that hurt me much. Even though such incidents are not frequent, they sting!

It's funny, but Nubian attitudes toward slaves are just as severe as Egyptian attitudes toward us. My feeling about the former slaves is that they are still slaves and nothing can change that. It is partly a racial thing. However, I personally have no objection to allowing a slave to marry my daughter, if she accepts. Islamic law views people as being equal. I don't think it can happen because, in general, I suspect people and I fear for my daughter's future. Regardless of the fact that the slaves have gotten houses in New Nubia and that they now own lands, the Nubians, especially in Diwan, still treat them as slaves. I suppose some changes will take place and their position will improve in the community, and perhaps they eventually will have rights to marry Nubian girls, but this won't happen for a hundred years!

Another problem is the big gulf between the Nubians and the Kenuz in the village. I have tried actively for many years to bridge this gulf, but it seems wider every day. Abbass was one of the big causes of the division between us. He insults the Kenuz and treats them as inferiors. Sheikh Muhammad is a fair man, but he also dislikes them. I have tried to point out disadvantages of this prejudice to him because he is a reasonable man. However, he explained that this is his feeling and he cannot help it. Hag Abdullah, on the other hand, also dislikes them, but because of the location of his shop he doesn't want to lose customers, so he acts friendly to them in his false way.

One of the Kenuz, Ali Gebril, comes to the club often, and he often stays with us on the *mastaba*. He tries to join our inner circle because he knows that he will gain much by associating with us. He also helps us when we need votes from the Kenuz or in getting information to them. Through our Nubian relatives, we arranged his transfer from the welfare office in Aswan to Daraw. This was a big help to him because his family is here and he appreciates it.

I am trying to figure out ways of getting the new generation of boys together—that is, the Kenuz boys and the Fadija—but I am fed up with trying to get the older men to cooperate. I think it is sad to find educated people like Hussein and Ahmed Kahlil still claiming superiority to other Nubians. This has been one of my greatest problems, to overcome this prejudice. When I went to Luxor last week for the meeting about Nubian problems, I told the people there that we are responsible for the development of the province of Aswan because it is our Nubian ancestors who built all these monuments and statues. When you see people like the

Kenuz here in the village carrying long genealogies in their pockets, tracing the descent to Muhammad, don't believe them. You will find that usually the fourth name back is a Christian one. The Nubians are really not Arabs; we are descendants of the original Pharaohs.

Another example of the bad influence of the tribal and ethnic feeling in this area was shown in the recent election. Hussein was running for the Arab Socialist Union, and the people of Daraw deceived us. They depend mainly on their kinship and ethnic ties for their support, and they consider us Nubians to be outsiders and, above all, a minority. In the previous election several years ago the people of our village asked me to nominate myself, but I refused. I know many people through my work at the hospital, but I knew that a Nubian's chance of success was not certain.

I do my best to be a friend of all the people, Nubian or non-Nubian. I know that we people of Kanuba must be friends with all the people of Daraw in order to survive until we are strong enough to stand alone. This time when I refused to nominate myself, Hussein said he was ready to nominate himself. I was sure that he would not succeed, although he is a good man. He is not well enough known. Even though he is a teacher in the intermediate school in Daraw, he is well known only to the pupils and their parents in a narrow circle. He has no political experience in how to deal with the other groups. However, when he nominated himself I did my best for him, and I got about 200 votes. I was on the committee in Daraw at the hospital where people came to vote, and I asked everyone to vote for Hussein. Actually, in the village we only have around 100 votes, so we agreed with other groups to exchange votes. If they had fulfilled their promises, Hussein would have gotten about 1,120 votes. We fulfilled our promises to them, but they didn't to us, so Hussein lost.

I had some ideas to strengthen our position, but the people didn't accept them before. One of them was to register all the women who were eligible to vote under the new Arab Socialist Union. Another idea was to strengthen the village by bringing more people in. In my view, Kanuba is still a baby. We are passing through a stage of construction. Gamal was the first to propose the idea of women voting. Many old men rejected the idea. So when Hussein wanted to nominate himself and the majority of the people did not listen to my idea of waiting till the next election, I found it an opportunity to let them live with the actual experience of failure.

When Hussein failed, they were awakened by the shock. They blamed themselves and began to discuss the possibility of women voting. They discovered their real place and position in this whole area—it is low! This is my way: when I propose an idea and it is overwhelmingly opposed, I keep quiet for awhile. Then I raise the idea again in another form. Sometimes I raise it indirectly and keep quiet again to give them a chance to discuss it. I do not want credit for any idea, I want to advance the village. I listen to their discussions to decide what is wrong and what is correct. I modify by suggestion. I avoid the bad and stress the good. I gain votes day by day, one by one.

You know Gamal the cripple? All the boys used to call him "the cripple," and he felt very bad. He wouldn't take part in village affairs. He always stayed away from the club. I knew he was intelligent and would be a good help to me, so I thought of another name by which he could be known in the village. I began to call him Rayis ["the boss"] so that he wouldn't feel inferior. Now everyone calls him that. It makes him feel good, and now he participates in all activities. Actually, he is one of the closest ones to me.

My plan is for joining the village administratively to New Nubia and to secede from Daraw. I have opposition in this from many of the Kenuz as well as from people in our village. Abbass, as usual, is against my plan. Today in the meeting I preferred not to face him when he opposed me directly. I want to avoid any trouble, so I left Hag Omar, Hag Abdullah, and Sheikh Muhammad to face him. According to my experience, arguments and oppositions do not lead to unified decisions. That's why I didn't join the group in the Kom Ombo coffee shop this morning when we were going to see the mayor and when Abbass was making the big trouble. According to the Koran, Allah says if you intend to do something, go ahead, since you are depending on God's help.

I am seeking the benefits of the whole village. I have no personal interests, although others do. They think only of themselves. Abbass opposes unification because his authority in Kom Ombo will be lost if our village is under new jurisdiction. Now he has connections in which he is able to get people jobs and influence various kinds of affairs. Sheikh Muhammad approved my plan in the beginning, but for some reason he changed his opinion. Probably he was influenced by Abbass. Abbass is a dominating character and can convince Sheikh Muhammad of many things, even though his arguments are weak. I think whoever opposes my plan is selfish and thinks only of himself. In my private talks with individuals, I stress that Abbass is not immortal but that Kanuba is. Sheikh Muhammad is more excitable and worries a great deal. He came to my house this afternoon and anxiously said to me, "You made a hasty decision." He would not take my explanations. I will try to convince him later because he could not listen to reasonable discussion when he was so excited. I try to avoid any confrontation with excited people because we lose more than we gain.

Actually, this morning the mayor welcomed us. I had taken the time to go and meet him before the group came. I got to Kom Ombo early and gave him a brief idea about our request and gave him logical reasons, which he accepted. Then he asked me to call the group to come in, so I sent a message to them in the coffee shop to come. The mayor was very clever.

He asked each individually for his reasons for wanting to include Kanuba in New Nubia. Then he wrote the report himself. Everyone in our group stressed a different point. I stressed nationalism. I said we are all Nubians, the other Nubians are related to us. President Nasser once said in a speech that we should gather together all the Nubians. Hag Omar stressed the idea that our lands are now closer to those of the Nubians than to the people of Daraw.

When we were finished, I told the mayor, "Insha Allah, you will be a minister but on one condition, that you fulfill our request." He smiled and said, "I don't want to be a minister; I want to be a healthy and wealthy man." I replied, "You will have all of that, Insha Allah." When we left, I proposed to the group that we send a telegram to the mayor for the warm reception and treatment that he gave us. I wanted to make a small *haraka* to keep him reminded of our request. Gamal didn't approve of the idea. He suggested that we use the money to buy soft drinks for those of us who went to Kom Ombo. The weather was hot and Gamal was very thirsty. That is how far they think ahead.

*Religion*  I like to read the Koran. I know only part of it by heart; but I used to read some of it every morning, so I'm familiar with most of its verses. Tomorrow I'll be able to listen to the Koran on the radio because a new station broadcasting only Koran and religious matters for twelve hours daily was just set up in Cairo. I don't like those reciters who sing more than they read. I don't like the way Umma Kalsum or Sheikh Abdul Baset do it. I like the way that Hosari recites. The way Mahmoud Kamel does it here in our own village is miserable, and I don't like the way Hag Abdullah, our imam, reads the Koran in the mosque. He is not a good sheikh or imam. He is not well educated, and that's why most of the people don't like to sit with him or to pray in the back of him or to listen to him preach.

Do you remember when Sheikh Maher came, how crowded the mosque was? If any good speaker comes to the village, the people crowd in because they think there is something to be heard, but from Hag Abdullah they gain nothing, so most of them prefer to stay on Sheikh Muhammad's *mastaba* gossiping rather than going to the mosque. They feel that going to the mosque is of no use to them. Besides they object to Hag Abdullah's strict, conservative, reactionary ways.

My own knowledge of the glorious Koran is not extensive, but I know by heart all "The Thirties," which is the last part. I have memorized other *suras* [verses or chapters] from other parts of the Koran, in particular the *suras* of the Cave and Yaseem and Marium. There's no one in the village who knows all of the Koran by heart, least of all our imam. In fact, there are few people in the village who know more than a few *suras*. However, old Hassuna knows many *suras* by rote, and even though he is illiterate he

*Entering mosque, Kanuba.*

can read the Koran because he learned it so well as a child. Sheikh
Muhammad also knows a lot. I doubt if there are more than two or three
people in the village who read some *suras* from the Koran daily. I know
that both Sheikh Muhammad and Hag Abdullah do it.

As far as the "Traditions" go, I only know a few of them, even though
I read a book about them once. Hardly anyone here knows any of the
"Traditions," although Hag Abdullah does know quite a few and can say
them on the proper occasions. Maybe Hag Ibrahim Bahrem knows more
than anyone else in the village. He lived in Saudi Arabia for two years.
Islam is historically recent in Nubia, so Nubians have used the Arabic
words instead of translating them into Nubian. However we sometimes
still use a few of our own words, such as *No* for God.

My first religious instructions were given to me by my grandmother
before I was twelve. My grandfather taught me a special formula to
prevent me from being bitten by scorpions and snakes. This is a formula
that invokes God to save a person from all bad creatures. Also, my
maternal grandmother taught me to recite the *sura* of "The Throne"

before going to bed. My father always advised me to recite the opening *sura* of the Koran whenever I feel bad. When I was an adolescent, he gave me excellent instruction in religion. God is the creator and sustainer of the universe and is described by the Koran by the ninety-nine most beautiful names. Hell is full of fire where non-Muslims will take their punishment. Heaven is a big garden where everyone lives an easy and comfortable life.

You know, Mahmoud Kamel here in the village said he was once married to a jinn girl in addition to his wife, and only two days ago he told us at the mosque that he had met a jinn as he was coming toward the mosque.

Once a strange thing happened to me, in 1936, when I was in Cairo. There was an accident in the street in which a car killed a foreigner. I went fairly close to see what was happening, and as I was returning home I suddenly noticed blood on my shoes. I was surprised because I had not been near enough to get any blood on me. The street was lighted and many people were going everywhere, but I became deathly afraid. The idea of ghosts jumped quickly into my thoughts, and I imagined the dead man's ghost following me. I began to run, and I ran all the way to the house. When I reached home, I began to shout and cry because I felt that the ghost was after me and was going to harm me. People often said that if one dies in an accident, his ghost wanders around the place of the accident and follows his blood wherever it is found. I finally got over my fear after many days, but I never was able to explain that strange happening.

You know that the supernaturals often appear to people in dreams, and I believe that dreams forecast the future. Also, I think many things that happen in dreams are really true. Once I saw a stranger in the street in Daraw with a torn gallabeya. I felt sympathy for him but I didn't talk to him. That night I saw him in my dreams, and I talked to him a great deal. Another time, in 1947, when I was working my pumps to bring water for our fields (during my pump-scheme period), I dreamed one night that the pumps stopped and I saw the land cracking with dryness. A week later the pumps stopped because there was no water.

Once when my mother was very sick, we all expected her to die. We began to prepare for the funeral, and I even bought the coffin. Then Sheikh Muhammad came to me in a dream and told me to be calm, that everything would be all right, my mother would not die. The next day I visited my mother, and I saw that she was beginning to recover, and she lived two more years after that. In another dream I saw President Muhammad Nagib, who is a Nubian. In my dream he came to Kanuba to our mosque and gave a speech to the people. I can't remember the subject, but the pulpit was upside down while he was talking. After the speech, all the people of the village waited outside the mosque to greet him. However, we were surprised when we saw him running from the mosque to the highway. I saw everyone running after him in a great crowd. Sheikh

Muhammad was calling to him to return and asking him what was wrong. Then all of a sudden he disappeared. Three days after that dream, Muhammad Nagib resigned from the government.

You can see why I believe dreams are true. They forecast the future accurately. I remember once, too, when I failed in my attempts to cultivate my ten feddans near the village, I had to look for a new job. I was out of money. I applied for the job in the Ministry of Health, and after several days I was about to lose all hope of getting the job. One night I dreamed that I met a doctor in the street. He told me to go the following day to see about the job because the ministry had approved it. In the morning I woke wondering what to do, and I hesitated as to whether to go or not. But I decided to follow the directions in my dream. I went and was surprised to find that my application was accepted.

Death occurs according to God's will. God gives birth and life, and he takes them away at a certain time known only to him. Death is a departure of the soul from the body. No one but God knows what the soul really is. But I believe that everyone has a second life that begins after resurrection. Until that time, the soul leaves the earth and goes to the sky until the Judgment Day. Everyone will die. It is Allah's will and man's fate. Maybe it is the lesser of the two evils. I feel that I will die soon.

I had a bad experience with death soon after I came to the village. It was in 1948, and I was eating dinner with a man called Gamal Muhammad Suliman. After we ate our dinner and were enjoying ourselves talking in the courtyard, I got up and went to get the tea inside the house. I came back to find Gamal asleep at the table. I tried to awaken him, but he was dead. I was so shocked that I cried for several days. He was my dear friend, and I had never seen death so close before.

Another death that made a great impression on me was that of Hassan Salah, our previous mayor. He was popular, kind, and good. A few days before his death we put him in a bier and mimicked a funeral without the least notion about the possibility of it ever happening. He was killed a few days later in a train accident near Daraw. The picture of this funeral is still in my mind. It is very vivid. When the village heard of the accident, men, women, and children ran wildly from the village toward the highway, which was at that time unpaved. Women were scooping up dirt and putting it on their faces and on their black dresses and veils. Even the Kenuz women went because he was well liked by everyone. It looked like a market without goods. People were wailing everywhere. Hundreds of people came from Daraw to give condolence here in the village. They came also from Ghabba, from Naga el-Kenuz in Daraw, and even Sheikh Issa came leading a huge group.

These two incidents taught me a lot about death. Nothing can be done to stop it. One must accept his fate and prepare himself for it. It's strange, although Islam preaches the inevitability of death and there are many sayings and *suras* about it, the human being can't help being sad about death. One of the traditions is: "You will die even if you protect yourself in castles."

It has struck me in recent years that there seems to be a lessening of grief about death. I think in our village this is due to Ansar al-Sunna. They want to follow the instructions of the Koran and *sunna* perfectly. One should regard death as something normal and not to be feared. However, even though these old customs have diminished does not mean that there are no people who maintain the traditions up to now. Many women do it exactly the same way they did it in Old Nubia. Recently, when his father died, Hussein's family wanted to put out the death mat to receive condolences for at least fifteen days just as they used to do it in Diwan. However, I made a suggestion to lessen the days. There is no need for such a long period now that we are obliged to feed so many people as before when people had to come from distant villages. Now it's possible to give condolences for an hour and then catch the bus back to one's village.

The women still insist on the old tradition of staying overnight with the grieving women of the family. Even if her husband takes the bus back, she still insists on staying overnight. Women maintain traditions much more than men. We try to stop these old traditions. For example, in that same funeral Abu Hanafi's wife put dust on her head and face in the old fashion. Hag Omar tried to stop her, but I advised him to let her alone as she is known to be a bit crazy. Some others in our group were saying that this would lead the other women to imitate her and thus revive the old traditions. However, it is impossible to stop her, and I felt we could gain more by pointing out that she was doing it because she is mentally unbalanced.

When I speak to the people about death, especially to the children and women in the mosque, I always say that it is Allah's will and man has to accept it without any discussion. There is no sense blaming Him, because God does the right thing and selects the best path for people. No one knows what might happen. When Hussein's father died, he cried like women and many people reproached him for it. The Ansar al-Sunna think this behavior is very bad. They claim that there is no necessity for grief because the person is going to a better world.

However, when my mother died last year, though I controlled myself throughout the whole funeral, when they began to bury her I failed to remember these principles and I wept. Hag Abdullah looked at me sharply and asked the people to take me away because weeping spoiled the burial procedure. Everything should go quietly according to Islam, but the death of my mother deeply affected me. When they were burying her, I remembered how her husband neglected her and her lifetime of troubles. A short film of my life with her passed before my eyes. A picture of my father arose in my vision, although he did not even attend the funeral. He

was again telling me to go to Kanuba because my mother needed someone
to live with her.

Despite the fact that in my heart I am with Hag Abdullah and the
Ansar al-Sunna, I cannot stop myself from believing in saints. When I visit
Cairo or Alexandria, I always visit one or two of them and even buy
incense. The reason is that I always see two sheikhs in my dreams, and
they are blaming me and accusing me. I don't want to see them. I never
send people to the sheikhs in Daraw because they have no real *baraka*, but
those great sheikhs' *baraka* cannot be denied or ignored. They are truly
close to Allah. I still venerate Sheikh Abu Shalashil, and I visit his tomb in
Diwan when I return there.

When I first came to the village, as I told you before, Sheikh Salama
and Ibn Sherif were the leaders of zikrs here. I found the people attending
zikrs often and everyone participating. People were sitting in the mosque
after evening prayer on Thursday, reading the *moulids* from the Mirghanni
book as well as doing the zikr chant. They frequently burned incense and
sprayed perfume. I wonder where they got this custom of spraying
perfume? Maybe it's from the Prophet's saying "God is *tayeb.*" *Tayeb*
means "to have a good smell." Anyway, for me zikrs are mostly nonsense
because most of the people who come are not serious about worshiping
God. To most of them the zikr is recreation and dancing for fun. I
remember one time when the "King," that is, Sherif's brother, got up
during the zikr and said loudly, "Look, people, I am the camel of the
Prophet." And he got down on his hands and knees and began walking
stiffly like a camel. I don't know what prompted me, but I immediately
jumped on his back, saying, "See people, I am riding the Prophet's camel."
Sometimes when people are saying *"Hoo, Hoo, Hoo,"* it changes to *"How,
How, How,"* and we turn into dogs.

I really like the "Bourda," which is a beautiful poem by the great
Sheikh Abu Siri in Alexandria. It praises the Prophet and is really
inspired. I think it is good if people read it, and that is one reason I
compromise and sometimes support these people who want to have zikrs
in the village. I know they like to dance. People everywhere like to dance
and sing, and in this way we can combine the singing and dancing with
reading something noble and inspiring. Maybe it's the only way we can get
them to read the religious poems, which are good.

Actually, as I told you, we are divided into two groups—the one that
is called Wahabis by the others (really the Ansar al-Sunna) and the other
we call Sufis. The leader of the Ansar al-Sunna in the village is now Hag
Abdullah, and the leader of the Sufis is Sheikh Muhammad. It's funny that
they are both from the Mundolab tribe and closely related to each other. I
am purposely in the middle in order to keep the sharp line between the
two groups from becoming a serious break and to help avoid quarrels. I
hold the stick in the middle. I want the village to be one unit. Therefore I

am trying to lessen the differences between the two sides. As to the women, they are mostly with the Sufi group. There is a woman called Horaya who is known in the village as being a strong Wahab, and Hag Abdullah's wife is one also. But what is funny is that most of the wives of the Wahabs are not Wahabs themselves. Women like dancing and show, and they adhere to the popular traditional beliefs and practices rather than to the orthodox.

I really follow the Ansar al-Sunna from my heart. I guess I got some of these ideas from the Muslim Brotherhood when I was in Cairo. However, in front of the people I do my best not to appear a fanatic. If I openly declared my belonging to Hag Abdullah's group, it would ruin my position because many people whose support I need belong to the Sufis. Their opposition is very strong. Actually, Hag Abdullah and Hag Omar would like to force me to declare my position in public, but this could put me in a hard position. What I reply is that Islam was preached by Muhammad, and Muhammad did not want any subgroups. He only wanted a single unified group which we called Muslims. We should follow the way of Islam. I uphold the view that the differences are not important, and what is important is that there should be union. The differences that exist are merely of interpretation. But for the Ansar al-Sunna, this kind of explanation is not strong enough. Nevertheless, I am not ready to go further at this time.

I am on good terms with the leaders of both religious groups in the village. However, I do not tell my most secret plans to either of them, although both of them individually think that I favor them. When I give speeches, I try to moderate Hag Abdullah's influence by emphasizing the dos rather than the don'ts. I say, "Eat, but don't eat too much because it hurts your stomach and is not good for the health." Hag Abdullah says: "God does not like those who eat much. They will go to hell." I say: "Allah likes cleanliness. If you can't take a bath, perfume yourself, enjoy your time." Hag Abdullah constantly preaches that Muslims must practice self-denial. He says that those who don't pray and follow rituals exactly will go to hell, and Allah will put obstacles in their path here on earth. I prefer simply to state it without reiterating the idea of punishment. I say, "Praying is good. Let's all pray now."

One of my characteristics that bothers me a lot is my fear of the dark. I am sure you have noticed that when I come to your house at night, somebody always accompanies me. I know they make jokes when someone has to go home with me from the *mastaba* in the evening. I have tried many times to cure myself of this fear. In the British Army I used to carry a flashlight in my pocket in spite of the fact that there were many lights. When I first came to Kanuba I always had it in my pocket until it wore out. When I came to the village in 1946 I tried to hide the fact from the people, but they soon noticed that I feared the dark, in spite of the different excuses I gave, because I always asked someone to accompany me to my house after sundown.

I even fear the dark during Ramadan when other people don't fear it. They believe that the ghosts and the *afreet* are in jail during this period. Even women and children can wander any time at the late part of the night without fear. But I fear even to go from my house to Hag Abdullah's store [about twenty yards] at night during Ramadan. Hag Abdullah always passes by for me when he goes to the mosque, or else some other man comes to pick me up.

Once during Ramadan, Abbass waited for me in the tree near Hag Omar's house. I was visiting his house, and for some reason I broke my rule and went back to my house alone. It's only a few steps. When I passed the tree Abbass jumped down shouting "How! How! How!" I screamed and fainted, and everyone thought I was about to die. Even Abbass did not expect this. This is one reason I hate him. Once I was in the mosque with

*Muezzin calling for prayer, Kanuba.*

164

all the people, and we were ready to pray the evening prayer. We found out that Hag Hassuna, the muezzin, was sick and had not come to the mosque that night. I volunteered to give the evening call to prayer, and I went out and climbed up to the tower. The people waited and waited and they didn't hear anything. Finally Aziz climbed up to see what had happened, and he found me sitting in the corner trembling. I was all right until I reached the tower and found darkness all around me. I lost my voice.

In Cairo I didn't usually fear the night in the street because of all the people, activity, and lights around me, but often when I entered my house and couldn't find the lights I became terrified. Once I visited my brother, and there was no light on the stairway of his house. I tried to act natural and took a few steps. Then I suddenly lost control and screamed, "Either come with me or light the stairs!" I couldn't restrain myself though I wanted to behave naturally, especially in front of my relatives. I remember that I hesitated a few seconds before screaming, but I failed to control myself. None of my children fears the dark, and I always warn my wife never to threaten them with darkness. It's good that my wife doesn't fear the dark at all. Sometimes she makes fun of me when I ask her to take me to your place or to some other house. She usually accompanies me until we can see the light, and then she goes back so that I can proceed alone.

Once, about two years after I came to Kanuba, around midnight I heard a loud knock at the door. I didn't dare open, but I had a pistol near my bed and I went to the courtyard. The moon was bright, and when I heard them knock loudly I fired a couple of shots. The man at the door thought that I had killed myself, so he rushed to Hag Abdullah and the whole village came running. That was very embarrassing when I had to explain to them what had happened. Another time I was walking in the evening and I saw a shape, so I pulled out my pistol and fired. It happened to be a man defecating by a wall. He was lucky that I was trembling and so scared that he didn't get hit.

After that, Sheikh Muhammad insisted on taking the pistol away from me, and he even broke it. He reasoned with me: "If you do not kill someone today, then maybe tomorrow. What makes you afraid? There's nothing to be afraid of in this village! I guarantee this." Maybe part of my fear is due to the Nubian belief that people close their doors after sunset to stop wandering ghosts from coming in. My grandmother used to say that.

*Memories and hopes*   I often go to Ballana these days. It has become the center of information since New Nubia was formed. One of my problems now is how to get the advantages of being a part of New Nubia without being under the control of those powerful leaders such as Sheikh Maher of Ballana. I think working through Maher will only give us an equal portion as is due to all the Nubian communities; but if we can be independent too, we will not have to share the profit. I would like to use Sheikh Maher but not be under his direction. This is difficult because his position is now high since he is a member of the National Assembly.

Due to his position, he cannot now openly oppose anyone in the government. His hands are more bound in this respect than they were before when he was simply a leader of all the Nubians. My hands are not bound, and I can send telegrams of complaint in many directions in which he now feels restricted. For example, all the Nubians in the new communities of Ballana and Adindan want electricity, and they send many complaints to the governor, and they try to influence Sheikh Maher on their behalf. I know that electricity will eventually reach us and that the government is doing its best already, so why waste telegrams and effort on this? It is better to ask for things that seem more remote and that will not come automatically, like the water for irrigation that we have waited for so long.

I fear the coming fight for power among the New Nubian leaders. If we attempt to join with them in obtaining our wants, we might find ourselves dominated by them. For example, new leaders are arising who will be chosen for such qualities as being a schoolteacher or a religious man, instead of the hereditary tribal leaders. I don't want to be a leader of all the Nubians, but these people who will come into power undoubtedly will not have the interests of Kanuba in mind, and I would like to see my hopes for our village realized.

I like Sheikh Salama, but I dislike the way he now treats me, as if I were not his equal. Actually, that's the way he treated me when I was younger and when he was a leader here in Kanuba. He still likes publicly to order me to do things, and he wants to give people the impression that he shaped me. In the past I admired him and viewed him as being very close to me, but now I don't like his way. I used to tell him my troubles, and he even selected my wife. I lived with him when I first came to Kanuba, while I was building my house, but I now try to avoid him and treat him more formally. However, he still orders me. Recently he said, "Shatr, I want my son to marry your daughter." He says things like this as if I have to obey. He demands everyone always to give him full attention, and he likes to have people around him following his orders. He delights in receptions and in having people coming to see him constantly. One of the main differences between him and me is that he likes to take all the credit whereas I like to be away from the lights. I think now that he is becoming only a symbol. I no longer tell him any of my hopes or feelings. If I did that, I know that he would tell me what to do, interfere in my life, and criticize me in public.

You know, we have a slight problem with the doctor whom the government recently has sent us for the Kanuba clinic. Before, we had Dr. Fikri, who was a Muslim and whom we liked very well. But now we have Dr. Magdi who is a Copt. He likes money. When he first came, we tried to include him in the village and to get him to participate in our activities, but he remained aloof. Ahmed Khalil and I paid him a visit when he first arrived and asked not to ask for money from any of the people of Kanuba; otherwise we would write a complaint to the government. We told him that he could do anything he liked to the people of Daraw but to be careful with the people from Kanuba. We asked him to be more friendly and more relaxed or informal. We didn't want him to insist on strict procedures in the clinic—that is, like taking tickets, standing in line, and making us go through examination before we get our medicine. We wanted him to relax the hours a little because the hours are now such that if a person comes at 2:00 P.M., he has to wait till the next day to be examined even though the doctor is inside there resting.

At first when Dr. Fikri came, he was the same way, very strict, but we molded him to our ways. But this doctor is stubborn; maybe it is because he is a Copt. His being a Copt also keeps him away from us. You probably remember how when Dr. Fikri came the first time, he immediately came to the mosque to attend prayers. He attended our *moulids* and other religious activities in the club. This gave him a chance to know the villagers and also a chance for us to know him as a person rather than just as a doctor. Dr. Magdi is clever, too, as a doctor, but cleverness is not everything. Actually, being friendly, helpful, trusting, and good is the more important thing. Because he lacks that, even though he is a good doctor, we do not have confidence in him, and he does not trust us. This doctor has the opinion that the people of Kanuba are troublemakers because they send complaints about many things to the government. He is very formal and cautious with his dealings with us.

My hope is to influence the chief doctor of the province through some of our other doctors who are Nubians in high positions. I want to get them to send a Nubian doctor to Kanuba. I think this idea will be well received because the plan for New Nubia and Nasser City is to transfer Nubians from other parts of Egypt to the area where they will be among their own people. There they will get cooperation from their relatives and friends.

You know, one of my plans for bettering our village is to create incentives for people to have high standards. We recently selected Sorraya as the "ideal lady" of the village. The committee at the club did this at my urging. The reasons we gave for our selection were that she knows how to organize her house, she has taste, she knows how to manage and educate her sons and daughters, she is not a troublemaker, and she understands the meaning of life. Actually, you know, without Sorraya, Shakr would be nothing. Most men of the village don't think he's worth a melleem even though he has that good engineering job in the pumping plant. Sorraya made him into a suit of a man. Sometimes we use this honor in giving positions to people who don't deserve it for reasons for keeping peace. For example, we once gave the honor to Abbass, and he does not deserve the position. We did it in order to keep him from making trouble and to get his support.

I never buy newspapers, but I read the club newspaper. I prefer *El-Ahram* because it reports the true news. I do not have any favorite authors, but I never like to miss Hassan Haikel's activities on Friday in *El-Ahram*. Sometimes I buy magazines and books like *Minbar Islam*, but I don't have much time to read. I usually read two or three *suras* of the Koran each day when I get up. Sometimes I don't even cut the pages of the religious magazines I buy. I lend them to Aziz Kalam or some other religious young men. I listen to the radio very seldom, but I listen when other people have it on in my house, at the *mastaba*, at work, or on the bus. What I like to hear best are religious programs or lectures on Islam in its contemporary setting. There is one program of this kind that comes on before I get to work. It's only ten minutes long.

The best time in my life was early childhood. After that, I had a bad time when I lived with my stepmother. I had good times again when I was working with the British Army . . . my youth. Then I earned much money and I had good friends. I built myself and my future. When I came to live in Kanuba, I had saved quite a bit of money in comparison to most people of those times. It was somewhere over 200 pounds. My father's ideas seemed good to me because I had always liked farms and land. I was impressed also by the farms I saw in American films and magazines. My father advised me not to move with the army, and, if I wanted to move from Cairo, he said that I should go to Kanuba where I could start a new work, invest my money, and take care of my mother at the same time. I have never regretted that decision.

In my father's letters, he always wishes my children and me good luck. He still continues to advise me to go into agriculture when conditions improve. He has always been against working in the government. When I was a child, I never visited my father in his office in Alexandria, and I only visited him once when he was working in Cairo. But I remember how delighted I was to see him as the boss of men. He was sitting at a desk in a clean room and telling other men to do this and that. Now I have not seen him for a very long time. In fact the last time I saw him was in 1962 during a major feast. For some reason, I went to Cairo at that time and visited all my brothers. Just a few months ago when my mother died, my father did not even come to Kanuba. He only sent a telegram and then he sent a letter.

In my work in Cairo as a welder I was very happy. I liked to work with tools and iron all day. I did not mind manual labor; in fact, I liked it. I would even now like to work in agriculture or to use my mechanical skills. When I failed in my pumping scheme, I wanted to open a welding shop in Daraw to serve the area, but everyone in the village advised against it. They advised me not to take another risk and to look for a job with a

168

steady income. Somewhere around that time, my half-brother found a welder's job with the Shell Company in Suez for a good salary, and he wanted me to come back and work with him. There were jobs for people with welding skills. I wanted to go and intended to, but my mother's illness forced me to stay in Kanuba. Also, after my failure I was in a bad frame of mind. I had lost all my money, and I was afraid to try anything at all.

I did apply for a job as a welder in Idfu, and I actually got the job. But when the notice came that I was accepted, I refused to go. Sheikh Ahmed and others talked to me. They said: "Here is your place. Here is your mother, your land, and your relatives. The village needs you, Shatr. You should sacrifice for the sake of your village." These words touched me, and I decided to stay in the village though I had no job. It was soon after that that the job in the hospital opened up, and many of my hopes have been realized. I have found my place.

I know that in the future Kanuba will be one of the leading villages in this area. I dream of a modern village. While crossing the tracks on my way home from work in the afternoon, I visualize the village as a whole, and I think of myself walking through a grove of palm trees. I see the new houses completed and unusual activity going on in the square. The background I see as green. Green is the color of paradise, and I want Kanuba to be green someday. Sometimes I imagine the pump working again and I hear its voice. When I cross the tracks by the kiosk where Ali Amin sits, instead of him in his dirty gallabeya I see a man in uniform, and I see an electric signal at the crossroad going "tic, tic, tic." I see a mechanic shop set up by the highway and a small market for vegetables grown by people in our village. I even think that eventually we will be able to make up little packets of produce containing the necessary materials to cook a dish of vegetables. I think our village will be a leader in this area, and we will have a special bus and a special train station. I hope I will be alive to see this, because sometimes I dream I will die soon.

# STRUGGLE FOR CHANGE

# 5

THE NEW KANUBA

Dr. Hussein Fahim, an assistant in the 1963–64 project who has been able to follow the village's progress at close range, has reported that Kanuba had undergone a major transformation by 1972.[15] In place of the harsh brown desert that had formerly surrounded it on three sides, waving fields of sugar cane now extend for several kilometers in one direction, while smaller fields of vegetables, wheat, barley, clover, peanuts, and sesame create a variegated pattern on the village's other sides. Newly planted palm, citrus, and guava trees will provide fruit as well as shade near the houses within a few years. Feeder canals flowing among the fields connect them with the large waterways that were built to convey water to the reclaimed lands of New Nubia.

The village itself has greatly changed in appearance. Some of the older, abandoned buildings have been replaced by new ones; new houses of stone surround a new school building and new community center (with a television set) on what had previously been an empty area in the middle of the village; and the government has agreed to build a large new mosque. The visitor is impressed by an atmosphere of prosperity and general well-being.

Kanubans today go to the Daraw market much less than they used to. In the evening, sacks of summer squash, cucumbers, tomatoes, green beans, cauliflower, and okra are brought to the village square, where women take what they need, paying a nominal amount of only two or three piasters if they have it, paying nothing if they do not have it. Some milk is being obtained from a small but steadily increasing herd of a dozen or more cows. The village consumes only a small percentage of what it produces, selling the surplus in Aswan, Kom Ombo, and Daraw. Although the communally shared profits are not yet great, they make a significant addition to incomes already relieved by the current availability of many foodstuffs at negligible cost.

In addition, the return of many men from the city has brought Kanuba's sex ratio into greater balance. The 1966 census revealed that the total population of the village had increased by one-third and that the sex ratio had shifted from 7 males to 10 females in 1964 to 9 males to 10 females in 1966. (According to our detailed study, the official figure of 8.8 males to 10 females in the 1960 census was incorrect.) Most of the returnees were men between twenty-five and fifty years of age, which also helped to normalize the population structure, and this trend seems to be continuing even though the basic occupational structure remains

*Kanuba women at the Daraw market.*

the same. The men still work at clerical and supervisory jobs, while the village hires farm labor from the surrounding area.

Such profound changes could not have occurred if the times had not been propitious for change, and the fact that the Nubians were given large tracts of reclaimed land adjacent to the village as a result of the resettlement was a most fortunate circumstance. Calling attention to a history of prolonged neglect and deprivation, the Kanubans petitioned the government to be included in the desert reclamation project of New Nubia, not only for irrigation water but also to have their houses rebuilt. Recognizing the legitimacy of their pleas and taking into consideration the relatively low cost of the project due to the large-scale work taking place nearby, the Egyptian ministries of agriculture and land reclamation appropriated the money for Kanuba, later assisting with drainage canals and a tile implantation project to relieve the village's problems with soil salinity.

Before these and other technical difficulties could be resolved, however, the Kanubans had first to cope with grave obstacles presented by the fragmentation of their land and problems of labor supply. During the 1930s, after resettlement, there were only 287 landowners in Kanuba, 92 percent of them holding plots of less than three feddans; indeed, 22 percent held a half-feddan or less, while only .5 percent held as much as fourteen to sixteen feddans. The land of Kanuba had thus been fragmented from the time of the village's founding. Even though more land has been purchased since then by men working in the city, inheritance has increased the number of landowners fivefold, until by 1972, 1,260 persons legally held property in the village, most of it in tiny plots.

Having long ago lost personal contact with agriculture and by now urban oriented to a high degree, the Nubians of Kanuba had also to confront the problem of finding a source of competent agricultural labor— a problem that was especially acute during the few years before any profit could be realized from the newly reclaimed land. An early proposal that the land be rented on a sharecropping basis to Upper Egyptian peasants from nearby villages was rejected after much debate. Although this might ensure a steady income from agriculture and deflect from themselves the necessity of facing the technical problems of farming, it was feared that Kanubans would later be unable to evacuate the tenants from the land and also that the tenants would not give them fair shares of the profits. A proposal that each individual cultivate his own land, with the assistance of other villagers, relatives, or hired labor when necessary, was also rejected on the grounds that these people had insufficient knowledge of farming and were too busy with their own jobs to oversee such work properly.

At the suggestion of Shatr Shalashil, an agricultural cooperative society was formed in Kanuba and chartered in 1969, its affairs placed

*Serving tea, Kanuba.*

Courtesy Samiha El Katsha.

in the hands of a board of directors elected from among the villagers and absentee landowners living in the city. As a result of the cooperative, large areas were planted with one crop, thereby reducing costs while yielding a greater output and profit. The society hires outside workers to do the cultivation but keeps the organization of labor and marketing tightly in hand. By obtaining a loan from the Kom Ombo sugar refinery, the cooperative was able to hire labor to cultivate sugar cane—something that individual farmers could not have done. The first sugar cane crop in 1971 yielded about twenty-eight tons per feddan; in 1972 the yield increased to thirty tons, bringing a substantial profit to the village, which also won first prize for quantity and quality of cane within the Aswan governorate. The cultivation of wheat, sesame, and vegetables has also been very productive, and these growing areas are being expanded. Poor results with clover, potatoes, and barley have led to their reduction or elimination in favor of the more profitable crops.

*173*

Thus, after some thirty-odd years of frustration, disappointment, and government neglect, Kanubans are prospering. They have kept their salaried jobs in Aswan Province at the same time that they are beginning to realize benefits from their land. They now have milk and abundant vegetables, and their leisure time has increased. Although Kanuba may still lack home electricity and its dreamed-of railway station, it was the first village in the region to register women to vote, with the result that its political importance has increased. Its reputation for progressivism has made it a chosen site for high officials and foreign experts to visit.

That much of Kanuba's development is the outcome of fortuitous historical forces, such as the events connected with the High Dam, cannot be denied. But its new prosperity cannot be attributed wholly to its good fortune at being in the right place at the right time since none of the other newly resettled communities of New Nubia has a progressive drive equal to that of Kanuba. Without its persistent struggle to be included in the resettlement scheme, this village would undoubtedly have remained a poor satellite of Daraw surrounded by barren desert. Repeatedly, however, the Kanubans forced an awareness of their village on the consciousness of authorities until the logic of its inclusion under existing circumstances finally became too strong to resist.

It is equally clear that opportunities have been seized in Kanuba by a small group of progressive village men whose central propulsive force has been the unprepossessing, unleaderlike, but highly effective Shatr Shalashil. It should be emphasized that Shatr's narrative was not an inflated fabrication aimed at impressing an outsider. By the time we began to take his life history we had been in the village for some eight months and already had an intimate knowledge of village events collected from other local informants. Even had he been so inclined, he knew there would be little point in deliberate distortion or concealment. This is not to say that he never exaggerated his role but only that we are convinced of the essential truthfulness of his story and greatly impressed by his part in translating and mediating on the level of his own community the changes taking place in Egyptian society as a whole.

## THE ROLE OF SHATR SHALASHIL

Although his early moving back and forth between Alexandria, Cairo, and the village of Diwan in Old Nubia, his frequent encounters with racial and ethnic discrimination, and his close relationship with his grandparents are common features of Nubian experience, Shatr Muhammad Shalashil is not a typical Nubian. Indeed, considering the number of atypical events and unusual features that distinguish his experience, it is

174

astonishing that he did not assimilate into Egyptian society.

Shatr's sense of himself as special, even as "called," seems to have begun during his early childhood in Nubia, when he was treated deferentially as a caretaker of the shrine of his saintly grandfather. Being a member of a family in which the father has two wives is not culturally unexpected, but it is infrequent among Nubians. Having an Egyptian stepmother is even more atypical, and his father's avoidance of other Nubians is most unusual. Since most Nubian boys of his time spent their early years in a village with exposure only to Koranic schools, Shatr's early educational experience in urban schools is unique. His job history, too, diverges radically from the ordinary Nubian pattern. To Egyptians, the very word "Nubian" connotes a servant; at the time of our study, 84 percent of the Nubian working population were still employed as waiters, messengers, doorkeepers, and cooks.[16] Shatr was never employed in a service occupation, however, and his British training as a welder and mechanic was substantially out of the ordinary.

It was not only his experiences at home, school, and work that took Shatr out of the usual Nubian life pattern and provided him with non-Nubian models. His teacher Muhammad Kamel; Birdley, his boss in the British Army; Muhammad Sayed, director of the acting company in Cairo; Anwar of the Muslim Brotherhood—all were non-Nubians. His experiences with Sheikh Shasli, the Muslim Brotherhood, and the theater group each provided him a learning environment outside the experience of most urban Nubians, and his cultivation of Christian friends both reflected and extended this pattern. In short, Shatr's long city experience provided him with a knowledge and understanding of the transformations taking place in the modern world far beyond the ken of any other Kanuban and helped to shape his vision of what the village could become.

At the same time, Shatr's account of his early life reflects a sustained pattern of rejection as well as a search for a place in which he could feel comfortable and secure. His many childhood moves, his isolation within the family, his separation from his real mother, the constant discrimination against him by his stepmother, and the many incidents of rejection of him as a Nubian—all induced in him a fundamental insecurity that would not be alleviated until he settled in Kanuba.

In spite of his intelligence and notwithstanding certain successes, Shatr was essentially an outsider to city life, and the prolonged, unsuccessful identification with Egyptian society made his eventual reidentification as a Nubian highly intense. He now parades his Nubianness with the excessiveness of a reaction formation, and it is this identification that has given him the special energy and force that have led to his successes. In a sense—with regard to his pumping scheme—his life in Kanuba also began in failure. But events of the late 1950s and early 1960s in Egypt,

*Evening on the village mastaba, Kanuba.*

and particularly the advent of the High Dam, brought about the circumstances that enabled his unique blend of personality traits and skills to flower.

Shatr's many failures in life have made him cautious, indirect, flexible, and able to sustain losses. Since he lacks the qualities commonly associated with charismatic leadership, he employs humor and persuasion instead, moving behind the shield of the prestige and personality strength of others, eschewing personal credit, and staying "away from the lights." Manipulation of existing wants, backstage maneuvering, and cajolery are his methods. He almost never attempts a direct frontal attack; rather, he carefully plants an idea in fruitful soil, gathers reactions, and assesses oppositon for counterattack before bringing the matter to the village for a formal decision.

Shatr's flair for the dramatic, revealed in the effective staging of his many *harakas*, was trained and channeled during his experience with the Cairo theater. He is adept at dramatizing success and downplaying failure, and his sense of timing is acute; he knows perfectly how to wait for evidence of frustration or failure before stepping forward with his own carefully prepared solutions. His descriptions of dealing with the new governor of Aswan illustrate this sense of timing. On one occasion, for another example, he correctly predicted that Kanuban candidates would lose in a local election. During the period of community dejection that followed their failure, he obtained village approval to register women to vote.

Shatr Shalashil's high degree of literacy and excellence in writing Arabic script are often enlisted in the furtherance of village goals, and his British Army experience makes him the ideal village representative to meet and deal with officials, foreigners, and visiting experts, to whom, one may be sure, he always presents a picture of village harmony. As an initiator and leader, however, his greatest strengths are his ability to infuse others with his dreams and give tangible shape to inchoate hopes, his persistence in stubbornly maintaining his objectives and pursuing his goals, and his farsightedness—the latter to be observed in his constant striving to promote village unity. The ethnic divisions between Kenuz and Fadija, the religious rift between the Ansar al-Sunna and the Sufis, and the generation gap have all at one time or another threatened his efforts in this regard. Realizing that nothing can be accomplished in a village the size of Kanuba unless the villagers pull together, he has made strong and persistent efforts to heal these breaches, with the result that the religious conflict is now almost dead and the other conflicts are diminishing.[17]

LEADERSHIP AND CHANGE

In its broader implications, this study aids us in understanding how significant social change may come about in traditional societies, and in that regard it is especially pertinent to the field of development anthropology— that is, among those specifically concerned with sociocultural change within the Third World. In the area of sociocultural change in general, the study touches on both the nature of leadership and the role of leaders in introducing innovations and mediating change. From a broadly methodological point of view, it attempts to combine an outsider's perception of the culture and society of a particular village with that of an insider.

Shatr Shalashil's account offers, among other things, a case study of a type of leadership that has had little attention to date in the literature of socioeconomic development. An indispensable leader who has operated without visible power or authority, he influences behavior in the style of a stage director, providing ideas for others from backstage though occasionally playing a principal part when called on to do so. If this type of leadership is widely to be found in the developing world—and close examination suggests that this may well be the case—it is a phenomenon that planners and administrators should better understand. In areas where charismatic types or strong executive leaders are lacking, or where such leaders obstruct the course of beneficial change, men like Shatr Shalashil could be keys to the future success of development programs.

Shatr's case also offers support for those who have observed that innovators are often psychologically and socially marginal.[18] The qualities of marginality may give the innovator the detachment to see things more clearly, the different perspective necessary for breaking out of a traditional order, the motivation to bring society and customs into closer conformity with his own vision, and the bit of recklessness that is often required in initiating change. Not all marginals are innovators, of course, but the cases presented here can help us to isolate the other qualities and experiences that may combine with marginality to produce such leadership.

The need to achieve—a psychological drive that predisposes individuals to accept innovations and take risks—is often invoked to account for change or the absence of change in a society,[19] and this drive is said to be greater in Western society than it is in the Third World. Even without psychological test data, however, it is clear that Shatr's motivation is exceptionally high in this regard; the actions of many of the villagers, especially among the younger groups and including some of the women, reveal that they, too, are high in achievement motivation. In addition, this drive is not a character trait that is instilled in them during childhood but appears to be an enduring enthusiasm that many of the villagers acquire in later life. In Kanuba, in any case, self-interest is fused with community spirit to a degree unusual among most of the Nubians in New Nubia, as well as among those in other, previously resettled communities.[20] Instead of being directed primarily toward individual advancement or entrepreneurial activities, in Kanuba the drive to achieve and excel s channeled principally toward improving the village.

Many studies of sociocultural change indicate what has changed while allowing the processes of such change to remain inferential—that is, how the change came about is anybody's guess. In contrast, Shatr's account of his life gives us an insider's view of: (1) which domains of experience are undergoing the greatest transformation; (2) how some Nubians feel about these changes; (3) some of the means by which customs still heavily invested with meaning, belief, and emotion may be changed; and (4) how situations fraught with emotional resistance and potential conflict may be redirected toward beneficial ends envisioned by a skillful, forward-looking leader. Such cases demonstrate that nonrevolutionary change is not always the mechanical, impersonal process that academic accounts often make it appear to be.

Shatr Muhammad Shalashil does not number among the great innovators or leaders in human history; yet, in the words of C. Wright Mills, he "has contributed to the shaping of his society, even as he was made by society and by its historical push and shove." During his boyhood and young manhood in the 1930s and 1940s, Shatr encountered on the personal level matters ranging in significance from World War II, the British colonial presence, and the rise of the Muslim Brotherhood to the relationships between such religious groups as the Copts and Muslims, the changing role of religion in education and the importance of Sheikhs and charlatans in the city. Thus, placing the events of his life in their sociocultural context and in historical perspective adds an illuminating footnote to the social history of modern Egypt. But by outlining the history and culture of a people, the dynamics of a changing village, and the life, personality, and roles of one of its leaders, and by showing how these lives, events, and processes interact, this book aims above all at suggesting something of what it means to be a Nubian in the modern world.

# NOTES

1. Thayer Scudder, *The Ecology of the Gwembe Tonga.*
2. See Robert A. Fernea and John G. Kennedy, "Initial Adaptations to Resettlement," pp. 349–54.
3. See L.L. Langness, *The Life History in Anthropological Science.*
4. C. Wright Mills, *The Sociological Imagination*, pp. 3, 6.
5. Rolf Herzog, *Die Nubier*, passim.
6. Johann Burckhardt, *Travels in Nubia*, p. 129.
7. William Y. Adams, "Continuity and Change in Nubian Cultural History," p. 12.
8. Bruce Trigger, *History and Settlement in Lower Nubia*, p. 17.
9. Robert A. Fernea, *Contemporary Nubia*, p. 273.
10. Burckhardt, *Travels in Nubia*, pp. 5–6.
11. Ibid., pp. 127–28.
12. For details, see John G. Kennedy, *Nubian Ceremonialism.*
13. Ibid.
14. Peter Geiser, "Some Differential Factors affecting Population Movement," p. 169.
15. Hussein M. Fahim and Omar Abdel Hamid, "The Cooperative Farm at the Village of Kanuba."

16. Geiser, "Differential Factors," p. 169.

17. Hussein M. Fahim, "Field Research in a Nubian Village."

18. Homer G. Barnett, *Innovation.*

19. David C. McClelland, *The Achieving Society.*

20. Fahim, "Field Research."

# GLOSSARY

Ansar al-Sunna movement   A movement of orthodox Muhammadans who accept the Sunna (a collection of precedents in Muslim law based on the actions and words of the Prophet) as being of almost equal importance with the Koran.

Baraka   Blessing, benediction. When used to refer to a person, it means a quality of blessedness, divine grace, or holiness.

Fadija   The southern group of Nubians.

Feddan   Land measurement roughly equal to one acre.

Gallabeya   Loose shirtlike garment worn by men in Egypt.

Haraka   A term meaning "movement," with the additional special meaning of creating a favorable climate of opinion in order to accomplish one's goals.

Imam   A leader; more particularly, a prayer leader.

Kenuz   The northern group of Nubians.

Koran   Sacred scripture of the religion of Islam which is supposed by believers to contain the words of God (Allah) as spoken to one of his prophets, Muhammad.

Kushaf   Hereditary rulers of Nubia from Mamluk times.

Kuttab   A Koran school (lower elementary school).

Mastaba   Outdoor stone bench, usually built into the side of a house.

Moulid   Birthday; used in a religious context to refer to saints' day celebrations.

Nakeeb (masc.)   Caretaker; used in a religious context to refer to the custodian of a shrine; nakeeba (fem.).

Nokout   Wedding presents.

Ramadan   The ninth month in the Muslim calendar during which believers maintain a daily fast from dawn to dusk.

Sakkia   Oxen-powered water wheel.

Shadouf   Primitive water-lifting device.

Sheikh   An elder or chieftain; in Sufi religion it refers to the master of an order.

Sufism   A sect of the Muhammadan religion that emphasizes asceticism and mystical practices and tries to keep within the Sunnas.

Sura   Verse, section, or chapter of the Koran.

Zar ritual   A ceremony to cure mental illness by making contact with the spirits thought to possess the victim.

# BIBLIOGRAPHY

Adams, William Y. "Continuity and Change in Nubian Cultural History." *Sudan Notes and Records* 48 (1967): 1–32.

Barnett, Homer G. *Innovation: The Basis of Cultural Change.* New York: McGraw-Hill, 1953.

Burckhardt, Johann. *Travels in Nubia.* London: J. Murray, 1819.

Fahim, Hussein M. "Field Research in a Nubian Village: The Experience of an Egyptian Anthropologist." Unpublished paper from Wenner-Gren, Burg Wartenstein Symposium no. 67, *The Theoretical and Methodological Implications of Long-term Field Research in Anthropology,* 1975.

_____, and Hamid, Omar Abdel. "The Cooperative Farm at the Village of Kanuba." Unpublished manuscript, n.d.

Fernea, Robert A. *Contemporary Nubia.* 2 vols. New Haven: Human Relations Area Files Press, 1966.

_____, and Gerster, Georg. *Nubians in Egypt: Peaceful People.* Austin: University of Texas Press, 1973.

_____, and Kennedy, John G. "Initial Adaptations to Resettlement: A New Life for Egyptians." *Current Anthropology* 7 (1966): 349–54.

Geiser, Peter. "Some Differential Factors affecting Population Movement: The Nubian Case." *Human Organization* 26 (1967): 164–77.

Harris, Marvin. *The Rise of Anthropological Theory*. New York: Thomas Y. Crowell, 1968.

Herzog, Rolf. *Die Nubier*. Berlin: Deutsch Akademie der Wissenschaften zu Berlin, Völkerkundliche Forschungen, Band 2, 1957.

Kennedy, John G. *Nubian Ceremonialism: Studies in Islamic Syncretism and Cultural Change*. Berkeley and Los Angeles: University of California Press and American University of Cairo Press, 1975.

Langness, L. L. *The Life History in Anthropological Science*. New York: Holt, Rinehart & Winston, 1965.

McClelland, David C. *The Achieving Society*. Princeton: Van Nostrand, 1961.

Mills, C. Wright. *The Sociological Imagination*. New York: Oxford University Press, 1959.

Scudder, Thayer. *The Ecology of the Gwembe Tonga*. Manchester, Eng.: Manchester University Press, 1962.

Trigger, Bruce. *History and Settlement in Lower Nubia*. New Haven: Yale University Publications in Anthropology no. 69, 1965.

# INDEX

Radio, 66, 157, 168
Rageb ritual, 31
Railroads, 24, 27, 89, 94
Rain, 19
Ramadan, 31–3, 65, 164
Rashayda (nomadic herdsmen), 50
Recreation, 150
Religion: Ansar al-Sunna movement, 31, 67, 68, 119, 161, 163; ceremonial life, 30–1; Christianity eradicated, 17; compulsory conversion in Egypt, 16; circumcision, 26; conflict reduced, 177; conversion by marriage, 17; edict of Emperor Theodosius I, 16; Daraw as religious center, 49; disputes between popular and orthodox Islam, 119; Friday break to attend prayers, 97; instruction, 158–9; Islam teaching equality, 154; magazines, 168; missions to Nubia, 16; men's knowledge compared with women's, 67; Muslim conversion of Nubia, 17; prohibition against adultery, 127; praying in mosque a must, 11; popular Islam, 31; popular vs. orthodox, 118–20; radio programs, 168; Shatr instructed by father, 86; Shatr's interest in, 101, 157–65; stories, 34; as veneer over folk beliefs, 17; women educated in, 119; women and pagan practices, 31. See also Islam; Muslim Brotherhood; Sufism; Sacrifice of animals
Relocation of Lower Nubians, 26
Research team members, 7, 8, 127, 137
Resettlement areas, 27
Roman-Merowitic period, 16

Sa'aidi clan, 24, 28, 59
Saber (Shatr's half-brother), 70, 81, 87, 91, 110, 115, 116, 117
Sacrifice of animals: 21, 34; at circumcision, 36, 37; at death ritual, 46; at sebua, 130
Sadeya (victim of rape attempt), 129
Saints' days, 89
Sakkia. See Waterwheel

Salah Muhammad, 116
Salinity, 4, 172
Samiha (research team member), 8, 127
Sayid Ismail, 59
Scorpions, 73
Sebua ritual, 130
Service occupations, 175. See also Occupations
Sexual equality, 131
Sexual segregation, 50, 63–6
Shaddi (bread), 111
Shadouf (water lifting device), 21, 23
Sharecroppers, 28, 172
Shatr Shalashil: accident to, 107; acting career, 103–5; in agriculture cooperative, 172; in Alexandria, 74; in Ansar al-Sunna, 163; Arabian language speaking, 74; bicycle riding, 97–8; Birdley influence on, 97–8; birth of, 69; birth control advocate, 131; British Army job, 90, 94 passim; boss of group at work, 95; Cairo life of, 80; childhood friends of, 77; children of, 82–3, 130–5; Christian friends of, 107; circumcisions of, 77; circumcision of children, 132; clever leader, 11; club policy of, 122; confrontations avoided by, 156, 176; Copts in life of, 95, 165; correspondence with father, 88, 168; costumes of, 71–2, 118; credit for progress, 174, 179; dairy plans of, 108; death of children, 130–1; death of grandfather, 86; death of mother, 161; education of, 74–5, 83, 87, 93, 106, 177; education plans for children, 131; English, his impressions of, 98; English speaking of, 106; father of, 69, 75, 78, 83, 87, 107, 159; father's shop, working in, 88–9; father's relationship with stepmother, 93; fear of dark, 73, 159, 163–5; farming interest of, 115; furniture of, 85, 86; grandparents of, 69, 70, 73, 80, 99–100, 134, 158; haraka, method used by, 121–3, 136–7, 149, 157, 177;